GUADALCANAL

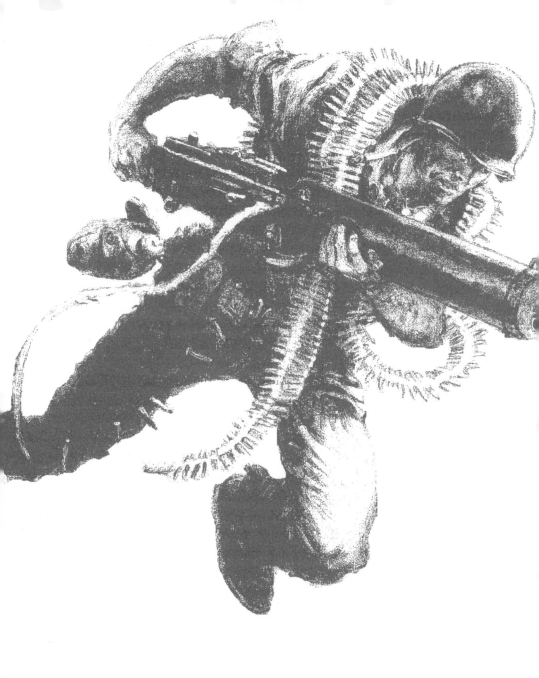

GUADALCANAL
AN AMERICAN STORY

Carl K. Hixon

NAVAL INSTITUTE PRESS   Annapolis, Maryland

Naval Institute Press
291 Wood Road
Annapolis, MD 21402

Library of Congress Cataloging-in-Publication Data

Hixon, Carl K., 1924–
    Guadalcanal : an American story / Carl K. Hixon.
      p. cm.
    Includes bibliographical references (p.) and index.
    ISBN 1-55750-345-1 (alk. paper)
     1. Guadalcanal (Solomon Islands), Battle of, 1942–1943.
   I. Title.
  D767.98.H59 1999
  940.54'26—dc21   99-25778

Printed in the United States of America on acid-free paper ∞
06 05 04 03 02 01 00 99   9 8 7 6 5 4 3 2
First printing

To Dory

CONTENTS

This is a story about a time in 1942 when a kind of magic happened to Americans: a story about the way we were. It is the account of an epic battle—the Battle of Guadalcanal—one we had no right to win, given the circumstances. One that any bookmaker would have bet against. It chronicles what young and untried Americans can do when it becomes necessary, and how they did it on Guadalcanal. It records a way of thinking, feeling, and acting that may be missing from our national life today, but that always returns with a rush when the chips are truly down. And it is about pulling up your socks when everything is going wrong for you.

ACKNOWLEDGMENTS

This book owes its existence to a great many people, living and dead, but out of this legion of contributors are those who were prominently helpful. I wish to thank Gene Keller, former U.S. Marine, Guadalcanal veteran, and a curator of the Guadalcanal Museum in Kalamazoo, Michigan, who opened the museum's files to me. I am also indebted to Harry Horsman, National Historian Emeritus of the Guadalcanal Campaign Veterans, who shared his more than fifty years of records with me and critiqued the manuscript: my obligation to him cannot easily be repaid. Ted Blahnik, editor of *Guadalcanal Echoes,* deserves my best thanks for opening his newspaper's files to me and vetting my work. My considerable gratitude as well to Gareth Bogaerde and the late Dick Marx, my collaborators in the earliest draft of a documentary film treatment that evolved into this book. A tip of my hat as well to Maj. Bill Fisher (Ret.) of the U.S. Marines, who read the manuscript and supplied me with many additional contacts. Mike Zello, past president of the Guadalcanal Campaign Veterans, went ashore on Guadalcanal wearing a World War I "tin hat"; to him I am grateful for a fund of anecdote and detail. My appreciation also to Col. John Sweeney (Ret.) of the 1st Marine Raider Battalion, who also read the manuscript. I also wish to thank the Guadalcanal Campaign Veterans organization. As an associate member, I attended several reunions, notebook in hand, and much of the color to be found in these pages derives from our late-night conversations. And lastly, my gratitude and love to Dory Hixon, my wife, gentle critic, coach, and computer expert.

GUADALCANAL

The Problem

"IT WAS GOD'S MERCY," wrote Adm. Chester W. Nimitz, "that our fleet was in Pearl Harbor on December 7, 1941." Had his predecessor known the Japanese were coming and sallied out to intercept their task force, Nimitz continued, the Japanese would have sunk many more of our ships, irretrievably, in deep water, at a far greater cost in American lives than the two thousand lost at Pearl Harbor.[1] It was *that* difficult to come up with anything resembling good news in the aftermath of the surprise Pearl Harbor attack. Both tactically and strategically, the United States was dead in the water. The Japanese had mounted history's first aircraft carrier strike, and in 110 minutes over Oahu they had forever altered the rules of naval warfare. Then in a matter of months they had gobbled up most of the Pacific Ocean and its western rim, including the United States's naval and military bases, our Pacific island territories, and our trading partners of long standing. The Pacific from Hawaii to Sumatra and north to Tokyo was now a Japanese lake, and our planet's greatest surface area ever under one empire's dominion.

In this explosive confrontation we were the undisputed underdog, our military establishment discredited and our peacetime industries six months away from conversion to anything like wartime production. By contrast, the Japanese had been on a war footing since their invasion of Manchuria in 1931. As unbelievable as it now seems, the United States could mount only a peashooter defense between this Japanese juggernaut and our West Coast. American military assets consisted mostly of a Gilbert and Sullivan army, part of it drilling with wooden rifles, and a Pacific fleet, half the battleships of which lay at the bottom of Pearl Harbor. Our traditional allies, the British, had been at war for two years and stood with their backs to the wall against the Wehrmacht. They needed more help than we did. Too late we realized that our image of the Japanese had been a fantasy. They were not a race of buck-toothed, nearsighted munchkins in kimonos who exported cheap goods for sale in Woolworth's. They were instead a proud warrior nation intent on having their way with us and off to a good start. It was a shattering truth, a disorienting experience, and it plunged the United States into a profound morale crisis. Overnight our feelings of superiority were dashed and our heroes became bums.

Wrote U.S. Secretary of War Henry Stimson in his diary, "I think it is quite within the realm of possibility that if the Japanese should get naval dominance in the Pacific, they would try an invasion of this country. If they did, we would have a tough time meeting them."[2] The chief of our naval intelligence unit on Hawaii declared that he was certain the Japanese planned another attack on Hawaii, this time with an invasion fleet. And some officials in corner offices of the War Department in Washington believed that the Japanese were headed for our West Coast to launch carrier strikes against the aircraft factories in southern California. When Admiral Nimitz took over the job of commander in chief, Pacific, and installed his headquarters (HQ) in Hawaii, he was appalled at the defeatist mindset of the headquarters staff that he inherited. "All of these [people]," he later wrote, "were in a state of shell shock, and my biggest problem at the moment was morale. These officers had to be salvaged."

To complicate matters, we were fighting not only the Japanese but also each other. As of 7 December 1941, the politics of war had been on the boil in Washington, D.C., as well as within our military command, and between ourselves and our Allies. Public officials in high places scrambled to seize the new wartime levers of power, while others maneuvered to cover their behinds. Gen. Douglas MacArthur was no sooner evacuated from the Philippines to Australia than he began his four-year minuet with Nimitz for control of our Pacific forces. President Roosevelt—like Alexander the Great with his frustrating Gordion knot—tried to solve the problem by splitting the Pacific down the middle, giving the western half to MacArthur and the eastern half to Nimitz. Our principal ally, British prime minister Winston Churchill, viewed the Pacific war theater as his arch competitor for U.S. manpower and other war-making assets and poured all of his persuasiveness into FDR's ear, successfully. Thereafter, the European theater of war would have first pick of American manpower and logistical resources; the Pacific theater would get the leftovers. Even Gen. Dwight D. Eisenhower, the U.S. Army's planning chief, was willing to let Australia go down the spout if necessary.[3] It followed that Nimitz and MacArthur must now slay the Japanese dragon using only the "B" team, and with smoke and mirrors somehow turn the Pacific war around. On Guadalcanal in the summer of 1942, the B team would turn out to be the tiny U.S. Marine Corps—a mere seventy thousand strong at the beginning of the war and the stepchild of our armed forces.

In the face of all these negatives, however, we had three things going for us. First, the surprise attack that had jolted us awake now unified us as nothing else could have done. Second, a mathematical wizard, Cdr. Joseph Rochefort, together with his team of U.S. Navy cryptographers, had cracked key portions of Japan's naval codes. As a result, we were now reading their mail. And third, we had still to learn of it, but Japan's military and naval officer corps, from the top down, was suffering from "victory euphoria." Their initial land, sea, and air battles had been won with such ridiculous ease that Japan's wartime leaders were giddy with success and took for granted that the U.S Marines on Guadalcanal would be a pushover. As a result the Japanese grossly underestimated American tenacity and resolve in a grisly fight to the finish.

The Players

Drawn into the Guadalcanal vortex were many remarkable individuals on both sides of the barbed wire, some famous, some not: Adm. "Bull"

Halsey; President Franklin Delano Roosevelt; the five Sullivan brothers, who went down with the torpedoed USS *Juneau*; and the wavering Vice Adm. Frank Jack Fletcher, who pulled his carrier task force out after the second day of the battle, before the transports had unloaded the last one-third of the marines' food, weapons, and supplies. It was he who inspired the marines' unofficial "George Medal"—on one side, a navy hand and sleeve dropping a hot potato into a marine palm, on the other side, a cow with raised tail backing up to an electric fan. The motto read *Faciat Georgius:* "Let George do it."

Then there was Joe Foss, marine Medal of Honor fighter pilot and later governor of South Dakota, at twenty-eight regarded as geriatric by his squadron and known as "Old Foos"; "Red Mike" Edson, the Corps' most enigmatic commander, who rallied and goaded his 1st Marine Raider Battalion to victory against atrocious odds at the Battle of Edson's Ridge; and "Manila John" Basilone, who coolly tuned his machine guns under showers of Japanese grenades and survived, only to die later on Iwo Jima. Basilone was one of the first enlisted men on the island to be awarded the Medal of Honor. "Chesty" Puller, the marine's marine, and Lou Diamond, rumored to have enlisted in the Marine Corps in 1798 and said to be two hundred years old, were also there. Master Gunnery Sergeant Diamond, according to marine legend, dropped an 81-millimeter mortar shell down the stack of a Japanese destroyer that ventured too near the beach. The destroyer speedily withdrew. Also in action was the valorous Company E of the army's 132d Infantry. The isolated company was nearly out of food and ammunition, and about to fix bayonets in the vicious fight for Hill 27, when it received a nick-of-time air drop that topped up its ammo and included a surprise bonus of chocolate bars. For the next three days the GIs lived and fought entirely on chocolate.

There were also many exceptional and gifted men on the Japanese side of the barbed wire: Col. Kiyanoa Ichiki, the George Armstrong Custer of the Japanese army and leader of Guadalcanal's first banzai attack on the U.S. Marines; Maj. Gen. Kiyotake Kawaguchi, who brought with him to the Battle of Guadalcanal a tailor-made white uniform in which to accept the surrender of Major General Vandegrift, commander of the 1st Marine Division; and Adm. Isoroku Yamamoto, his nation's most gifted naval strategist and the architect of the Pearl Harbor attack. Present as well were the Japanese fighter pilot ace, Saburo Sakai, who gave the United States its first posthumous Medal of Honor winner, and the resourceful and infinitely patient commander of the historic Tokyo Express, Rear Adm. Raizo Tanaka, who throughout the six-month battle zigzagged dexterously around the whistling 1,000-pounders of American dive bombers and the sometimes puzzling orders of his superiors.

The Marine Corps

There is the rest of the world and there is the United States Marine Corps, a one-off organization if ever there was one—salty, patriotic, hard-assed, colorful, sardonic, and uncompromisingly professional, possessing a collective state of mind unfathomable to civilians. In 1939 the Marine Corps was smaller than the New York City Police Department. By 1942 its numbers had increased to seventy-five thousand and consisted largely of newly volunteered and hastily but mercilessly trained American kids, average age nineteen, equipped with World War I hand-me-down weapons but inspired by a cadre of hard-core veterans known as the "Old Breed." Marine brigadier general Samuel B. Griffith II (Ret.), a Guadalcanal veteran, defined the Old Breed in his book *The Battle for Guadalcanal*:

> These were the professionals. Many had fought "Cacos" in Haiti, "Bandidos" in Nicaragua, and French, English, and American soldiers in every bar in Shanghai, Manila, Tsingtao, Tientsin, and Peking. They were inveterate gamblers and accomplished scroungers, who drank hair tonic in preference to post exchange beer, cursed with wonderful fluency, and never went to chapel unless forced to. Many dipped snuff, smoked rank cigars or chewed tobacco. They could live on jerked goat, the strong black coffee they called "boiler compound" and hash cooked in a tin hat. They knew their weapons and they knew their tactics. They knew they were tough and they knew they were good. There were enough of them to leaven the [1st] Division and impart to the thousands of younger men a share of the unique spirit that animated them and the skills they possessed.

The Japanese officer corps had been at war for eleven consecutive years and had never been defeated. Most marine officers, however, would need to learn their trade on the job, with help from the Corps' World War I veterans and the handful who had fought in Haiti and the Banana Republic wars. In the entire Marine Corps, fewer than one in ten of the men who would soon be locked in combat with the Japanese had ever seen an enemy over their rifle sights.

The Japanese

The Japanese commanders had every right to believe that they would swiftly crush the ill-prepared and ill-equipped American venture at Guadalcanal, just as they had rolled up every other allied stronghold in the Pacific during the previous six months, and before that the Chinese army. More so than even the Germans, the Japanese in 1941–42 were world-class military professionals, having scored many of their major victories on the Asian continent while the Wehrmacht was still in short pants. Their battle-proven navy was not only state of the art and astutely commanded but also skilled in the expertise soon to be found wanting in the U.S. Pacific Fleet—night fighting and the use of torpedoes; the Japanese air force was distinctly superior to ours in combat hours flown and aircraft performance; and their vast army with years of hard and victorious fighting behind it was the most formidable in the hemisphere. Their ace in the hole, however, was the low-slung Japanese infantryman, whose morale was always high and who could march thirty-five miles a day on a palmful of rice, humping a rifle, bayonet, grenades, canteen, full field pack, and several heavy mortar shells, then fight a forty-eight-hour battle in the mud. He was indisputably the most aggressive and dedicated foe the U.S. Marine Corps would face since its formation in 1798.

The Warbirds

The Guadalcanal story is also about some heroic aircraft and what they did: our stubby little F4F Wildcat fighter, nicknamed the "Knock-kneed Bumble Bee" for its rotund fuselage and improbable looking landing gear; the SBD, our rock-steady marine and navy dive bomber known affectionately as the "Slow But Deadly," the "Speedy-D," the "Barge," and the "Clunk"; and the TBF, a combination torpedo plane and level bomber, referred to as the "Pregnant Beast" because of its bloated midsection. Our big but graceful Catalina PBY—"Dumbo," named after the flying baby elephant in Walt Disney's animated film—plucked hundreds of downed fliers out of the sea and once at Guadalcanal, with two torpedoes rigged under its wing, broke the back of an enemy transport. It returned safely with more than fifty bullet holes. The sleek and deadly Mitsubishi Zero was the Pacific war's best fighter plane in 1942. One of them flashed down the beachhead on landing day and slow-rolled out of sight, while scores of marines leaped like prairie dogs from their holes and gave it the finger. The twin-engine Japanese "Betty" bomber arrived over Guadalcanal daily by the dozens to plaster marine positions at lunchtime—you could almost set your watch by them; and "Louey the Louse" and "Washing Machine Charley," two Japanese float planes, dropped ghastly green flares and scattered small bombs over the marine perimeter at night to keep everyone awake. To the young pilots on both sides who flew these warbirds, they had potent symbolic meaning. "I believed," wrote one Japanese ace, "that the Zero fighter was to me what the sword was to the samurai—and I felt that I must control my plane as if it were my own body."

The Island

In August 1942 all of these dynamic forces collided with shuddering impact on an obscure South Pacific island. The Japanese called the island "Gadarakanaru." To the natives it was "Pua-Pua." The marines called it "Guadal," "the 'Canal," or just "the Island." It had been christened "Guadalcanal" in 1566 by its discoverer, Alvara de Mendana, after the Spanish hometown of his expedition's troop commander. Lying some 550 miles east of New Guinea and sharing its hellish climate, Guadalcanal was the southernmost-but-one major island in the Solomon Islands chain. Think of it as a slightly smaller Puerto Rico, ninety miles long by twenty-five miles wide, dominated by an eight-thousand-foot volcanic cone that rose like a great green carbuncle above its Rousseau-like rain forest. Near the sea, the rain forest gave way in places to grassy, humpbacked ridges that meandered like giant mole hills, and to steep ravines, choked with jungly undergrowth. Down these ravines snaked the island's many rivers on their way to the sea, draining off the day's rainfall. Visible in their brackish inlets were the gnarled snouts and bulging eyes of submerged crocodiles. (Marine advice: if one chases you, run zigzag; they can't change direction.)[4] The humidity most days approached 100 percent, and the afternoon temperature seldom fell below ninety degrees. Annual rainfall totaled 165 inches. "Nothing stood against it," recalls Robert Leckie:

> A letter from home had to be read and reread and memorized, for it fell apart in your pocket in less than a week. A pair of socks lasted no longer. A pack of cigarettes became sodden and worthless unless smoked that day. Pocket knife blades rusted together . . . pencils swelled and burst apart. Rifle barrels turned blue with mold and had to be slung upside down to keep out the rain. Bullets stuck together in the rifle magazines and machine gunners had to go over their belts daily, extracting and oiling and reinserting the bullets to keep them from sticking to the cloth loops.[5]

Moisture conspired with heat to make Guadalcanal's jungle the ideal incubator for every form of life but human. It housed scorpions that stung like tetanus shots, wriggling leeches, huge homicidal wasps, psychedelically colored spiders with webs like tennis nets, and countless buzzing things that tickled or bit your sweaty neck in the perpetual green twilight of its rain forest. Over sixty varieties of malaria-carrying mosquitoes spawned in its puddles, and marines would learn to wrap their heads in blankets at night for sanity's sake. Land crabs the size of dinner plates scuttled through the underbrush, sounding like infiltrating Japanese. When they tumbled into a foxhole at 2:00 A.M. they were frantically beaten to death with an entrenching tool by the unnerved occupant. A sweat-soaked skivvy shirt left hanging on a bush would be half eaten in the night by God knows what. From this great steaming greenhouse, manured with the excrement of a million life forms, there arose a stench like hot, ripe garbage laced with rotten eggs and used diapers. Naval historian Samuel Eliot Morison described the odor as "fecaloid." Most of Guadalcanal's estimated population of ten thousand Melanesians wisely chose to live as near to its beaches as possible. The only sociable terrain to be found was the few level miles east of the Lunga River delta on the island's north coast, where for many years Lever Brothers and a French concern had maintained well-groomed coconut plantations and fenced in acreage for livestock. The Marine Corps would target this strip of coast as its landing zone.

He Shaved with a Blowtorch

Japan's attack on Pearl Harbor was only the first of a series of rude shocks to the United States and its Allies. Others swiftly followed as Japan moved to exploit its advantage. On 23 December the small marine garrison on Wake Island was overrun by a Japanese landing force. On Christmas Day, Hong Kong fell. Manila was occupied on 3 January. In the next two weeks, Japanese armies swarmed through the East Indies, then blitzed the strategically important Bismarck islands, jumping off point for New Guinea and site of one of the Pacific's most secure harbors. Next, Borneo. Then, with now accustomed ease, Japanese forces scooped up Singapore, Britain's key naval and military stronghold, capturing thousands of British soldiers and civilians, many of whom would perish from starvation, exhaustion, and maltreatment building the infamous "River Kwai" railroad. On 6 May came another solar plexus blow to U.S. morale. The American-held island of Corregidor in the Philippines capitulated, and with it sixteen thousand American and Philippine troops—more grist for the empire's forced labor camps. There remained as Japan's phase-one priority only the conquest of New Guinea, which would serve as a staging area for the invasion of northern Australia.

Meanwhile, the United States and its Pacific Rim allies, Australia and New Zealand, had begun showing signs of life. One of the first was the appointment of Adm. Ernest King as Chief of Naval Operations. It was said of the tall, granite-faced King that he shaved with a blowtorch. President Franklin Roosevelt solemnized the legend by giving King a blowtorch for his sixty-fourth birthday. And when a Washington official complained that King was behaving like a "son-of-a-bitch," King snarled, "They always call on the sons-of-bitches when they're in trouble!"[6] King appointed Adm. Chester W. Nimitz as commander in chief, Pacific (CinCPac in navalese). Flaxen-haired, with calm, horizon-blue eyes, his freckled face etched by sun and salt, Nimitz was just what the doctor ordered. Under his unflappable aegis, the U.S. Navy rallied and began to fight back. The first effort was a joint Army-Navy long shot—the 18 April 1942 Doolittle air raid on Tokyo. Launched in stealth from the aircraft carrier USS *Hornet* close aboard Japan's home islands, sixteen of our twin-engine B-25 bombers caught Japanese air defenses with their pants down and, to the embarrassment of Japan's military establishment, bombed and strafed their way across Nippon, ending up in China. When asked by the press from where Doolittle's bombers took off, Roosevelt grinned and said, "Shangri-La." The raid was a token strike and did little damage, except to Japanese hubris. But it worked wonders for American morale and was hailed by the U.S. media as an audacious thrust up the enemy's nose. Several of our airmen were shot down and taken prisoner, then tried as criminals. Three were publicly beheaded.

At a Poignant Sacrifice

Then, on 7 and 8 May, in the Coral Sea off of Australia's northeastern coast, a U.S. carrier task force intercepted a Japanese carrier task force en route to Port Moresby, New Guinea, which it was about to seize from the Australians. Our aircraft carriers punched it out with theirs across 170 miles of sparkling blue water. We sank their light carrier, the *Shoho*, but Japanese dive and torpedo bombers sank our fast fleet carrier, the USS *Lexington*. It was a tactical success for the Japanese, as they gave better than they got, but a strategic victory for the United States because the Japanese task force commander, fearing the loss of his crowded troop transports, aborted the Port Moresby invasion and returned to base.

On 3 June there occurred the most decisive seagoing engagement of the Pacific war—the Battle of Midway. Japan's equivalent of Ernie King, a brilliant and charismatic naval officer named Isoroku Yamamoto, planned a two-step move against the United States. He would send a powerful carrier force with troop transports to attack U.S.-held Midway Island in the central Pacific. The U.S. Navy, what was left of it, would hasten to its rescue (Yamamoto reckoned) and be brought to battle by the superior Japanese force, which would sink it. Japanese troops would then seize the island. The Midway victory would open wide the door for step two—the invasion of Hawaii and the West Coast of the United States.

Yamamoto might have succeeded, but for one reason—we were reading his mail. Forewarned, the remains of the U.S. Pacific Fleet ambushed the Japanese invasion force northwest of Midway. At a poignant loss of sixty young American lives, our dive-bomber pilots sank four of Yamamoto's carriers in an epic air-sea battle that cost us only one carrier—the USS *Yorktown*. Meanwhile, many leagues to the south, there were promising developments.

The 4th Marines Went over the Top, Parlez Vous

On 10 April 1942 the first Marine Corps expeditionary force of the war sallied from Norfolk, Virginia, through the Panama Canal and into the Pacific. The 7th Marine Regiment, thirty-four hundred strong, was headed for Samoa. It would act as a deterrent in the event of a Japanese thrust into the South Pacific.

At the same time, Vice Adm. Robert L. Ghormley, an intellectual and cultivated naval officer with no recent seagoing experience, was appointed South Pacific Area commander and installed at Auckland, New Zealand. Ernie King, in tandem with Nimitz and the Marine Corps commandant, then activated the 1st Marine Division, which until now had existed only as a fluctuating and widely dispersed collection of regiments and battalions. On D-day the 1st Division would arrive at Guadalcanal shorthanded, its absent regiment, the 7th Marines, still under canvas at Samoa. (It was Marine Corps doctrine to refer to its regiments as, for example, the 1st Marines, the 3d Marines, the 5th Marines, and so on, a holdover from days when the Corps thought only in terms of regiments, being too small to field an array of twenty-thousand-man divisions. Hence the World War I trench ballad: "The 4th Marines went over the top, parlez vous, the 5th Marines went over the top, parlez vous . . .")

Another admiral who would figure importantly in the battle for Guadalcanal was at this moment scratching impatiently in a hospital bed on

Oahu, suffering from a severe case of eczema. Vice Adm. William F. "Bull" Halsey was to the navy what "Chesty" Puller was to the Marine Corps. Soon he would be giving eczema to the Japanese.

The Coastwatchers

The Royal Australian Navy, with some nine thousand miles of coastline to defend, had already put in hand one of the Pacific war's most colorful and eccentric establishments: the coastwatcher network. It consisted of more than a hundred hidden observation stations stretching from eastern New Guinea across to the Solomons, down the island stepping stones to Guadalcanal, then south as far as Vila in the New Hebrides group, a distance of twenty-five hundred miles. The stations were manned by an assortment of rugged loners, men who knew the islands intimately, who did not scare easily, and who were fluent in pidgin, an imaginative mixture of bastardized English and Melanesian words (a PBY "Dumbo" translated into pidgin came out "Alla same big fella bird"). These stations were tucked away high in the jungle hills, many behind enemy lines. Each was equipped with a ponderous shortwave radio, a pedal-powered generator, and an antenna, all of which could be packed up in minutes and wrestled farther into the rain forest at the first sign of a Japanese patrol, for there was no doubting a coastwatcher's fate in the event of capture: kubi o kiru— beheading. Because the coastwatchers were there to spy, not to fight, their code name was "Ferdinand," after the pacifistic, flower sniffing bull of children's literature. For broadcasting their early warnings of enemy ship and aircraft movements, the coastwatchers would soon be numbered among the 1st Marine Division's best friends; and in the months to come they would fish 120 marine and navy airmen out of the sea and spirit them back to Guadalcanal under Nipponese noses.

Staik and Aiggs

At the island of New Britain, just east of New Guinea, was one of the finest deep-water harbors in the Southwest Pacific. The Imperial Japanese Navy had seized the island during its initial southward plunge, and now, at its capitol city of Rabaul, the Japanese established an advanced naval base and air arm complex. Rabaul would shortly become the Japanese reciprocal of Guadalcanal, close enough at 565 miles for Japanese bombers and fighters to reach Guadalcanal, spend a few violent minutes over the marine perimeter, and return.

To secure the flanks of their Rabaul stronghold the Japanese hastened to establish a picket line of island outposts, including one at Tulagi, Guadalcanal's little sister island. It was just visible on the horizon from coastwatcher Martin Clemens's hidey-hole on Guadalcanal's north shore. Tulagi's government station had for several days been receiving radio intelligence reports that a small but sinister Japanese naval force was moving in its direction. Should the Japanese appear, advised the Royal Australian Navy, Tulagi radio was to come on the air with its emergency evacuation code, "Steak and eggs," then run! This prospect was soon made flesh by the appearance over Tulagi of Japanese bombers, who lay waste the naval dockyard and damaged a PBY. The PBY was patched up by Clemens and towed across to Guadalcanal, where it was camouflaged under palm fronds by Clemens's native irregulars.

In the early hours of 3 May from his perch high in a banyan tree, Clemens's native lookout blew a mighty blast on his conch shell, signaling trouble. Through his binoculars Clemens made out four warships approaching Tulagi Harbor, and assorted Tulagi-based craft departing at flank speed. He sprinted to his radio shack and spun the dial to the Tulagi frequency. Reception was poor, but between crackles he could hear a distressed Australian voice exclaiming, "Staik and aiggs, goddamn it, staik and aiggs." The Japanese were on Clemens's doorstep.

On the eighteenth Adm. Robert Ghormley, commanding officer (CO), South Pacific, moved his HQ north from New Zealand to Noumea on the French island of New Caledonia. There arose an immediate problem with office and living accommodations. The French, many of whom were Vichy government sympathizers, ignored Ghormley's courteous request to set up his headquarters ashore in the vacant Japanese embassy. Rather than make a fuss, Ghormley chose instead to establish his HQ in the harbor aboard the USS *Argonne*, the antiquated and sweltering naval vessel that served as his flagship.

On 8 June a considerable number of Japanese troops came ashore on the north coast of Guadalcanal near the coconut plantations, erected a tent city, and began building a wharf. Clemens reported this by radio, theorized on its meaning, and a few days later added that the Japanese were burning off grass on an inland plain, as if to clear it for some new enterprise. On 6 July a twelve-ship Japanese convoy dropped anchor off the mysterious wharf. Then, as the ships began unloading specialized construction equipment—heavy duty tractors, steam rollers, generators, an ice plant, and a miniature railroad with two toylike locomotives and a dozen hopper cars—Clemens's suspicions were confirmed. Guadalcanal was about to become a Japanese air base.

Come Out of the Fort and Fight

Clemens's prognosis was correct, but the news was already forty-eight hours old. An Allied reconnaissance plane snooping the area on 4 July had spotted the Japanese at work and immediately spread the word of an enemy airfield in the making deep in the southern Solomons.[7] Ernie King, however, wasn't having it. The time was ripe, he told Nimitz, to come out of the fort and fight. King's case for going over to the offensive was airtight. Whoever owned the airfield on Guadalcanal owned the sky around it for a flight radius of six hundred miles. And whoever owned this vast blue dome of sky owned the islands and sea beneath it. If the U.S. Navy permitted Japan to operate an airfield that dominated this zone of the Southwest Pacific, Japanese warbirds would descend like Furies on the sea and air lanes linking the United States with Australia, denying the United States access to the Down Under continent and isolating Australia for easy pickings when the time came for Japan to invade—which King knew would be damned soon. And once the Japanese airfield on Guadalcanal had become operational, landing U.S. assault troops on the island could only be done—if done at all—at a grim cost in American lives.

Time was now exceedingly of the essence. Therefore, on 24 June, while the Japanese on Guadalcanal were laying out their airfield perimeters, King in Washington directed Nimitz in Hawaii to prepare to capture "Tulagi and adjacent positions." Three days later King added a postscript, advising Nimitz that he would not have use of the U.S. Army.[8] The job would have to be done by the U.S. Navy and Marine Corps. And quickly, ordered the impatient King. Then on 5 July, he specified "Guadalcanal" as "the adjacent position."

On the eighth Ghormley flew to General MacArthur's HQ in Australia to discuss King's order. Ghormley, on whose shoulders would fall responsibility for the operation, worried that it was not doable. MacArthur, none of whose business it was, commiserated, and together they composed a rebuttal to the U.S. Joint Chiefs of Staff in Washington: "The initiation of this operation at this time without a reasonable assurance of adequate air coverage would be attended with the gravest risk." Students of the MacArthur ego would recognize the general's elegant prose style in the message. It reminded the Joint Chiefs that MacArthur had recently proposed his own much riskier plan for leaping northward to Rabaul and beyond with no more air coverage than Ghormley could count on. They took no action. For his part, the fire-breathing Ernie King shot back a message to Ghormley to the effect that there would be no postponement of the landing—period. It turned out to be one of the most pivotal decisions of the Pacific war.

Just Five Weeks Hence

The newly constituted 1st Marine Division was commanded by Maj. Gen. Alexander Archer Vandegrift, a Marine Corps professional since 1909.[9] Vandegrift at fifty-five was a quiet but steel-willed man with a dimpled chin and a gentlemanly Virginia accent. He sailed off to war from Norfolk, Virginia, on 20 May 1942, with the first echelon of his new command, having been told to expect no combat assignment until the following year. The Pacific crossing was uneventful, with one exception. As the troop transports neared the equator, the suffocating heat made it necessary to open all hatches and skylights to cool off the thousands of marines crammed below decks. The arrangement had the desired effect until a rising sea caused Vandegrift's transport to stuff its bow into a large wave and take aboard several tons of green water, which cascaded through the open hatches onto the troops below. For a moment Vandegrift feared a panic among his tightly packed marines, but tension evaporated when a voice from the depths of the transport's holds shouted, "Women and children first!"[10] Vandegrift's second echelon sailed in June from San Francisco and a month later would join the first echelon at Wellington, New Zealand. Not a single marine, from Vandegrift on down to the cooks and bakers, had the slightest notion of why they were there or what would happen next.

Vandegrift's arrival in Wellington touched off a series of calamities large and small that would breathe new life into the proverb "Haste makes waste," beginning with a meeting in Auckland, New Zealand, to which Admiral Ghormley summoned the marine general. The admiral glumly advised Vandegrift of King's orders to capture Tulagi and Guadalcanal, and explained the strategic reasons for doing so. In place of his absent 7th Marines, Vandegrift would be assigned the 2d Marines, presently staging at San Diego. He would also be given the Marine Raider Battalion, the Marine Parachute Battalion, who had yet to make a combat jump, and various other elements of engineers, tanks, amphibious tractors and drivers, medics, and communicators—none of whom were on hand at the moment. And, Ghormley added, Guadalcanal would hereafter be referred to by its code name "Cactus." Then Ghormley dropped the bomb. D-day on Cactus would be 1 August—just five weeks hence. It was like commissioning Michelangelo on Thanksgiving Day to paint the Sistine Chapel ceiling in time for Christmas.

Vandegrift has recorded that words failed him. (Where the hell was Tulagi? he silently wondered.) He had no maps of the Solomons, no up-to-date charts of the surrounding waters, no intelligence estimates of enemy strength or disposition. His men had left the States taut and trim but had softened aboard ship. His second echelon was still at sea, not to arrive for another two weeks. Furthermore, even as he pondered, his troops back in Wellington were struggling to unload the cargo ships that contained the division's supplies, equipment, and weapons. It had been pouring rain for days in Wellington, and the New Zealand dock workers union had forbidden their "wharfies" to unload in inclement weather. As a consequence, Vandegrift's men were working a twenty-four-hour schedule, operating the cargo winches, humping the bags, crates, and boxes off of the pallets and stacking them on the dock. In the cold, soaking downpour, hundreds of boxes came unglued and fell apart. The scene—slanting rain under dim dock lights—soon became a Dali-esque quagmire of sodden corn flakes, trampled chocolate bars, and mountains of soggy clothing. One dripping, shivering marine scrawled his sentiments on a latrine wall for posterity: "All wharfees is bastards!"[11]

A Caveat of Iron

Once back in Wellington it was immediately clear to Vandegrift that in no way could he make good on his Cactus assault date. He asked for and got a six-day extension from King, but with a caveat of iron: the 1st Marine Division would hit the Guadalcanal beaches at dawn on 7 August, the Chief of Naval Operations said, or Vandegrift and staff would have failed in their duty to King and country. The awful deadline pressure now took its toll. No item could be brought aboard that was not essential to living and fighting for the first days ashore. The division's gear and provisions would be pared to the bone. All excess clothing and equipment would be stored in Wellington, including most of the heavy vehicles. Even ammunition was cut back to ten days' reserve in expectation of speedy resupply—far too optimistic an assumption, as it turned out.

One cheerful bit of news did reach Vandegrift. General MacArthur's intelligence chief in Australia had assembled a detailed aerial map of Guadalcanal from photo-recon studies of the island's landing beach and was sending it to Vandegrift. But the jinx was still working. The photomap, packed in boxes and mailed from Australia to New Zealand, was wrongly addressed and wound up in the dead letter department of the Auckland post office. Vandegrift's intelligence section would have to fall back on its collection of century old British Admiralty charts, and the hand-drawn maps made for marine intelligence in Australia by former Guadalcanal residents.

The 1st Marine Division, seventeen thousand strong, filed aboard troop transports, cast off hawsers, and eased out of Wellington Harbor on 22 July 1942. The convoy was led by the flagship of Kelly Turner, the brilliant, peppery admiral who commanded the transports and escorting warships of what was designated "the amphibious force." Turner was Vandegrift's commanding officer. Where the convoy was headed only they knew, but fresh rumors swept the decks every hour, one to the effect that the convoy would make for European waters, where the 1st Marine Division would be brigaded with Russia's Red Army for an assault on Germany.[12]

Four days later the convoy rendezvoused at sea with an aircraft carrier task force commanded by Vice Adm. Frank Jack Fletcher and meant to provide the crucial air umbrella for the Guadalcanal landings. Fletcher, who reported to Ghormley, was Turner's boss, making for an awkward command structure. If Vandegrift wanted to query Ghormley, his question was bicycled from Turner at sea to Fletcher at sea to Ghormley at Noumea —and Ghormley's response was routed back via the same zigzag channel.

The two task forces had met in the waters offshore of Koro, an obscure isle in the Fijis, for the purpose of rehearsing the 7 August landing on Guadalcanal. The rehearsal was a shambles. Navy tide tables for the area proved useless, and the marines' landing craft grounded on the island's barrier reef, banging in their bottoms and denting their propellers. In the end, the rehearsal was called off in hopes that all would come right on the day. Following the debacle, Fletcher called a meeting aboard his flagship attended by Vandegrift, Turner, and Ghormley's chief of staff, Ghormley being too busy to come.

How long, Fletcher asked, would it take to unload the marines and their baggage at Cactus?

About five days, declared Turner.

"Fletcher then stated that he would withdraw his carriers—the Marines' crucial air umbrella—from the Solomons after two days because of danger of air attacks against his ships, and because of the fuel situation; if the troops could not be landed in two days then they should not be landed. In any case, he would depart at that time."[13]

Once again, Vandegrift could not believe his ears. He pleaded for more time. Fletcher begrudged him one more day, then declared the meeting adjourned.

CHAPTER TWO

Thrust! Withdraw!
Horizontal Butt Stroke!

LATE IN THE AFTERNOON of 31 July the combined U.S. task forces, now under the flag of Vice Adm. Frank Jack Fletcher, heaved up their anchors and stood out from the island of Koro on a spurious heading of southwest, in hopes of deluding any snooping Japanese submarine or scouting aircraft into thinking that they were Australia-bound. Fletcher's armada was the largest and mightiest ever assembled for the purpose of landing on a hostile shore,[1] and this knowledge buoyed the spirits of the thousands of marines sweltering in the armada's fat and vulnerable transports. It helped anesthetize their fear, the rancid lump that lay in the pit of each man's stomach and was his constant companion—fear not only of death or mutilation but also of the unknown, and how well or poorly he would acquit himself in combat among his peers.

Lounging in small groups on the hot transport decks, the shirtless young marines fought their angst in the same way that warriors have always dealt with fear on the approach of battle. They looked to their weapons—field-stripped, cleaned, oiled, and reassembled them, honed their bayonets to a needle point, and slathered each cartridge with grease to prevent jamming. The weapons themselves were totems against fear; it was second nature for a marine to regard his rifle not only as an extension of his arm but also as the holiest of objects. While they fussed with their weapons, the talk flowed. Much of it was about sex: who did what, where and when, with which girl, how was she persuaded, did she like it, how many times did they do it, and would the teller mind divulging her address and phone number for the benefit of his buddies home on leave. At seventeen and eighteen, the youngest of the marines were probably virgins (this was 1942), but they nonetheless had their tales to tell. All of them knew that most of what they were hearing was wishful thinking, but it distracted their minds from the great question mark toward which the transports churned. Another favorite topic was the enemy— the "Japs," "Nips," or "Shambos." Were they really little twerps with thick glasses, and such lousy shots? Were they as tricky as rumored? Did they play dead, then rise up and shoot you in the back? Were they as good with the bayonet as they looked in the newsreels? ("They have those big hooks on their bayonet hilts to twist your rifle out of your hands!") At this mention, one of them would invariably leap to his feet, grab his rifle, and with manic energy run through the marine bayonet drill, yelling, "Thrust, withdraw, horizontal butt stroke, slash, vertical butt stroke, smash!" while his chums looked on approvingly.

"I'm gonna get me some Jap gold teeth and make a necklace," boasted one marine.

"I'm gonna take back some ears," promised another. "Pickled!"

"What'll you do if a Jap jumps out of a tree on you?" someone asked.

"Kick him in the balls!" was the answer.

Someone else was sure to ask if it were true that the Japanese brought prostitutes with them to battle, and another round of enthusiastic sex talk would start up.

At night on the blacked-out decks in the cool wind of passage the talk hushed down. From various directions came the occasional wheeze of a mouth organ and the sounds of singing:

Ship me over, Sergeant Major, ship me over
I'm a fightin' son-of-a-bitch!

As we go marching, and the band begins to P-L-A-Y,
You can hear them shouting, "The Raggedy-ass Marines are on parade!"

Belowdecks a marine officer in charge of planning told Richard Tregaskis, a news wire service correspondent, that the landing would probably be hotly contested. One man in four, he estimated, would become a casualty. A colonel briefing his officers read from an intelligence report that stated that the Japanese were on Guadalcanal in force, equipped with artillery and automatic weapons. But, he told his audience, there will be concentrated naval gunfire on the beach before we land, and dive-bomber attacks against Japanese shore installations, launched from Fletcher's carriers. Next, a lieutenant stood up and read out General Order Number Three, specifying that marine graves would be suitably marked and all bodies must bear identification tags. The colonel then gave his officers a chalk talk about the hazards they would face on hitting the beach. There is only one way to do it, he told them. Get out of the boat, yell "Follow me," run like hell, and take your people with you. The colonel concluded his remarks by emphasizing that the whole world was watching them, and they must not fail.[2]

Down in one of the steamy holds under a dim light, a first lieutenant was filling in his machine-gunners on last-minute details of the D-day assault plan. When he had finished, he paused, grinned, and suggested they take along a change of skivvies. Everyone laughed. Noncoms were more blunt about it. "When the shooting starts," they advised their men, "keep a tight asshole."

On 5 August the task force abandoned caution and headed north for Guadalcanal. The following day, D-day minus one, Frank Jack Fletcher's three carriers, the USS Enterprise, USS Saratoga, and USS Wasp, with their support vessels, eased away from the convoy and stationed themselves one hundred miles south of Guadalcanal, close enough to provide air cover for the marine landings but far enough from the Japanese airfields at Rabaul to be beyond reach of their dive bombers and torpedo planes. The transports and their escorts, slipping through the South Pacific night under a squally overcast, continued to close on Guadalcanal and Tulagi.

In the predawn hours of Friday, 7 August, the convoy tiptoed silently around Cape Esperance at the northwestern corner of Guadalcanal and split into two assault forces. The smaller would veer northward across Sealark Channel to assault Tulagi and its tiny satellite islands of Gavutu and Tanambogo, neither of them much bigger than a city block. The larger force would drop anchor four and one-half miles offshore of Guadalcanal in what would soon become known as "Iron Bottom Sound" and ready itself for the morning's work. It would be the first amphibious assault by American troops since the landing at Vera Cruz in 1914. The Tulagi landings were reckoned by Major General Vandegrift and his staff to be relatively easy and would be undertaken by a mixed force that included the 1st Marine Raider Battalion; the 2d Battalion, 5th Marines; the 1st Marine Parachute Battalion; and the 2d Marines. But according to Vandegrift's latest intelligence estimate, the assault on Guadalcanal would be opposed by as many as five thousand veteran Japanese infantry, against which he would pit his unblooded rifle regiments. And for all Vandegrift knew, the enemy would confront his young American marines at the water's edge and drive them back into the surf on their bayonet points! This he would find out at 9:10 the next morning when the first assault craft grounded on the sands of Guadalcanal. If, during the long watches of that fearful and oppressive night, Archer Vandegrift spoke to his Maker, his words may have echoed those of another troubled commander on the eve of his own historic battle, Henry V at Agincourt, who prayed:

> O God of battles! Steel my soldiers' hearts;
> Possess them not with fear; take from them now
> The sense of reckoning, if the opposed numbers
> Pluck their hearts from them . . .

Start Engines

At 6:14 A.M. on 7 August 1942, at the bivouac of the 13th Japanese Naval Construction Unit on Guadalcanal, there arrived a shrilling in the air, a vindictive orange flash and a hovering incubus of smoke, then another and another as a salvo of 8-inch shells from the heavy cruiser *Quincy* plowed up the tent camp's topsoil and sent the palm fronds flying. Within minutes all of the assault force's guns had registered on their assigned targets, and the booming of naval cannon merged with the crash of incoming shells into one continuous hell's orchestra of sound. The men of the 13th Construction Unit, most of whom were there not to fight but to build an airstrip, dropped everything, sprinted for the safety of the jungle, and vanished into its tangled green twilight.

An hour earlier, Fletcher's carriers had swung into the wind to launch aircraft. "Start engines!" rasped the loudspeakers. Several dozen F4F Wildcats and Douglas SBDs, their canopies pushed back and the cloth-helmeted heads of their pilots and aircrews silhouetted against the faint loom of dawn, barked clouds of exhaust smoke until their plugs burned clean and their three-bladed props revved smoothly into yellow-banded disks.

The Wildcats and SBDs had flown against the Zeros before at the Battles of Coral Sea and Midway. The SBDs (Scout, Bomber, Douglas—the latter the manufacturer's name), having learned the hard way that in union there is strength, would fly in tight, stepped-up formations to bring the concentrated fire of their rear-facing gunners to bear on the flashing, banking, skidding Zeros. Built like a fire hydrant, the sturdy dive bomber could soak up a lot of lead before it quit flying, and the steel shield behind the front seat made life sweeter for the pilot, improving his concentration on the job at hand—delivering his bomb to the target. Japanese warships under dive-bomber attack would jink and curl, and hitting them required finesse. In the words of one SBD pilot, it was like trying to drop a marble on a scared mouse from eye level. He could have added, "while the mouse is shooting back." After its howling, ear-popping dive from two miles up and its bomb release at two thousand feet, each SBD was on its own, streaking naked across the wave tops, hell-bent for home. That was when the Zeros dropped like falcons on the lone aircraft and its crew. Many SBDs never returned, and others hobbled back to the carriers barely ticking over, their wounded pilots fainting with pain, their rear gunners slumped dead in their bucket seats behind the twin 30-caliber Brownings—or, lost and their fuel tanks empty, they ditched in the sea, scrambled out of the sinking aircraft, and inflated their yellow life rafts. Some were spotted hours or days later and picked up by searching PBY "Dumbos," but many were not, instead ending their days as tiny specks bobbing in the Pacific ocean fastness, dead of thirst and exposure.

The F4F fighter played a different role. It was meant to engage and destroy the fabled Japanese Zero. For this task it was singularly ill designed. Its adversary, the Zero, was fully one-third lighter than the Wildcat, could climb like a homesick angel, and could turn so tightly that a 360-degree tail chase that began with the Wildcat behind the Zero would end with the Zero behind the Wildcat, all guns blinking. But for this weight advantage the Zero pilot often paid with his life. His aircraft had neither self-sealing gas tanks nor an armored pilot's seat. Both had been sacrificed in the interests of speed and maneuverability. It was thought in Japan's aeronautical circles that the pilot's superior skill and his sense of divine mission would make up the difference. Indeed, the Japanese fighter pilots of this early period were the world's most experienced, some with thousands of hours of combat time over China. They had trained like olympic gymnasts, somersaulting from a high diving board to the ground, swimming underwater for a minute and a half, supporting their weight with one hand for ten minutes while hanging from a vertical pole, and wrestling in matches where the loser was summarily dismissed from the program.[3] In a typical flight training syllabus, one that could take as long as seven years, two-thirds of the hopefuls were weeded out before graduation day. By contrast, U.S. Navy fighter pilots, so desperately needed in the Pacific war theater, received only twenty-four months of training, and some entered combat with as few as 225 solo hours in their flight logs. But they were proud and determined. And at Guadalcanal they learned to make the most of the Wildcat's strengths and to minimize its weaknesses. The cardinal principle was never to go one on one with the Zero. Rely instead on hit-and-run tactics—a diving pass at the enemy aircraft from out of the brassy Pacific sun, a burst of fire at the unprotected pilot or his gas tanks, and a quick getaway. When properly stitched by the F4F's sextet of 50-caliber machine guns, the gossamer Zero flew apart in its attacker's face or blossomed into an orange fireball; whereas the Wildcat, slower and clumsier by virtue of its sturdiness, could take a carnal pounding from the Zero's guns and still fly (Wildcat pilots alluded to their aircraft's manufacturer, Grumman, as the "Grumman Iron Works"). Many an F4F flew jauntily home after a bullet riddling that would have demolished a Zero on the spot, a classic example of tortoise versus hare. The Wildcat's self-sealing gas tanks were reasonable proof against fire, and its thankful pilot, shielded by the heavy armor behind his seat, would live to fight another day. Even so, the aircraft was not imperishable, and a great many F4Fs and their pilots were lost.

From the decks of the *Enterprise, Saratoga,* and *Wasp* that cool August morning rose the SBDs and the Wildcats that would batter Tulagi's shore installations, bomb and strafe Japanese strongholds near Beach Red on Guadalcanal, and establish a protective air umbrella over the marine landing force. Their arrival over Tulagi, Gavutu, and Tanambogo came as a complete surprise to the Japanese garrison. Most of its seaplane squadron was machine-gunned and sunk on its moorings, and the few Japanese float planes—"Petes" and "Rufes"—that tried to launch were flamed like kitchen matches by the scorching tracers of the Wildcats before they could lift off. The beached pilots of the sunken float planes would pick up rifles and fight as infantrymen alongside the island's garrison. Taking hastily to the airwaves, the Tulagi radio operator informed Rabaul: "Enemy landing at Tulagi in great strength. We will defend to the last man. Pray for our success on the field of battle."

Australian coastwatcher Martin Clemens at his hideaway in the Guadalcanal hills awoke at dawn to the rip-snarl of diving SBDs and the thudding of naval cannon. He snatched up his binoculars, but his view of the task force was blocked by Guadalcanal's Koli Point. Twiddling his radio dials, he could hear the carrier pilots' eager chatter and the voices of airborne spotters adjusting naval gunfire. "Calloo, callay, oh what a day!" Clemens recorded in his journal. "I hear Tulagi is taken and the marines have landed on Gavutu. Wizard!" His long and lonely vigil was over.

Land the Landing Force

At 6:41 A.M. there sounded over the loud speakers of the transports the scalp-tingling summons to battle that the Marine Corps would hear again and again for the next two and a half years until the Pacific war was won: "Now hear this—land the landing force." The men of the 1st Marine Division began shuffling from their crammed-together assembly stations on deck toward the landing craft that would carry them to Guadalcanal's Beach Red. There was no overt excitement and little talk. The marines had already done what needed doing—written letters to parents, wives, and girlfriends, knelt at divine service, seen to their weapons with exquisite care, helped one another shrug into harness—and now they moved slowly forward, heavy with the accoutrements of their trade.

They were dressed for battle in faded sage green, herringbone dungarees (today called "utilities"): loose fitting pants and jackets with copper buttons, large side pockets, and a breast pocket on which was stenciled in black the Marine Corps eagle, globe, and anchor over the initials USMC. Their pants were tucked into tan canvas leggings that laced around their calves and covered their boondocker tops like spats. Hung, slung, and strapped on their persons were two full canteens, a belt of six-round clips of 30-06-caliber ammunition, a blued-steel bayonet, grenades, entrenching tool, first-aid kit, toothbrush for rifle cleaning, combat knapsack containing extra socks, skivvies, picture of wife or girlfriend, and food rations that included several cigarettes, a bite-resistant chocolate bar, and yellow powder for making a doubtful kind of lemonade. Also carried was a mess kit, Zippo cigarette lighter, shelter half, poncho, and blanket. On one shoulder was slung their weapon, a nine-pound 30-06-caliber Springfield bolt-action rifle patented in 1903 and beloved by the Marine Corps, or a 30-06-caliber Browning automatic rifle, also venerated by the Corps and referred to as a "BAR," weighing twenty-one pounds with bipod and flash hider, plus six twenty-round magazines carried in pouches on a web belt. On the heads of most rode one of the new pot-style helmets, but a few units still wore the basin-shaped World War I "tin hats." The average marine rifleman's burden came to approximately fifty pounds. Weapons specialists carried more—machine-gun barrels, tripods, and ammo boxes, 60- and 81-millimeter mortar tubes, shells, and base plates.[4] Day-to-day survival as a nineteen-year-old World War II marine infantryman was not so much a question of brawn but of how much physical punishment you could take, and for how long, without collapsing. Few did. It would have meant letting down their friends.

The Higgins boats were swung out on booms and lowered to the water, where they clustered and bumped like big water beetles around the sheer sides of the transports. Each flew a small U.S. flag at its stern. On the transports, the cargo nets were flung over the side and uncoiled themselves to the water line with a splash. Down these perversely swaying, sagging webs of hemp clambered the burdened marines, their equipment bumping and shifting, each man trying not to step on the fingers of the man below and hoping the man above would extend the same courtesy. It was stickier yet at the bottom. Release of the net had to coincide with the downward plunge of the bobbing boat. If, alas, you met the boat coming up it could mean a broken ankle, or perhaps a visit to the wonders of the ocean floor.

As the marines struggled down the cargo nets, a swelling cadenza of battle sounds smote their ears. Higgins boat engines thrummed and burbled as their coxswains jockeyed for position. Ships' loudspeakers crackled with indistinct commands ("marine garbage detail, lay aft"). Men on all sides muttered profanity, prayer, and the F-word. From the escorting warships erupted *barooms* of naval gunfire, followed by visible shock waves and the whooping of 8-inch shells on their way to the beach, then a succession of distant *clump-clump-clumps* as the shellbursts stomped along the tree line like giant footsteps. Audible over the din were grace notes—the yapping of the rapid-fire 20-millimeter cannon and the staccato *tak-tak-tak* of the 50-caliber machine guns as their smoking tracers arched shoreward, probing for targets. At intervals could be heard the whistle of the SBDs' perforated dive brakes and the basso *ba-boom* of their 1,000-pound bombs cratering the strike zone.

Landing Unopposed

At the end of the second hour the ear-banging overture sputtered out.
The Higgins boats and amphibious tractors with their tense, adrenaline-
pumping passengers opened their throttles and churned in line-abreast
waves toward Beach Red, leaving windrows of white wakes in the aquamarine water. To Vandegrift's enormous relief, none of the problems that
had afflicted the Koro rehearsal reoccurred on this day of days. No reefs
tore out the bottoms of the landing craft and mangled their propellers,
no boats capsized or conked out five hundred yards from shore. Best of
all, and most thought provoking, there was no return fire. Braced in one
of the landing craft, Lt. Col. Merrill Twining, Vandegrift's assistant operations officer, lowered his binoculars, turned to his crouching, adrenaline-
pumping marines, and said, "There goes the signal from Hunt's boys.
Landing unopposed!"[5] The war gods had granted Vandegrift the most
precious of military advantages: total surprise. Eight months to the day
after Pearl Harbor, Vandegrift's marines had hit the beach on the Japanese
held island of Guadalcanal—standing up.

Rabaul reacted instantly. The moment Tulagi's dramatic radio message
hit his desk, Vice Adm. Gunichi Mikawa, whose responsibility it was to
oversee Guadalcanal operations, began assembling a naval striking force
for rendezvous at Rabaul and immediate redeployment to Guadalcanal
waters. Simultaneously, the general commanding the 25th Air Flotilla at
nearby Vunakanau ordered his planes to scratch their pending raid on
Milne Bay, New Guinea, and head for Guadalcanal, there to bomb and
sink the U.S. transports and their escorts. All submarines were directed to
concentrate on the Solomons. The Americans were to be swatted like flies.

Ashore on Beach Red, the still-suspicious 5th Marines began staking out
a beachhead perimeter and extending it westward toward the Lunga River
delta. The 1st Marines, landing in the next few waves, filtered through
them and into the jungle, heading for Mount Austen, a brooding eminence
to the south that appeared to dominate the airfield. Identified on marine
maps as "Grassy Knoll" and thought to be two miles inland, it turned out
to be several times that distance over hell's own acreage of tangled, gullied
rain forest. It was the marines' first encounter with General Jungle. Before

long they would also meet General Rain, General Mud, and General Malaria. Heavily laden, out of shape after their long sea voyage, scant of water and salt pills, the 1st Marines bogged down far short of "Grassy Knoll" and dug in for a night of formless fears and mosquito slapping (hoarse whisper by platoon sergeant: "Don't slap for Chrissakes, you'll give away your position!" followed by more uncontrollable slapping, then, "Goddammit, you ate today. Now let them!"). No contact had been made with the Japanese.

Half a mile west of Beach Red, the 1st Battalion of the 5th Marines under Col. LeRoy Hunt were also struggling with heat, humidity, and their imaginations. Ordered to push westward toward the Lunga River delta, they found it heavy going, due partly to the terrain but mostly to their excessive caution. It seemed to the jumpy nineteen year olds that the jungle had a thousand eyes and teemed with shadowy, flitting Japanese, on which apparitions the spooked marines wasted good government ammunition. In spite of these distractions, Hunt's marines by nightfall had reached and dug in at their first objective, the east bank of a tepid, murky backwater called Alligator Creek. Vandegrift was less than pleased by their performance and blistered the 1st Battalion command for its timidity.

Twenty-four Bombers Headed Yours

The Japanese air strike ordered that morning by Admiral Mikawa at Rabaul consisted of twenty-four Betty bombers and seventeen Zero fighters. They lifted off their runways at 9:30, pointed their noses at Guadalcanal, and trimmed for a slow climb. Cruising at 180 knots, the formation would arrive at Iron Bottom Sound around noon. By 10:30 they were over the south coast of Bougainville. Sixteen thousand feet below them, Australian coastwatcher Paul Mason heard the distant droning, counted the stately V formations of Japanese aircraft through his binoculars, and radioed to anyone listening, "From STO [Mason's code name], twenty-four bombers headed yours." His message was picked up by Nimitz's powerful receiver at Pearl Harbor and relayed to the fleet. When the Australian cruiser *Canberra* on picket duty near Guadalcanal received the transmission, its loudspeakers announced matter-of-factly, "The ship will be attacked at noon by twenty-four torpedo bombers. All hands will pipe to dinner at eleven o'clock."[6]

Back on the beach, the logistical situation had gotten out of hand. Tall stacks of crated equipment, gasoline drums, and boxes of supplies had piled up faster than they could be hauled inland, until all sixteen hundred yards of Beach Red resembled a monster garage sale. Confused navy coxswains brought boatloads of aviation fuel to landing zones reserved for medical supplies, and foodstuffs to the ammunition dump. Scores of Higgins boats loaded to the gunwales with essential cargos bobbed offshore, waiting for a place to unload. The three-hundred-man shore party sweated far into the moist tropical night but made scarcely a dent.[7] It would be days before the mess was sorted out.

Like a Gangfight in West Chicago

The air battle for Guadalcanal began shortly after noon on D-day and continued around the clock for six months. All morning on 7 August combat air patrols of Wildcats from Fletcher's carriers had flown sentry duty in the overcast sky above Admiral Turner's transports in Iron Bottom Sound. At 12:30 P.M. the radar operator of the cruiser USS *Chicago* picked up some oncoming blips forty-five miles out and sounded the alarm. Lt. Cdr. Lou Bauer, division leader of the *Enterprise* combat air patrol on station over Iron Bottom Sound, was advised of the approaching bogies and given a heading meant to vector his four-plane division onto a collision course with the approaching Japanese bombers. It did not. Instead, it sent them straight back to the carrier task force. The fighter director officer had muddled his reading of the radar scope.

While Bauer and company headed back, wondering what the hell was going on, a second four-plane division of Wildcats was dispatched from the *Enterprise* to Iron Bottom Sound to replace Bauer's. As they approached at sixteen thousand feet—"Angels 16"—each man performed the fighter pilot's ritual head dance: look up, look down, glance right, glance left, as if trying to free up a stiff neck. At 1:10, the ritual paid off. "Tally ho!" one of them exclaimed into his throat mike, and there were the Japanese, barely visible motes in the immense Pacific sky, twenty-four Betty bombers arrayed in a constellation of Vs and shepherded by many Zeros. The four Wildcats banked in unison, shoved throttles to the stops, flicked on their electric gunsights, and dived to the attack. What followed was like a gang-fight in west Chicago. The Wildcats slashed through the Betty formation at a relative closing speed of five hundred knots, pulled up in a wing-over, then curled back to strike again while the brown-bodied, yellow-winged Zeros swarmed around them like killer bees, pumping bullets and 20-millimeter cannon shells into the lead-absorbent F4Fs. The action took place with such frenetic video-game swiftness that no single pilot saw it whole. Each was able to snatch only glimpses of his target, of his own tracers darting forward, of his hard-pressed wingman, of smoking tracers streaming past his own canopy, of the sky below, the sea above, or the vertical horizon as the opposing teams of fighters scuffled across the heavens.[8] On the ground the antiaircraft guns fell silent and an audience of thousands craned their necks to watch the show, hoping each time one of the tiny aircraft fell blazing from the firmament that it was one of theirs, not ours.

The Ordeal of Pug Southerland

Lt. "Pug" Southerland of *Saratoga*'s Fighting-5 group was one of the Wild-cat pilots in the swirling melee. In two diving runs against the Bettys he had left a pair of them smoking and exhausted his ammunition. His four-plane division had then been "bounced" by Zeros, who shot down two of Southerland's wing mates. The other *Saratoga* division in the scrap had riddled two more Bettys before losing two of their own number to the Zeros. Of the four downed Wildcat pilots, only one escaped death.

Southerland, his gun boxes empty, found himself defenseless among the gladiators and dived away but was set upon by yet another Zero. The Japanese pilot clung to Southerland's tail, firing burst after burst into the Wildcat's vitals without noticeable effect on plane or occupant. Souther-land had lowered his seat, slid his lanky frame forward, and hunkered down behind the seat's steel-plated back, against which the Zero's bullets bonged impotently. A moment later the Zero was joined by two mates who took turns diving at Southerland's F4F with all guns spurting, but the

American continued to cheat death by second-guessing their approaches and presenting them each time with his tattered derriere, or turning across their flight path, giving them a maximum deflection shot, the most difficult of all aerial gunnery angles. Then the firing ceased as Southerland's three tormentors fell back to make room for one of Japan's leading aces— Saburo Sakai, a fighter pilot with fifty-six verified kills. It was he who had given the United States its first posthumous Medal of Honor winner of World War II: Capt. Colin Kelly's B-17 had fallen under Sakai's guns in the Philippines.

Now Sakai prepared to create another posthumous U.S. hero. But Southerland wasn't buying it, and he set out to give the Japanese ace a few lessons in the art of evasion. This he did so expertly that in five passes Sakai was unable to fire a single round. Southerland, anticipating the other's every gambit, simply refused to appear in Sakai's gunsight while continuing to plod on toward Guadalcanal in his see-through Wildcat. After a fifth attack it dawned on the Japanese ace that Southerland was out of ammo and could be approached safely from any angle. Sakai's next pass, therefore, would be the coup de grâce. Before performing it, he pulled up alongside Southerland and shot a photograph with his Leica camera for his trophy collection. Then, dropping back and taking his time, Sakai executed a picture-book pass at Southerland and for the sixth time was faked out by the American. In amazement, Sakai again drew alongside and peered over at Southerland, who showed him his clenched fist and was shown Sakai's fist in return,[9] after which the Japanese ace chose a position from which he could not possibly miss, switched on his pair of 20-millimeter cannon, and fired a killing burst. Sakai saw Southerland's cockpit suddenly puff smoke and flame. An instant later the indestructible American emerged from his demolished Wildcat and pushed off into space. Then Sakai saw Southerland's parachute open and his form swinging safely under the big, white mushroom as it drifted toward the Guadalcanal jungle and came to earth somewhere west of the marine perimeter. Soon after, Southerland was located by a native and guided back to marine lines. In his after-action report he wrote:

> Flaps and radio had been put out of commission. . . . The after part of my fuselage was like a sieve. She was still smoking from [an] incen-

diary [hit] but not on fire. All of the ammunition box covers on my left wing were gone and 20-mm explosives had torn some gaping holes in its upper surface. . . . My instrument panel had been shattered, my rear view mirror was broken, my plexiglass windshield was riddled. The leakproof tanks have apparently been punctured many times as some fuel had leaked down into the bottom of the cockpit even though there was no steady leakage. My oil tank had been punctured and oil was pouring down my right leg and foot.[10]

After the war Sakai would record that Southerland was the most skillful opponent he had ever flown against.

Later that day Sakai himself cheated death. In a rare lapse of judgment, he mistook a flight of TBFs for Wildcats and approached the U.S. formation from behind. The cone of fire from their eight 30-caliber machine guns in the hands of the TBFs' tail gunners sent him spinning toward the sea with multiple wounds that left him nearly blind and in agony. With great effort, Sakai regained control of his Zero at the last moment, and, striking his throbbing head wounds to keep himself from passing out, was able to fly his perforated aircraft back the 565 miles to Rabaul. Sakai's wounds cost him an eye and kept him out of action for two years.

In the first day's air battle for Guadalcanal, half of the U.S. Wildcats were shot out of the sky and several American pilots died. The Japanese lost five Betty bombers, nine Val dive bombers, and two Zeros with their pilots and aircrews. Japanese bombs had damaged one U.S. destroyer, but for all of their skill and aircraft superiority, the Japanese had failed in their mission: they had not derailed the U.S. landing.

Lollypop

By nightfall on 7 August the marines had dug a beachhead perimeter of two- and three-man foxholes and wired themselves in. Each platoon dangled K-ration cans from the barbed wire on its front. The cans contained pebbles that would rattle when disturbed by a creeping Japanese or the occasional wild pig, stray cow, or other 'Canal fauna. Fire lanes for machine guns and BARs were cut through the undergrowth and stakes pounded into the ground on either side of the machine guns to limit their traverse, a precaution against firing down the marine line in the bedlam of a night attack.

When everything had settled down, the password was circulated. Marine folklore had it that the Japanese could not pronounce the letter "L," as in "London." Instead, they said "Rondon." Accordingly, the password for the first night ashore was "Lollypop," and the countersign was "Lollygag."[11] The ridiculous words, passed sotto voce down the line of foxholes in the jungle dusk, heightened the sense of unreality felt by the edgy nineteen year olds. All of them had volunteered to be there (the Marine Corps accepted only volunteers), but this was no help at the moment. From the surrounding jungle came the squawks and screeches of a Tarzan movie, a cosmic humming of mosquitoes, and the distant grunt of a bull crocodile. Robert Leckie describes the experience in his book *Helmet for My Pillow*: "It was darkness without time. It was an impenetrable darkness. To the right and the left of me rose up those terrible formless things of my imagination, which I could not see, but I dared not close my eyes lest the darkness crawl beneath my eyelids and suffocate me. I could hear the enemy everywhere about me, whispering to each other and calling my name."

It came as a welcome relief to hear the parade ground bellow of a marine colonel ripping strips from a rifleman who had noisily left his foxhole to fill his canteen in a stream. "The next son-of-a-bitch I hear," yelled the colonel, "I will personally blow his goddamn head off!"[12] Two of Vandegrift's men died that night, both killed by friendly fire. One was a navy medical corpsman who left his foxhole to relieve himself. The other was a sergeant in L Company, 5th Marines, shot dead by a jittery sentry.

We'll Get Your Body Out

To everyone's surprise the 7 August assault on little Tulagi by the 1st Marine Raider Battalion and the 2d Battalion, 5th Marines had been everything that the Guadalcanal landing was not—a bloody showdown between combat-hardened Japanese troops and highly motivated but unblooded Americans. It began favorably enough. The landing beach at Tulagi was undefended,

except for a lone sniper who brought down one marine before being fer-
reted out and killed.[13] The northern half of the two-mile-long island was
then reconnoitered by the 2d Battalion, 5th Marines without a shot being
fired. But the marine Raider columns fared otherwise. Their orders were
to head south through the jungle gloom toward the knobby hills at Tulagi's
southern tip and secure that end of the island. When they emerged from
the rain forest, blinking in the sunlight, the manure hit the fan.

In happier colonial days, Tulagi had been the seat of the British Solomon
Islands Protectorate, complete with an imposing residency, cricket pitch,
and, curiously, an insane asylum.[14] It was here that the Raiders exited the
jungle; and it was the high ground just beyond this abandoned settlement
that the Japanese had chosen to defend. From it, they could look down
the throats of the advancing marines. Tucked away in the steep-sided hill
were several dozen man-made caves and rock embrasures concealing
machine guns with mutually supporting fields of fire. Verifying this fact
cost the Raiders their next five casualties. D Company's commander was
critically wounded, and a young navy doctor, Lt. Samuel Miles, was sniped
and killed as he worked over three fallen marines. It was Japanese military doctrine to use wounded marines as bait, sniping one and waiting
for another to come to his aid. Then the rescuer was himself sniped, and
the deadly game extended. Unless it struck a vital organ, a slug from the
6.5-millimeter Japanese Arisaka rifle or 7.7-millimeter Nambu machine
gun was more apt to wound than kill, which was consistent with the
Japanese practice of encumbering the enemy with the care and feeding
of as many wounded as possible. Ironically, this tactic thrived on the
promise made by the Marine Corps to every marine: if you are wounded,
we'll get you out; if you are killed, we'll get your body out. Many marines
were killed or wounded making good on this commitment, but the Marine
Corps seldom broke its promise. The knowledge was comforting, and one
of the many things that bonded marines together in and out of battle.

Stymied for the moment by the Japanese defenses and the failing light,
the Raiders' commander, "Red Mike" Edson, chose to dig in and renew
the attack at dawn. The Japanese would surely counterattack during the
night, Edson told his marines, so they had better dig deep and stand by

for a ram. Everyone was hungry, but unlike the men on Guadalcanal who had gone ashore with several days' rations in their packs, Edson's Raiders were traveling light. "Don't worry about food," the wolf-eyed Edson had assured them on the eve of the landing. "There's plenty there. Japs eat too. All you have to do is get it!" This was vintage Edson humor. But apart from his flashes of grim levity, the man behind the wolfish eyes was unknowable to most. Richard Tregaskis had this much to say about him in his book, *Guadalcanal Diary*:

> He was a wiry man with a lean hard face, partly covered by a sparse, spiky growth of grayish beard; his light blue eyes were tired and singularly red-rimmed in appearance . . . [and] his red eyebrows and red eyelashes, being almost invisible, heightened the effect. But his eyes were as cold as steel, and it was interesting to notice that even when he was being pleasant they never smiled. He talked rapidly, spitting his words out like bullets, his hard-lipped mouth snapping shut like a trap. Hardly a creature of sunlight and air; but I could see that he was a first-class fighting man.

Counterattack

Edson was right. At 10:30 that night under a pale Pacific moon, the Japanese counterattacked, howling like maniacs from hell. They punched through the Raider lines at the juncture of two companies and surrounded one of them. It was a dirty, gouging, no-quarter alley fight. Leaping and shrieking, the Japanese came at them with long bayonets, samurai swords, hand grenades, and Nambu 8-millimeter pistols. Edson's marines jumped out of their foxholes and met them with bayonets, Colt 45 automatics, steel-reinforced rifle butts, sharpened entrenching tools, thumbs, and fingernails. Six of the attackers crawled under the residency building and fired into the backs of the nearest marines, killing three before they were grenaded to death. Another group fought to within fifty yards of Edson's command post, at which an extraordinary rage rose up in the Raiders and they rallied and drove the Japanese back to where the machine guns could get at them.[15] Three more times the screaming Japanese attacked with the bayonet, and three more times Edson's Raiders checked them at the perimeter before the night battle finally flickered out. Marine casualties were heavy; in the hand-to-hand fighting, one machine-gun company had lost half of its noncommissioned officers.

The sun rose on a grisly still life. Twenty-six Japanese corpses sprawled in the dishevelment of death along the marine perimeter. Already the iridescent-blue flies were bustling noisily around their eyes, nostrils, and mouths. In one of the foxholes lay an American teenager, marine PFC Edward H. Ahrens, BAR-man.[16] His eyes were closed and he was dying. With him in the foxhole were two dead Japanese. Thirteen more lay scattered around his position. Clutched in Ahrens's hand was a Japanese officer's sword. He had been shot twice in the chest and bayoneted. Capt. Lew Walt, his burly commanding officer, gathered Ahrens up to carry him back to the battalion aid station. "Captain," Ahrens whispered, "they tried to come over me last night, but I don't think they made it." "No they didn't, Eddie," Walt said. "No they didn't."

Death Is Lighter Than a Feather

That morning, concerned with mounting casualties in what was supposed to be a mop-up operation, Vandegrift dispatched a battalion of the 2d Marines to Tulagi and committed reserve units to Gavutu and Tanambogo as well. The Marine Parachute Battalion's struggle on these two mini-islands had been even bloodier than the Raiders' experience on Tulagi. Now Edson and his men, stiffened by reinforcements, began the dicey process of cave-busting on the steep hillside overlooking their positions. Each of the concealed strongholds had to be demolished with high explosives, together with its occupants. The Japanese, however, had positioned them so logically that every cave was protected by the supporting machine-gun fire of its neighbors. It was hands-on work, perilous and nerve racking. The men who did it had great sangfroid, were slightly mad, or simply didn't give a damn. It was no good standing off and hurling grenades into the openings—they sailed right out again to explode in the hurlers' faces. Doing the job properly meant slithering up on elbows and knees to one side of a cave entrance under cover of smoke grenades, towing a wooden pole. On the business end of the pole were wired several blocks of fused

TNT. From inside the cave could be heard the sound of Japanese voices. Meanwhile, the riflemen of the attacking squad banged away at the entrance of adjacent caves to keep the occupants' heads down. At the critical moment, assuming the cave buster had survived the stabbing crossfire, he yelled, "Fire in the hole!" and lit the fuse. Some did it stylishly with a cigar butt. The business end of the pole was then thrust into the cave and jammed hard against the side of the entrance, thwarting any attempt by the occupants to eject the fizzing TNT. There followed a hollow explosion, a blast of smoke and debris issued from the entrance, and the voices within fell silent. It was folly, however, for the cave buster to presume the occupants all had perished and go in for a look. Until marines learned better, several were killed by seemingly "dead" Japanese who rose from the tangle of bodies to shoot the perpetrator. The first half-dozen times this scene was enacted, the caves' occupants were invited via megaphone to surrender by the battalion's Japanese-speaking interpreter and were promised safe conduct to the rear. But they invariably chose to die.

This same stoic behavior had puzzled marines the previous day, when the Raiders were threading their way through Tulagi's braided jungle. At intervals from somewhere in their rear was heard the high, flat crack of an Arisaka rifle, and a marine would flop down heavily with a grunt and a 6.5-millimeter slug in his back. Then the column would take cover while the bypassed sniper was sought out and killed, usually in a leafy treetop where he had waited for a going-away shot. It was a career with no future for the sniper. None escaped the marines' wrath and, once spotted, the spraying of his leafy hideaway by a BAR. Then down would tumble his rifle and the sniper would be left hanging by his harness in the treetop, a carnival for flies. This suicidal tactic was routine in the Japanese army, an effective way to delay and demoralize an advancing enemy. It was the marines' first encounter with bushido, the self-sacrificial code of Japan's armed forces. A Japanese soldier was obligated by his culture to chose death in preference to surrender. His surrender would stain not only his own honor but also that of his family, who would become social lepers.

The nineteenth-century Emperor Meiji spelled out this obligation in an Imperial Rescript addressed to Japan's armed forces: "Death is lighter than a feather, duty is heavier than a mountain." The souls of those who died in the service of the emperor would join the hallowed spirits of warriors from ancient times, whose task it was throughout eternity to safeguard the emperor and the nation. It was a useful incentive in the hands of Japan's military commanders, who practiced it themselves. And it worked. Of the estimated one thousand Japanese soldiers on Tulagi, all but three fought to the death. On Gavutu and Tanambogo, defended by five hundred Japanese, there were no survivors. By late afternoon on the second day of the Tulagi-Gavutu-Tanambogo landings all three islands were proclaimed "secure," although a smattering of snipers and cave dwellers remained to be dealt with. Casualties for the two-day campaign were estimated at fifteen hundred to two thousand Japanese killed, not counting those entombed in caves. The Raiders, the Parachute Battalion, and their reinforcing units lost 108 killed in action and 140 wounded.[17]

On Tulagi, Gavutu, and Tanambogo, all of the surviving marines had one thing in common: they were filthy, stubble-bearded, and red-eyed with exhaustion; they stank like goats; the knees and elbows of their dungarees were ripped out from crawling; there were salty white rings under their armpits and on their backs; their hair was plastered to their heads with sweat; their socks were slimy in their boondockers; and their hands and faces were blotched with mosquito bites. But there was another look to them as well, one of quiet élan. They had come ashore as novices, but they stood there now as authentic "Raggedy-ass Marines." And what was reckoned to be a sideshow had become instead a rehearsal for the firestorm battles soon to be fought by the Marine Corps in the Hieronymus Bosch landscapes of Tarawa, Peleliu, and Iwo Jima. Vandegrift, summing up the Tulagi-Gavutu-Tanambogo assault, described it as "a storming operation . . . unremitting and relentless . . . decided by the extermination of one or another of the adversaries engaged. Soldierly behavior was manifest wherever the enemy was encountered . . . and there was an unflinching willingness to accept the . . . hazards of close and sanguinary combat."[18]

Having weathered one crisis, the landing, Vandegrift now faced a second in the form of Fletcher's threat to pull his carriers out in another forty-eight hours. Without Fletcher's protective air umbrella, Turner's thin-skinned, lightly armed transports would be sitting ducks for the bombers and torpedo planes of Japan's 25th Air Flotilla. It was an unacceptable risk, and Turner would be forced to pull the transports and their escorts out as well. But with Turner's fleeing transports would go the weapons, equipment, food, and supplies as yet unloaded—fully a third of Vandegrift's war-making inventory.

CHAPTER THREE

Under New Management

D AY TWO ON Guadalcanal dawned bright and beautiful—fine bombing weather. Coastwatcher Jack Read in his hidey-hole on Bougainville was first to hear the undulating roar of many aircraft engines and looked up to see wave after wave of twin-engine bombers and single-engine torpedo planes flash by close overhead, red circles on their wings, their propeller blades strobing in the sun. Quickly counting them, he raced to his radio shack and transmitted, "Forty-five bombers now going southeast."

In the deep blue waters some one hundred miles south of Guadalcanal, Fletcher's orbiting carriers swung into the wind and launched all available aircraft. Most of them were vectored by the fighter director officer onto a collision course with the oncoming Japanese air strike. The rest would fly protective air cover over the carriers. Aboard his flagship in Iron Bottom Sound, Adm. Kelly Turner passed the word to his transport skippers to stop unloading, up anchor, and find some sea room in which to maneuver. But before the transports and their warship escorts could make good on the order, the Japanese pounced. Turner's gunners had a surprise for them. Unlike the obsolete Chinese, British, and U.S. warships the Japanese airmen had so effortlessly sunk in the heady days leading up to Guadalcanal, Turner's escorting destroyers and cruisers were armed with new antiaircraft guns that would depress to fire point blank at the low-flying torpedo bombers. The Bettys bored in at masthead height, each with its fearsome "Long Lance" torpedo, powerful enough to break a destroyer in half and sink it in two minutes with all souls. But they flew into a vortex of fire and moments later were cartwheeling into the sea or etching black smears across the blue sky as they fell under the guns of Fletcher's diving Wildcats. Two U.S. ships were damaged in the attack, one of them later to be scuttled. Seventeen sailors and marines were killed. Twenty-two Bettys and two Zeros with their pilots and aircrews would never see Rabaul again. All of Fletcher's Wildcats returned safely to their carriers. The Japanese now knew that they were in a war.

Earlier that morning, the 5th Marines, still too cautious for Major General Vandegrift's taste, arrived at the abandoned camp site of the Japanese airfield construction troops. It looked postnuclear. Teacups, chopsticks, and half-filled rice bowls lay where their owners had dropped them and bolted when the first naval salvos arrived in their midst. Lying helter-skelter around the ripped tents and smashed huts were parts of uniforms, helmets, blankets, and rifles, much of which the marines appropriated as souvenirs.

Vandegrift had given the 1st Marines a change of orders. Forget about reaching "Grassy Knoll," he told their CO, and push west toward the Lunga River. In their path lay one of the most precious pieces of real estate in the Pacific: the airstrip. Presumably it would be heavily defended. At 4:00 that afternoon leading elements of the 1st Marines halted in the shade of a coconut grove, peered out into the open, and there before them lay the prize, a dirt-surfaced, east-west airstrip, 2,600 feet long, 150 feet wide, and shimmering in the equatorial heat. An officer with field glasses had a long, careful look. Nothing stirred. Perhaps it was an ambush. A noncom stepped into the open. Nothing happened. He was joined by a few riflemen. Again, nothing happened. The regiment silently deployed, enveloping the runway. Still nothing—no sound but the wind, no enemy movement. The priceless airstrip was deserted. For reasons known only to them, the Japanese had failed to defend one of their most valuable South Pacific assets, and the 1st Marines took it over in a walk. A few days later, Vandegrift would name it "Henderson Field" in memory of marine SBD pilot Lofton Henderson, who died attacking a Japanese carrier in the 3 June Battle of Midway. The dusty little airstrip with its potholes, ruts, and undulations would shortly become the white-hot focal point of one of World War II's most suspenseful dramas.

The airfield securely in hand, two battalions of the 1st Marines pressed on toward the Lunga River delta to see what they could see. Snipers were encountered and sprayed with BARs. Two prisoners were taken and escorted back to where the 1st Division interpreter, Lieutenant Cory, could grill them. Correspondent Richard Tregaskis described them as "a measly lot," adding that they were puny, sallow, and only five feet tall. The prisoners told Cory that they belonged to the naval labor battalion at work on the airstrip. Most of these sad little chaps who kept turning up in the jungle were Koreans, shanghaied into Japan's forced labor battalions. They were given all of the dirty work but did none of the fighting and had no scruples about surrendering. The marines named them "termites." Their interrogation by Cory and the division's intelligence officer, Lt. Col. Frank Goettge, provided Vandegrift with the first indications of enemy strength and whereabouts,[1] including the fact that the labor battalion had been guarded by two hundred well-armed troops of the Special Naval Landing Force (SNLF), the Japanese version of marines. These had yet to be heard from.

At the mouth of the Lunga River, the 1st Marines came upon the second of the day's miracles, an Aladdin's Cave of booty. The inventory included a Japanese electricity plant, an ice-making plant, a huge motor transport pool containing more than one hundred assorted trucks, most of them Japanese knockoffs of Chevrolets, and two tiny gasoline-powered locomotives with hopper cars for hauling landfill, which the marines promptly christened the "Toonerville Trolley" after a popular newspaper cartoon strip of the day. Further exploration revealed a deserted tent city containing hundreds of iron bed frames, baroque French-style telephones, elegant riding boots, a huge shortwave radio transmitter-receiver, bicycles on which a few marines leaped and wobbled off, a prodigious amount of food, including such Japanese delicacies as tinned oysters, marinated plums, crab meat, cases of bubbly pop labeled "Mitsubishi-champagne Cider," and—yahoo!—enough beer, wine, and sake to pickle the regiment. The luckiest find, however, was rice—bags and bags of it. In the months to come, the marines would think themselves lucky to be eating it. An unrecorded quantity of sake and tinned delicacies found their way into dungaree pockets, and some of the other niceties were also put to good use. Letters were written home on Japanese rice paper. A sergeant announced with a straight face that he would conduct classes in flower arrangement, using as his text a splendidly illustrated book that he had liberated. The scholarly Merritt Edson found an English translation of *A Short History of Japan* and, for authenticity of mood, perused it while listening to Japanese records on a hand-cranked phonograph. The official takeover of the ice-making plant was proclaimed by a sign at the front door reading "Tojo Ice Plant, now under new management, J. Genung, Sgt. USMC, Mgr."[2]

At sundown on the second day, twenty-four hours sooner than he had agreed with Turner and Vandegrift, Frank Jack Fletcher turned his back on Guadalcanal and steamed away from the sound of the guns. With Fletcher's carriers went seventy-nine Wildcat fighters and SBD dive bombers, the whole of U.S. air power at Guadalcanal. A critical shortage of flyable aircraft and fuel were the reasons Fletcher gave his superiors for renouncing the fight, but his logs later showed that he had fuel enough to operate for several more days without risk, nor was he seriously short of aircraft. On Fletcher's behalf it can only be said that the three aircraft carriers in his keeping—*Saratoga, Enterprise,* and *Wasp*—represented 75 percent of U.S. naval air power in the Pacific, and Fletcher evidently placed a higher priority on preserving these key assets than he did on supporting the Guadalcanal adventure, of which he was frankly skeptical. Fletcher had already lost the *Lexington* at the Battle of the Coral Sea and the *Yorktown* at Midway. Were he to lose even one more of the three operating U.S. carriers (the Japanese had eight), he could be blamed for handing the enemy a virtually no-contest Pacific victory, opening the door for their invasion of Hawaii and the West Coast of the United States. History would lay rough hands on him. The admiral was between a rock and a hard place, but the Marine Corps found it difficult to forgive him.

Fletcher's departure would trigger an exodus from Guadalcanal of all but the marines, their navy corpsmen, and some shore-based naval detachments. Without Fletcher's air umbrella, Turner had no choice but to flee with his fragile transports and their escorts. With Turner would go eighteen hundred men of the 2d Marine Division as yet unloaded, all of the long-range artillery and earth-moving equipment, and tons of other weaponry, barbed wire, foodstuffs, and ammunition, leaving the orphaned marines with rations enough for just thirty-seven days of two skimpy meals daily, most of it captured Japanese rice, and ammunition for only four days of heavy fighting. Moreover, without Fletcher's fighter cover the marines would be sitting ducks for Japanese air power until they could complete the runway at Henderson Field and fly in marine fighters and dive bombers. The Bettys, Zeros, and Vals would savage them by day, and the Imperial Navy would stand offshore and shell them silly by night. But to Adm. Kelly Turner's eternal credit, he agreed to hang in and unload the transports for one more day, and to hell with the gun-shy Fletcher and his vanishing aircraft carriers. Reticence was not Turner's style. On the eve of his departure he could be heard throughout the camp, making small talk, joking and laughing. And when a Japanese destroyer began lobbing shells ashore in his immediate vicinity, Turner yelled, "What are they doing to my boats? That's what worries me!"

By the time the smoking lamp was declared out on that hot, oppressive evening, the 1st and 5th Marines were dug in along the east bank of the Lunga. They hadn't a clue to what lay on the other side, nor, as the night wore on, what to make of the violent yellow flashes that played like heat lightning along the horizon to the north, or the rolling kettle drum thunder that accompanied them.

Calamity at Sea

What the marines ashore were witnessing was the Battle of Savo Island, the most humiliating defeat in U.S. naval history. A powerful Japanese task force of cruisers and destroyers had slipped undetected through New Georgia Sound, the island-enclosed waterway connecting Bougainville with Guadalcanal, soon to become famous as "the Slot." In the black of night, the Japanese attacked an equally powerful but disorganized and unready American force, the warships whose task it was to guard Turner's precious transports. As they had at Pearl Harbor, the Japanese achieved total surprise, and for the same reason: the U.S. Navy's unpreparedness and what Turner later described as "a fatal lethargy of mind."[3] In "a bar room brawl with all the lights shot out," the Japanese sank four U.S. heavy cruisers and one destroyer, suffering scarcely a dent in return. But their task force commander, Adm. Gunichi Mikawa, then committed a cardinal sin. He took the money and ran. Had Mikawa followed through and sunk Turner's helpless transports as his orders specified, Japan's battle for Guadalcanal would have been won, then and there. Seventeen thousand U.S. Marines would have been starved out, mopped up, and the few survivors taken prisoner. By dawn's early light the surface of Iron Bottom Sound was a black oily soup in which floundered, like wretched sea birds in an oil spill, more than a thousand burned and wounded sailors, together with the bobbing corpses of hundreds more. None of them were Japanese.[4] Combing the wreckage for survivors, the sailors and marines in landing boats shot a dozen sharks busy at their grisly trade. That same day, the citizens of Japan opened their morning papers to headlines that trumpeted the news of a historic victory over the Americans at Guadalcanal. According to the Japanese press, thirty five U.S. vessels—eleven of them crammed with marines—had been sunk by the Imperial Navy. There was still plenty of room at the bottom of the Pacific for more of the U.S. fleet, taunted Tokyo Rose. But Yamamoto, aboard his flagship in Japan's inland sea, was furious with Mikawa for his failure to capitalize on his victory. A shocked Ernie King, on his flagship in the Washington Naval Yard, got the bad news in a radio dispatch from Turner. "That, as far as I was concerned," King later admitted, "was the blackest day of the war."

By 12 August, Vandegrift and his marines had brought some order out of chaos. He had begun by setting out three immediate tasks for the 1st Division. The first was to complete Henderson Field, their reason for being there. The second was to organize a perimeter defense of the airstrip, and the third was to move everything of value within the perimeter—to circle the wagons. This all had to be accomplished with blinding speed, before the Japanese could marshall their considerable South Pacific assets and react with crushing force, which Vandegrift knew would be soon in coming. Due to the 1st Division's slender resources, an offensive was out of the question. For the moment they would have to dig in and settle for aggressive patrolling. In the frenzy of preparation and landing, Vandegrift had come ashore with only the dimmest notion of enemy strength and disposition. Probing by patrols would at least furnish some clues, and perhaps keep the Japanese on their back foot. Just now it appeared that they were somewhere west of him. A patrol thrust in that direction on 10 August had backed off after provoking heavy firepower from the far bank of the Matanikau River, some three miles west of the Lunga.[5] On the same day, the Japanese air-dropped badly aimed packages to their troops, seven of which were recovered by marines. Done up in green wicker baskets with long red tassels, the packages contained tins of goulash, biscuits, candy, maps with directions for attacking Henderson Field, and messages of encouragement. One of them read, "The enemy are collapsing before your eyes . . . relief is near . . . we are convinced of help from heaven and divine grace."

With eighteen thousand yards of beach, jungle, and airfield to defend, no amount of manpower juggling afforded Vandegrift the advantages of an unbroken line of defense. There would have to be huge gaps in his perimeter. Only along the beach and the eastern flank of his establishment were the foxholes within whispering distance of one another. Barbed wire was in short supply, most of it having gone south with Turner. But Vandegrift's marines, like all marines since 1798, were accomplished scroungers and quickly stripped the local cattle fences of enough rusty barbed wire to shore up likely hot spots along the beach and the banks of the Tenaru River. As a result, mooing cattle wandered dreamily in and out of the perimeter day and night, provoking shouts of "Who goes there?" and on one occasion stampeding through 1st Division Headquarters like the climax of a John Wayne western. The rest of the perimeter was defended by a loose network of strongholds, between which night-crawling Japanese could easily slip. Well out in front of the lines and strongholds were lonely listening posts, positioned there to give early warning of an enemy attack. These were manned by jittery marines with one hand on the field telephone and one finger on the trigger. Few survived when a listening post was overrun.

Getting the airfield in shape to land marine fighter and dive bomber squadrons was a gut-busting job for the 1st Marine Engineer Battalion. The Japanese had worked from both ends of the strip toward the middle but had decamped leaving 160 yards of the center unfinished. Vandegrift ordered the battalion to complete the work on a twenty-four-hour schedule, and while they were at it, to lengthen the runway another one thousand feet. As nearly all of their heavy equipment had sailed away with Turner, the marines simply picked up at the point where the Japanese had downed tools and fled, using their abandoned earth tampers, steamrollers, air compressors, hand carts, and shovels, the last two items powered by "marine steam." Thus equipped, marines humped one hundred thousand cubic feet of earth from a nearby ridge to fill the huge hole in the middle of the runway. Japanese troops would later be told by their officers that, if taken prisoner by the marines, they could expect to have their arms and legs cut off and what was left of them flattened on the runway by the marines' captured steamrollers. They had been exposed to similar disinformation in their training manual, which stated that "Westerners—being very haughty, effeminate and cowardly—intensely dislike fighting in the rain or mist or in the dark. They cannot conceive night to be a proper time for battle—though it is excellent for dancing. In these weaknesses lie our great opportunity."[6]

On 12 August, navy lieutenant William Sampson talked himself onto the pages of World War II history by radioing Henderson that his PBY was running rough. Could he please make an emergency landing? "Be our guest," replied the marines, and a few minutes later Sampson set his big Dumbo down on Henderson, the first pilot to land on the world's most newsworthy airfield. He then pronounced the airstrip fit to receive fighters, which was a shade optimistic as Henderson was still a giant mud puddle when it rained and a dustbowl when it didn't. Puzzled marine mechanics found nothing wrong with Sampson's engines and realized they had been conned: Sampson's "rough" engines had cinched him a historical first.[7]

On Friday, the fourteenth, the Japanese inaugurated what would become their daily lunchtime raid on the marine airstrip, announced by the clanging of the air-raid alarm, a battered dinner bell borrowed from one of the deserted coconut plantations. In the absence of Fletcher's carrier-based fighters, nothing stood between the marines and the Japanese bombers overhead but the antiaircraft guns of the 3d Marine Defense Battalion. Col. Robert H. Pepper and his gunners were good at their work, but not magicians, and their best efforts brought down only the odd Betty, although they holed a great many more. Pepper's gunners did, however, breed a healthy enough respect among Betty pilots to keep the bombers at twenty-five thousand feet. From this altitude their bombing of Henderson Field was hit and miss, although lethal enough to any marine caught above ground wherever the bombs landed. Even Vandegrift's 1st Division HQ, located some distance from the airstrip, suffered several close calls and became known as the "Impact Center." In mock desperation at their lack of air support, Pepper's gunners wrote a Christmas letter to the Piper aircraft company, makers of the small puddle-jumping Piper Cub:

From: the Antiaircraft Artillery
To: Mr. Piper, Piper Cub Company U.S.A
Subject: Piper Cub, request for
    Dear Mr. Piper, I hate to bring this to your attention, but we would like one of your little Piper Cub airplanes. We got a pilot but no airplanes. We forgot to bring ours. The Japs got both, real big ones (the airplanes, not the Japs).
    We also got some AA guns, but they is not enough, and too late.
    If you can't help us out please bring this to the attention of Mr. S. Claus. Xmas is only four months away. The Japs is two hours away. Signed,
The A.A. Boys
PS—Do you have any kites?

A *Sub* Named *Oscar*

By way of dramatizing their control of both air and sea, the Japanese began a routine of round-the-clock harassment. To murder sleep, the Imperial Navy flew single-plane sorties over the perimeter in the after-midnight hours, dropping flares and scattering small bombs. The flares turned marine faces a pukey green, and the bombs got everyone up and running for dugouts. There were two of these night visitors—"Louey the Louse" and "Washing Machine Charley," the latter so named because his engine made a churning sound that reminded marines of the washing machine at home in the basement. Japanese destroyers and the occasional cruiser stood arrogantly offshore, just out of artillery range (the marines' heavy guns having left with Turner), and flung random shells into the perimeter. It is marine folklore that this so incensed one of the Corps' most eccentric and terrifying noncoms, M. Gun. Sgt. Lou Diamond, that he set up his 81-millimeter mortar—a hand-carried piece of ordnance not recommended for coastal defense—and registered it on a close-in piece of water used nightly by one of the prowling destroyers. When it sailed into range one dark night, ready to shell the sleeping marines, Diamond astonished its captain and crew by dropping a mortar shell down one of their destroyer's stacks.

But the most provocative harassment was inflicted by a submarine called "Oscar." Oscar would pop up close at hand from the depths of Iron Bottom Sound, and out of its conning tower would spill a half-dozen white-clad figures who would run to Oscar's deck gun and fire off a round or two at the perimeter before tumbling back down the hatch. Oscar would then vanish to pop up somewhere else. Apart from the lethal effect of its shelling, Oscar's surprise performances added a touch of show business to the Japanese routine.

One especially suspenseful episode took place on 12 August, as three small craft manned by marines were chugging across the aquamarine waters of Iron Bottom Sound on their way to Tulagi. They had nearly reached the halfway point when up from the blue depths three thousand yards off their port side rose the sinister black shape of Oscar, glistening in the sunlight like some sea monster come to eat them. The boats' occupants, including two war correspondents, spotted him immediately and shoved throttles to the fire wall, but their effort was feeble compared with the sub's 20-knot surface speed. On came Oscar with a bone in his teeth, rapidly closing the range as the white-clad figures boiled out of the conning tower and ran to the deck gun. Now marines ashore spotted the drama and began shouting encouragement to their fleeing comrades. Suddenly one of the boats' engines coughed blue smoke and lost speed. A watcher ashore, his voice choked with emotion, said, "Jesus, her engine's conked out!" Without hesitation the lead boat chopped its throttle, circled and slid alongside the other, whose frantic occupants scrambled over the gunwales and into their rescuer's boat just as a whistling shell from Oscar geysered the water one hundred yards astern. Another shell screeched close overhead and spouted one hundred yards ahead of them as the rescue boat picked up speed. The tension heightened, with Oscar closing in and shells dropping closer and closer to the fleeing marines until, without warning, four tall waterspouts straddled the submarine and drenched the gunners. In the heat of the chase, Oscar had charged into waters commanded by the 11th Marines' beach defense artillery. A second salvo was nearly on target, prompting the white-clad figures to abandon their deck gun and scramble back down the hatch as the sub's dive warning went *a-ooga, a-ooga,* and Oscar retreated beneath the waves to the cheers of the watching marines.

Swords Flashing in the Morning Sun

On a probe into the unknown country west of the Matanikau River, a marine patrol reported seeing a white flag waving in the distance. This sighting coincided with the testimony of several termites, who had told of starving and demoralized Japanese troops west of the river and ready to surrender. A few days later another patrol in the same area captured a Japanese naval rating. Plied with brandy, he confirmed the termites' story. To the 1st Division intelligence chief, Lt. Col. Frank B. Goettge, it all added up to a possible intelligence breakthrough. If he could coax in an enemy infantry officer or noncom with precise knowledge of Japanese disposition and intentions, he could at last furnish Vandegrift with a reliable picture of what they were up against.

With Vandegrift's reluctant approval, Goettge organized a lightly armed twenty-five-man patrol consisting largely of clerks and intelligence specialists, plus 1st Lt. Ralph Cory, the division's Japanese-language officer, and an adventuresome navy doctor who was itching for excitement. The party set out by boat at dusk on 12 August, skirted the shore, and arrived by moonlight at a beach just beyond the Matanikau. A few yards offshore, the boat grounded on the coral bottom. While several marines tried to rock it free, Goettge hopped over the side and waded to the beach with the rest of the party, including the Japanese informant, who was guarded by Plt. Sgt. Denzil Caltrider. After a brief conference on the beach, Goettge, followed by most of the others, set off through a coconut grove to reconnoiter the ground but had taken only a few steps when a burst of automatic fire struck him in the face, cutting him down. The tree line then erupted in a firestorm of lead. Sergeant Caltrider immediately shot the Japanese naval rating. The navy doctor knelt to aid a wounded marine and was himself shot through the chest.[8] The remaining marines were caught in the open. There was nothing to do but wriggle their bodies into the sand and return the fire. As the hours went by, they were picked off one by one until only the three marines nearest the water's edge were left alive and unwounded. At dawn, when it was obvious that hope was gone, they slipped into the sea and, swimming and crawling over four miles of razor-sharp coral, made their way back to the perimeter, arriving exhausted and gashed from head to foot. One of them, Sgt. Frank L. Few, had looked over his shoulder as he swam away and seen samurai swords flashing in the rising sun as the Japanese hacked the wounded and dead marines to pieces.[9]

The disaster might have been even greater. Lieutenant Cory, the Japanese language specialist, had worked in central U.S. intelligence and was privy to the knowledge that the United States had broken the Japanese code. Had he been taken alive and tortured, he might have revealed one of our most precious wartime secrets. A few days later, a patrol from the 5th Marines investigated the area and found arms and legs sticking out of the sand, marine helmets, and the doctor's empty first aid bag, but before they could return to recover the remains, a fierce storm swept through the Solomons and obliterated all traces of the Goettge patrol's fate. The white flag glimpsed by the earlier patrol may have been simply a Japanese battle flag, its red circle folded inward, and not a flag of surrender. But Guadalcanal marines believe to this day that the Goettge patrol had been cunningly entrapped by the Japanese. True or not, it hardened the hearts of many and marked the beginning of an unofficial "take no prisoners" policy exercised at severely trying times by individual marines. A similar "no prisoners" philosophy had for centuries been a fixture of Japan's *bushido* military culture, and in World War II it found a worthy hate object in the U.S. Marine Corps.

Coming in Out of the Cold

The marine sentry squinted incredulously up the beach and drew a bead with his rifle. Advancing toward him on the morning of 15 August was a column of sixty natives, marching briskly in step. Leading them was a white man in disreputable shirt and shorts, wearing on his head a scruffy bush hat, and on his stockingless feet a pair of highly polished black, pointed-toe shoes, fashionable in Britain and known there as "winkle-pickers." At his heels trotted a small black dog. Coastwatcher Martin Clemens was coming in out of the cold. Clemens, a Scot with a Cambridge University degree, was tall, blond, and fit-looking despite his loss of forty-five pounds to jungle living. With him was a singular appearing man, a bare-chested Guadalcanal native who would a few years hence be knighted for his services by order of the king of England. His name was Jacob Vouza. He was a forty-six-year-old retired policeman who had come along to volunteer his considerable talents to the marines. Stocky and heavily muscled, with a broad Melanesian face and bushy hair, bleached pinkish blond in the Solomon Islands fashion, Vouza would turn out to be one of the most durable human beings on either side of the barbed wire. Martin Clemens, with his encyclopedic knowledge of the island, would prove a valuable intelligence consultant to the 1st Division. Jacob Vouza, acting as

Clemens's number two, would head up the constabulary force of Clemens's native irregulars and pass into Marine Corps legend as a superb tracker, patrol leader, and jungle fighter.

Also on the fifteenth, a naval detachment of 180 enlisted sailors and 3 naval officers[10] came ashore with orders to report to Henderson Field and help marine engineers sort out their many problems. CUB-One had arrived. Untrained for combat, but equipped to the teeth with helmets, Springfield rifles, and bayonets, they turned to with a will. In the coming weeks, CUB-One would comprise Henderson Field's sole resource for the seemingly nonstop job of fueling and arming the marine aircraft soon to arrive.

Two days after the appearance of CUB-One, Adm. Robert Ghormley in Noumea, having never set eyes on the island, informed the Joint Chiefs of Staff in Washington, D.C., that there was reason to doubt Guadalcanal could be held by the marines.

CHAPTER FOUR

Japan Man 'long Here?

IN THE IMPERIAL JAPANESE ARMY, Col. Kiyanoa Ichiki was a rising young star who operated along the lines of U.S. general George Patton. The dynamic Japanese colonel had made his reputation in China at the head of his crack 28th Infantry Regiment, waging bold, swift, and victorious war against enemy units many times his strength. Ichiki, whose 28th Regiment was seasoned in night fighting and the bayonet attack, had been given the honor of assaulting the marine garrison at Midway Island, once the remnants of the U.S. Navy had been destroyed. That had fallen through, and now, as a consolation prize, Ichiki had been singled out for another honor, that of crushing the U.S. Marines on Guadalcanal and retaking the airstrip.

Rear Adm. Raizo Tanaka, the naval officer who would oversee Ichiki's delivery to Guadalcanal, had carefully studied the problem of how to move Ichiki's 28th Regiment to the island without detection. He concluded that the convoy must move by night, proceed by the shortest possible route to minimize sea time, and be within range of friendly fighters for protection against any enemy carriers within striking distance. Only one route met these requirements: Tanaka would use New Georgia Sound—the Slot.

At midnight on 18 August, marines crouching in the listening posts on the perimeter's beach heard a curious new sound, a gentle wash hissing on the sand at the water's edge. The wash was created by the passage through Iron Bottom Sound of six Japanese destroyers bound for Taivu Point.[1] There they would offload Colonel Ichiki and his advance unit of nine hundred shock troops. The remainder of his regiment would be delivered in a week. The wash was heard again at 3:00 A.M. as the destroyers withdrew, pausing to lob a few shells at the marine establishment on Tulagi. Once ashore, the serenely confident Ichiki immediately marched his advance force westward along the coast, toward the marine lines on the Tenaru River. Misinformed by Japanese intelligence that only two thousand Americans held the airstrip, Ichiki saw no reason to wait for the rest of his regiment; besides, the fewer men, the greater share of honor. He would accomplish the job in his usual brisk fashion, using only the advance unit. By daybreak on the nineteenth Ichiki's column reached Tetere, nearly halfway to the Tenaru. There they filtered into the jungle to rest and hide from American aircraft, a needless precaution as none existed on Guadalcanal.

Meanwhile, Jacob Vouza and his native irregulars had been busy outside of the perimeter, slipping through the rain forest like ghosts, climbing trees for a look-see, and asking every native they met, "Japan man 'long here?" Returning to the perimeter, they ventured an educated guess that Japanese reinforcements were ashore in large numbers somewhere east of the marine lines and moving toward the Tenaru. Major General Vandegrift immediately ordered a patrol to reconnoiter the eastern approach to the perimeter. The patrol, led by Capt. Charles H. Brush, set out the same day and marched east along the coast on a collision course with Ichiki. Four of Vouza's men marched with them as scouts. Vouza himself led a second patrol of native irregulars for a walkabout farther inland, in case the Japanese had taken to the jungle. As the Brush patrol neared Koli Point, the native scouts up front signaled "visitors!" and the patrol hit the deck. Through the trees Brush could make out a group of Japanese walking casually through the coconut palms in his direction, with no point man or flankers for security. Oblivious to their danger, they were laying telephone wire.[2] It was a textbook ambush opportunity. The marine patrol silently deployed, each man chambered a round in his Springfield and waited with thumping heart until the Japanese party had strolled into his sights. Then the marines squeezed their triggers and worked their bolts for a mad moment of firepower as their targets staggered, toppled, and died.

The surviving Japanese quickly rallied and fought back, but the marines had them boxed. After an hour of close combat, the fight was over. Five Japanese escaped to tell the tale to Ichiki's debriefers. Twenty-nine others were sprawled among the coconut palms in the broken-toy attitudes of death. The first thing Brush saw as he bent to examine an officer's corpse was the insignia on the man's mushroom-shaped helmet. It was not the anchor and chrysanthemum worn by the Japanese naval troops encountered to date: it was the star of the Imperial Japanese Army. This was a wholly new adversary, the enemy's varsity, the same army that had descended on China, Malaysia, and the Philippines, swallowing everything in its path. Now it was here on Guadalcanal. Further search of the bodies confirmed the fact. The four officers were dressed in new and carefully pressed uniforms. Their boots were polished. They carried swords and field glasses. Their map cases contained detailed maps of Guadalcanal. Brush and his men hurried back to the perimeter with the evidence. It was obvious that the patrol had ambushed the advance party of a much greater force, one headed for the perimeter and soon to arrive.

Okay to Land

Late in the afternoon of that day, marines in the Guadalcanal perimeter stopped whatever they were doing and listened. The sound was unmistakable: the droning approach of many low-altitude aircraft. Men looked at one another with raised eyebrows or eyeballed the nearest dugout. What was it? The Japanese always bombed at noon, or was this some new outrage? Then the marines nearest Henderson saw them, a diamond-shaped formation of twelve blue-gray aircraft with large white stars under their wings and on their fuselages—marine SBD dive bombers!—their landing gear lowering as they queued up for an approach to Henderson.

On the hood of a jeep parked at the downwind end of the runway stood Maj. "Fog" Hayes with his arms stretched out like wings in the signal for "Okay to land." The first SBD floated in over the coconut trees; its pilot sized up the battered airstrip, decided it was land-worthy, opened his throttle for another go-around, then made a perfect landing in a swirling cloud of Guadalcanal dust. In a few minutes, the entire SBD flight was on the ground. Close behind them was another welcome sight— nineteen Grumman F4F fighters. Marine Air Group 223 had arrived, and so was born the Cactus Air Force. It was an emotional moment. Some marines jumped for joy, cheered, and threw their helmets in the air, others looked on wordlessly with tears on their cheeks. Archer Vandegrift leaped from his jeep, trotted the few steps to the first of the SBDs, and pumped the hand of its pilot, Maj. Richard Mangrum. Vandegrift later confessed that his own eyes were moist. It was, he recorded, "one of the most beautiful sights of my life." Only one man of this first detachment of SBD pilots would be able to walk to the navy transport plane that would eventually carry him away from Guadalcanal.

A Quarter-Ton of Lead

As more evidence of a new and oncoming Japanese force filtered in to 1st Division HQ, Vandegrift gave orders to strengthen, with the few resources at hand, the patchy line of resistance that ran along the bank of the Tenaru. (Historians have given this watercourse three different names—the Tenaru, the Ilu, and Alligator Creek. But to the marines on Guadalcanal at that time, it was the Tenaru.[3]) To stiffen defenses, tanks were put on alert and several 37-millimeter antitank guns dug in. The plantations were scrounged for more rusty barbed wire to string, and hundreds of Japanese rice bags were hastily filled with the red earth of Guadalcanal by sweating marines and stacked up at strongholds. Forward observers from the division's artillery regiment, the 11th Marines, registered their 75s and 105s on the river's far bank and the sandspit that at low tide connected both banks at the river's mouth.[4] Here the Tenaru was a slender lagoon, shaped like a giant leech with a long oval body and tiny head where it emptied into the sea. Its water was mucky and evil smelling. It was, as Mark Twain said of the Missouri River, "Too thick to drink, too thin to plow." Cruising just beneath its surface and sunning on its banks were ten-foot crocodiles.

As tropical darkness swiftly fell on the evening of 20 August, men of the 2d Battalion, 1st Marines, peering over the edge of their foxholes near the sandspit, could sense a malevolent presence gathering shape in the coconut grove across the river. Around midnight, marine listening posts crouching on the opposite bank reported sound and movement just inland, metallic noises, and hushed voices. They were told to pull out, pronto, by Lt. Col. Edwin A. Pollack, who commanded the 2d Battalion. Soon their dim silhouettes were seen trotting back across the sandspit. Now the only sound was the gentle swish of waves against the shore, the occasional click of a rifle bolt as a tense marine rechecked the action on his weapon, or an order being relayed down the line. Sgt. Robert Cally, sitting in his two-man foxhole, heard one coming and cocked an ear toward the foxhole on his left. The message, hoarsely whispered across fifteen feet of river bank, sounded like "Eat a can of beans, pass it on." Cally looked at his foxhole partner, shrugged, and whispered to the occupants of the next foxhole, "Eat a can of beans, pass it on." He could hear the order being repeated on down the line until it faded away. Neither Cally nor his partner had a can of beans to eat, and wondered how the order had originally read. Probably, reasoned Cally, it was something to do with the "1st Marines." They never found out.[5]

It grew late. The luminous hands on Cally's wristwatch read 1:39. For one minute more the night was hushed and black, then the marine positions nearest the sandspit were bathed in green psychedelic light as Japanese parachute flares popped and swung overhead. An instant later the line of marine foxholes was drenched in spouting mortar shells, and nine hundred Japanese throats on the opposite bank began to scream in unison, "Banzai! Banzai! Banzai!" "Come and get it, you sonofabitches!" yelled a marine. In the weird green light of the flares, marines of the 2d Battalion could see a dense body of Japanese infantry, bayonets thrust forward, running toward them across the sandspit, their feet splashing in the shallows and their officers urging them on with glinting swords. The marines let them have it with everything at hand: barking Springfields, rattling BARs, chugging 30- and 50-caliber machine guns, and grape-sized buckshot spat from two 37-millimeter antitank cannon. Up and down the line, marine noncoms calmly chanted, "Line 'em up and squeeze 'em off, line 'em up and squeeze 'em off."[6]

The quarter-ton of flying lead smote the front rank of oncoming Japanese like the fist of an angry god and flung it to the sand. But Ichiki's men were living up to their reputation as elite troops. Behind the first wave, a second and third kept coming, leaping over bodies, soaking up the marine firepower. Sheer momentum and guts carried many of them up to the barbed wire and over, where the fight swirled into the marine lines and broke up into small knots of frantic action. A marine corporal firing a BAR was surrounded by three Japanese when his weapon jammed. One jumped into his foxhole, shouting, "Marine, you die!" Grabbing his machete, the corporal chopped at his first attacker and decked him. Then with manic swiftness he hacked the other two down before they could react. Pvt. Al Schmidt, firing his machine gun from a dugout near the river bank, saw the Japanese charging through the ankle-deep shallows on his front like stampeding buffalo and fired burst after burst into their midst. Moments later his dugout was overrun by the enemy. One of them, running by, tossed in a grenade that blinded Schmidt with white-hot splinters. Schmidt yelled for help and was heard by Pvt. Whitney Jacobs, who jumped into Schmidt's dugout and wrapped his bleeding face in a bandage, then bandaged the mangled hands of Schmidt's partner, Cpl. LeRoy Diamond, who had been wounded by a burst of fire in the first minutes of the attack.

Schmidt and Diamond now pooled their resources. Schmidt could fire the gun but couldn't see to aim. Diamond could see to aim but couldn't fire the gun. Together they were in business. Schmidt fired, Diamond called the shots, and between them they carried on cutting down attackers on their front. As the battle progressed, marines near the sandspit could hear what sounded like ripping bursts of Nambu machine-gun fire behind them and worried that the Japanese had surrounded them, cutting off their line of retreat. A check of their rear disclosed nothing but the battalion reserve hunkered down and waiting to be summoned forward. They later found that the attackers had created the machine-gun illusion by lobbing strings of giant firecrackers behind marine lines. Maj. Bob Luckey was coordinating the support weapons at the 1st Battalion command post when messages began arriving to the effect that his mortar fire was falling short and landing on marine positions. As he snatched up the phone to order firing corrections, he was stopped by Col. Clifton Cates, 1st Marines' CO. "That's an old trick," Cates told him. "Keep right where you are." Cates knew that the Japanese mortar teams were timing the arrival of their shells to create this impression. Skillful deception had been a specialty of Japanese arms for centuries.

The Japanese continued to surge against the marine positions like surf on a beach—a mob of howling infantry bristling with bayonets, followed by small groups that filtered across the forty-five-yard sandspit in the darkness between dripping flares, followed by lone Japanese who crept through the heaps of still-warm bodies, then rose from the dead to rush the nearest foxhole with only a handheld bayonet. During lulls, bleeding Japanese survivors crawled back to the far bank, while the marines evacuated their own dead and wounded, called for water and ammunition, and worked to clear jammed weapons. Then another shouting wave would break against the marine wire, followed by another silence, broken only by the murmuring of the wounded on the sandspit and the slatting of palm fronds in the onshore breeze.

Eighteen-year-old Pvt. Harry Horsman and a fellow squad member, Pvt. Charles Carter, both riflemen, noticed that the 37-millimeter anti-tank gun on their left was silent, evidently knocked out. Leaving their foxholes and crawling over to it, they found it empty, its dead or wounded crew apparently evacuated but the gun itself undamaged. Horsman takes up the story: "[We figured that] maybe we could get this thing going again —so as the Aussies say, we gave 'er a go! and with good effect." Horsman and Carter then noticed some crimped-nose canister shells stacked in a corner and fired these into the charging Japanese, blowing large holes in their ranks. "[The Japanese then] set up a machine gun directly opposite us; we saw it and fired a high explosive shell across the river and smack into them. [Then] in came Corporal DiPetroantonio and Sgt. Jim Hancock, who had some artillery experience. . . . Down the line some Japs were getting into the abandoned amphib tank a little farther upstream, we fired another high explosive at it, and it worked! But now came a shower of mortar shells and Hancock was hit."[7] Horsman and the other ad hoc gunners then turned their gun over to a special weapons crew and rejoined the firing line.

Toward morning, Ichiki made one last attempt. He sent a company-
strength sortie on the desperate mission of outflanking the 2d Battalion
from seaward. They were quickly spotted wading through the surf with
their rifles at high port, and the marines opened up on them with everything in their arsenal, including pack howitzers and a 75-millimeter half
track. Again, a quarter-ton of whizzing lead churned the water to foam
in which most of the attackers perished. The few survivors swam away,
their bobbing heads a target for marine sharpshooters.

With the coming of light and the sputtering out of Japanese fire from
the opposite bank, Vandegrift and his operations officer, Col. Gerald
Thomas, knew that the initiative had passed to them. Thomas spelled it
out: "We aren't going to let those people lay up there all day."[8] The 1st
Battalion, commanded by Lt. Col. Leonard B. Cresswell, was dispatched
into the jungle with orders to cross the Tenaru upstream of the Japanese,
then hook back and take the Ichiki force from the flank and rear. Cresswell's men would next squeeze the remnants of Ichiki's battalion into a
pocket in the coconut grove at the river mouth, and, with the help of
artillery, mortar, and small-arms fire from the marine perimeter, annihi-
late the Japanese force. By midmorning, marines on the west bank could
hear sounds of battle to the rear of Ichiki's position and see Japanese soldiers running in all directions, like ants in a demolished anthill. Even the
newly arrived Cactus Air Force got a piece of the action. They had been
awakened in their tents at 2:00 A.M. by the din of battle, listened a while,
and gone back to sleep, thinking it was simply a typical night on Guadalcanal. A few hours later they were taking off from Henderson Field to
strafe the cornered enemy.

Vandegrift, determined to close the books on the Battle of the Tenaru
by sunset, sent six light tanks across the sandspit to hurry the process. One
was knocked out by a resolute Japanese rifleman who threw himself and
his magnetic mine against the tank's hull. Two others bogged down in the
soft ground, and the remaining three went to work flushing Japanese
from cover and butting palm trees to shake out the snipers.[9]

By 3:00 in the afternoon watchers on the near bank could see marines
stepping cautiously into the coconut grove that sixteen hours ago had sheltered nine hundred of Colonel Ichiki's superb shock troops. The marines

walked like western movie gun fighters, slowly, rifles at the ready, eyes flicking from body to body, looking for movement or an aimed weapon. Nothing stirred. Suddenly one of the corpses, its face smeared with blood, rose on one elbow and flung a grenade at the nearest marine. It fell short and the grenade thrower was instantly riddled. Out on the sandspit, Colonels Pollack, Twining, and Cresswell were inspecting the morning's work when a seemingly dead Japanese noncom sat up and fired a pistol at them, missed, then shot himself in the head. The lesson was obvious— dead Japanese were dangerous. The word was passed to kill them a second time, to shoot or bayonet the bodies of all fallen Japanese.

The body of Colonel Ichiki was identified by a member of the Japanese construction battalion, Hajime Yamamoto, who was pressed into service by the marines to help bury the Japanese dead. According to Yamamoto, he buried Ichiki on the east bank of the Tenaru.[10] A handful of Japanese survivors trickled back through the jungle to Taivu, eating roots and chewing their leather rifle slings. The marines counted 777 Japanese dead on the sandspit and in the coconut grove.[11] Their bodies, already putrefying in the heat, were buried by bulldozer. The two marine battalions lost thirty-five dead and seventy-five wounded, a profitable exchange in the cruel mathematics of war. But the Battle of the Tenaru had far greater significance. For the first time since Pearl Harbor, the Imperial Japanese Army had been beaten in a fair fight by American arms. The lesson for Vandegrift, Nimitz, and King was that Japanese heroism and willpower could be bested by marine coolness and firepower. The lesson for the Japanese high command was stated by Rear Adm. Raizo Tanaka, who wrote, "This tragedy should have taught the hopelessness of 'bamboo spear' tactics." And it did. After Guadalcanal, the Japanese would fight a very different kind of war.

Tougher than a Boiled Owl

At 7:00 that morning Martin Clemens had been sitting in the operations dugout, listening to the crump of mortar fire along the Tenaru when the phone rang. It was a call from the 2d Marines command post, informing him that a severely wounded native had crawled out of the jungle and

was asking for him. It was Vouza. Clemens hopped into a jeep and sped
to the scene. He recalled:

> [Vouza] was an awful mess, not able to sit up. I could hardly bear to
> look at him. We dragged him behind a jeep, and he told his story as
> best he could in spite of the gaping wound in his throat. He had
> gone out on his patrol, taking with him a miniature American flag,
> which had been given him as a souvenir. Going to hide it in a house
> at Volonavua, he had walked slap into three or four platoons of Japs.
> They were dispersed all round the village and he had no chance
> of escaping with his American flag. He was caught red-handed and
> hauled before the commanding officer.[12]

What then happened to Vouza was reported by Don Richter in his book
Where the Sun Stood Still (Richter, a marine who had fought in the Guadalcanal campaign, returned after the war as a missionary and became Vouza's
close friend). According to Richter, the Japanese bound Vouza to a tree
with straw ropes and interrogated him, demanding details of American
strength and disposition. Vouza maintained a tight-lipped silence. The
officer in charge told Vouza that he would be killed here and now if he
would not talk. Still Vouza was silent. The officer spoke and a rifle butt
smashed into Vouza's face, then a flick of the officer's sword opened a
deep slash on his arm. He stiffened with pain, but his mouth remained
shut. Vouza was then subjected to a series of torments, forced at bayonet
point to lie on a nearby red ant heap until bitten hundreds of times by the
large, venomous insects, then hanged from a tree by his arms, his feet off
the ground. At nightfall, Vouza was cut down and led stumbling away to the
west by the patrol that had captured him. Soon they joined Colonel Ichiki's
assault force, which was advancing westward to the attack. Moments later
firing broke out and one of the Japanese soldiers with Vouza was killed.
Vouza was now in the way, and an officer ordered him bayonetted to death.
The first thrust drove up under his armpit and out his throat, splitting his
tongue and leaving a gaping wound. Another bayonet under his other
armpit penetrated his chest. After a few more perfunctory jabs at his chest
and abdomen, he was left to die. In agony but rational, Vouza summoned
up the last of his adrenalin and began to make his way toward the sound

of the firing, where he knew he would find the marine perimeter. Staggering along until he fell, then crawling, drifting in and out of consciousness, he navigated an incredible two miles through the rain forest and somehow across the Tenaru until he was challenged, then rescued, at the marine lines.[13]

Vouza, who proved to be tougher than a boiled owl, made a complete recovery and before long was back in business as a patrol leader. Vandegrift, mightily impressed, ordered that the three chevrons and rockers of a marine sergeant major be sewn on Vouza's shirtsleeve, then awarded the pink-haired Guadalcanal native the Silver Star Medal for his gallant services to the 1st Marine Division.

I Feel Like Hell about It

On 19 August, the day that saw Colonel Ichiki and his men marching confidently to their rendezvous with destiny, an event of little note took place in Tokyo. Imperial General Headquarters (IGHQ) shifted the responsibility for obtaining a Guadalcanal victory from the navy to the army, and in doing so raised the Guadalcanal issue one notch on the IGHQ priority scale, from a piddling annoyance to a second-rate, but official, problem. Maj. Gen. Kiyotake Kawaguchi, who commanded the 35th Infantry Brigade, victors of the Borneo campaign, was ordered to proceed to Guadalcanal with his three thousand veteran troops and take charge of all Imperial Army and Navy units there. He was then to eradicate any marines Ichiki may have overlooked. Meanwhile, Admiral Tanaka, operating under previously issued Imperial Navy orders, was already at sea with his night-running destroyers, transporting the second echelon of Ichiki's ill-fated 28th Infantry Regiment and the Yokosuka 5th SNLF to Guadalcanal. Simultaneously, Admiral of the Fleet Yamamoto, the loser at Midway and now taking no chances, had assembled two powerful task forces, one of battleships and another of three aircraft carriers. These he pointed at Guadalcanal with instructions to locate and sink Vice Admiral Fletcher's carriers, neutralize the Cactus Air Force by battering Henderson Field with 14-inch naval salvos, bombard the marine perimeter, and support the landing of the troops en route to Guadalcanal in Tanaka's destroyers.

As a result, the ether over the Pacific was soon crackling with Japanese radio transmissions, attentively monitored by U.S. Navy intelligence. By the twenty-third they had advised Vandegrift of what looked like a massive buildup of Japanese land, sea, and air forces for the ostensible purpose of putting an end, once and for all, to the U.S. presence on Guadalcanal. One element of the Japanese armada, Tanaka's five transports and their warship escorts, had already been sighted that morning by a scouting U.S. Navy "Dumbo," and its position, course, and speed relayed to all concerned.

On beleaguered Guadalcanal, Vandegrift agonized over his options. He had no confidence that Fletcher, far to the south, would attempt to defend Guadalcanal with his carrier aircraft by attacking Yamamoto's force at sea. Yet if no resistance was offered, it seemed certain to Vandegrift that his orphaned marines would be overwhelmed and immolated. His alternative was to send the tiny, four-day-old Cactus Air Force on a mission impossible against Tanaka's transports and, for all Vandegrift knew, Yamamoto's entire fleet, to do what they could with the few aircraft they had. Delivering a crippling blow against so powerful a seaborne enemy required strikes by a hundred or more dive and torpedo bombers. The Cactus Air force could muster only nine SBDs and twelve F4F fighters.[14] It was, however, Vandegrift's only option. With pain in his heart, he ordered them to go, knowing that it was likely to be a suicide mission.

The little force took off at 4:30 that afternoon. Vandegrift stood beside the airstrip and watched them leave, fearing that he would never see them again. But fate put her hand in. A hundred miles out, the Cactus Air Force flew into a turbulent, zero-visibility weather front. Lost in the cotton-wool mist, unable to see one another and maintain formation, they turned back to Guadalcanal with heavy hearts, believing that they had lost the Battle of Guadalcanal and maybe the Pacific war. "I feel like hell about it," mourned a squadron leader, "but we just couldn't get in there." "I came back from Tulagi two feet over the water, trying to get under the overcast," said an SBD pilot. "Even then I couldn't see anything."[15] Waiting for them at Henderson Field was a deeply concerned Archer Vandegrift, who assured them, while trying to conceal his own emotions, that the failure had been no fault of theirs.

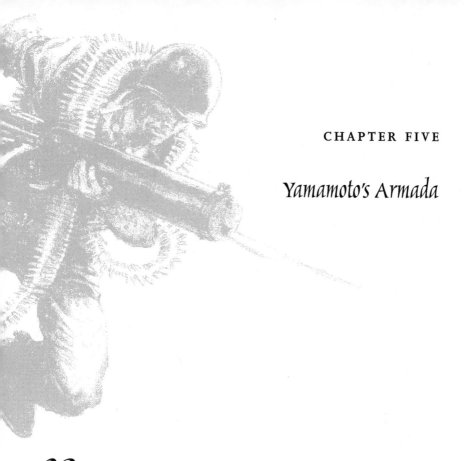

CHAPTER FIVE

Yamamoto's Armada

23 AUGUST 1942: The fifty-eight warships of Admiral of the Fleet Yamamoto were three hundred miles north of Guadalcanal, bearing down at seventeen knots on Maj. Gen. Archer Vandegrift and his marines. Assuming no alterations in course or speed, they would arrive in Guadalcanal waters in fewer than eighteen hours. The armada consisted of two divisions —a powerful striking force built around three aircraft carriers and commanded by Adm. Chuichi Nagumo, and a second force of battleships, cruisers, and destroyers, commanded by Adm. Nobutake Kondo. Nagumo's mission was to locate and sink Frank Jack Fletcher's three carriers, the *Saratoga*, the *Enterprise*, and the *Wasp*. Kondo's orders were to bombard Henderson Field and the marine perimeter in support of the Japanese landing, scheduled for the following night.

On a parallel course one hundred miles west of these two formidable task forces was a third element, Adm. Raizo Tanaka's five troop transports and their warship escorts. Into Tanaka's troop holds were crowded the second half of the unfortunate Colonel Ichiki's 28th Infantry Regiment and five hundred men of the Yokosuka SNLF. They were the first of thousands of reinforcements scheduled for delivery to Guadalcanal by Tanaka in the coming weeks. It was Tanaka's transports that had been spotted by a snooping navy PBY and reported to the worried Vandegrift. Tanaka, having glimpsed the distant, cloud-hopping PBY and thus aware that his position was known to the Americans, immediately advised Rabaul. He was ordered to turn around and steam north until further notice.

The same radio report that alerted Vandegrift also reached Fletcher, whose carrier force was orbiting three hundred miles southeast of Guadalcanal. This time Fletcher rose to the occasion. He ordered *Saratoga* to mount an air strike. By 2:45 that afternoon, thirty-two SBD dive bombers and six F4F fighters led by Cdr. Harry D. Felt were on their way to attack Tanaka's crammed transports. After battling the same vicious weather front that defeated the Cactus Air Force but somehow punching through, the flight arrived at the PBY's reference point but found no transports. Tanaka was now many miles to the north. With gas gauges trembling toward zero and the sun rapidly setting, Felt and his group headed for Henderson Field, which lay fifty miles closer than *Saratoga's* flight deck. They reached it just at nightfall and for the next half hour, with sweaty palms and straining eyes, landed on the unfamiliar and nearly invisible dirt strip, dimly outlined by an improvised system of jeep headlights and flashlights hastily rigged by the marines. Felt later recorded that they were "distracted somewhat by occasional machine gun tracer fire streaming astern from either Japanese snipers or doubting marines." All got down safely.[1] At that point the newly arrived navy ground crew, CUB-One, took over. Working until dawn, they refueled the navy dive bombers, straining the gritty but only available aviation gas through chamois (there was no filtration equipment) and pumping it by hand into the SBD's fuel tanks. When the navy pilots took off the next morning to rejoin the *Saratoga*, they left as a welcome quid pro quo for marine hospitality the first half-ton bombs that Henderson armorers had seen since leaving the States—twenty-seven 1,000-pounders.

While *Saratoga's* strike group had been searching in vain for Tanaka and his transports, the Japanese admiral had received a second order from Rabaul. He was directed to turn around again, head for Guadalcanal, and execute the troop landing as originally planned. This was nonsense, objected Tanaka. The timing was now wrong. It would mean approaching Guadalcanal and disembarking fifteen hundred troops in broad daylight under the guns and bombs of the Cactus Air Force. Execute the order, he was told. Tanaka, one of Japan's most competent and experienced admirals, bit his tongue and again turned south. Aboard Fletcher's flagship, the *Saratoga*, an equally suspect order was given. The carrier *Wasp* was directed by Fletcher to leave the task force and head south to refuel. Admiral Ghormley, Fletcher's superior, had originated the order from his desk at Noumea, many hundreds of miles away. The *Wasp* represented one-third of Fletcher's striking power, and her departure would tip the scales in favor of Nagumo and his three carriers in the battle now taking shape. Yet Fletcher did not protest, and away went the *Wasp*.

An hour before dawn of the following day, 24 August, Nagumo made the opening move of what was to become the Naval Battle of the Eastern Solomons. He ordered *Ryujo*, the smallest of his three flattops, to detach itself from the carrier force and speed ahead toward Guadalcanal. Its mission, he told *Ryujo*'s commander, Capt. Tadao Kato, was to bomb Henderson Field and cover the troop landing. But Nagumo had a secret agenda. He intended to troll the mini-carrier under Fletcher's nose as bait. If Fletcher took the bait and struck at *Ryujo*, the American admiral not only would reveal his location but also would have to commit much of his strike force to attacking the expendable *Ryujo*, leaving Fletcher's own carriers, the *Saratoga* and *Enterprise*, dangerously unprotected. They could then be ravished at leisure by Nagumo's dive bombers and torpedo planes. When the U.S. carriers had been sunk, the two Japanese task forces would proceed to Guadalcanal, shell and dive bomb Henderson Field to neutralize the Cactus Air Force, and get on with the landing that would recapture the airfield. All this in exchange for little *Ryujo*.

At 10:17 that morning a sharp-eyed PBY pilot spotted the *Ryujo* and radioed her position and speed to Fletcher. Skeptical of the sighting, Fletcher ignored the report. But the elephantine Dumbo continued to shadow the small Japanese flattop and at 11:58 updated details of the sighting. This time Fletcher took the bait. He ordered a search and destroy mission to find and sink the *Ryujo*. At 1:00, the summons to "flight quarters" was sounded throughout the *Enterprise*. Pilots, rear gunners, and radiomen trotted to the ready rooms for briefing and were assigned search sectors.

Their aircraft, gassed and armed for the strike, were spotted on the after flight deck in order of takeoff. When all was in readiness, the ship's loudspeakers clicked on and rasped, "Pilots, man your planes." The pilots clambered into their cockpits. There, fussed over by their plane captains, they performed the rite of preparation for takeoff: first buckle on the seat-pack parachute, then click into place the complex web of body constraints, the straps that would resist the Newtonian forces of gravity, inertia, and centrifugal pull, all of which would tug at the pilot as his horizon rocked from side to side, inverted, and vanished altogether in the frenzied business of attacking and being attacked. The air crewmen enacted a similar ritual in the rear-facing seats of the SBDs and torpedo-carrying TBFs. On the bridge, the steering order was given that would point the bow of *Enterprise* into the wind's eye. The helmsman spun the ship's wheel, and the eight-hundred-foot carrier swung ponderously onto the new course. "Start engines," ordered the scratchy voice of the loudspeakers. Forty engines spluttered and coughed blue smoke, then merged into a ragged internal combustion chorus. A seaman in a yellow jumper, hands beckoning, extracted a waiting F4F from the huddle of aircraft and prompted it forward into takeoff position. The flight deck officer, a small checkered flag in his hand, signaled the F4F pilot to stand on his brakes and open the throttle. Then, dropping to one knee, he pointed his flag theatrically at *Enterprise's* bow. With a shattering roar the Wildcat streaked down the flight deck, became airborne, and climbed away, wobbling a bit as its pilot's right hand made the obligatory thirty-eight and one-half turns of the crank that tucked up the Wildcat's knock-kneed landing gear. This drama was repeated until the flight deck had been cleared. Sixteen of the F4Fs would fly combat air patrol over the *Enterprise*. The rest, together with the SBDs and TBFs, would form up in pairs and head out on their assigned search sectors. When one of the pairs spotted the *Ryujo*, all would home in for the kill.[2]

Hank, They're Attacking ENTERPRISE

Before leaving port, Nagumo had been advised by Japanese intelligence that Fletcher was cruising somewhere in the Coral Sea, south of Guadalcanal. Now, on the early afternoon of 24 August, Japanese search planes were combing the area where Fletcher was thought to be prowling. One of them, a Kawanishi flying boat searching a sector southeast of Guadalcanal, had failed to return to base. The big amphibian had flown onto *Saratoga's* radar scope at 12:22 and been reported to *Sara's* combat air patrol. There followed this exchange, filtered through the throat mikes and earphones of the pilots and their fighter director officer aboard ship:

> "Scarlet 7, Scarlet Base. Bogey ahead 15."
> "Wilco."
> "On the port bow, Dave."
> "Up or down? ...Tallyho, one Kawanishi. Repeat, one Kawanishi.... Follow me."
> "Go below the clouds, go below the clouds, Hank."
> "Below you, I see him."
> "Box him in, box him in."
> "A little to the right and down, to the west of you. ..."
> "I'm going in now."
> "In the clouds, I got him, Hank. Bingo!"
> "Nice going, Dave."
> "Boy, look at him burn."

The Kawanishi was enveloped in flames before it could radio news of its sighting. Only one of its crew escaped incineration, a lone figure who leaped from a hatch without a parachute and cartwheeled through space. At 1:20 a second Kawanishi flew onto Fletcher's radar scope and, like the first, was unable to make radio contact with Nagumo before suffering the same fate. Then, shortly after 2:00 P.M., a float plane from the cruiser *Chikuma* sighted the U.S. carriers but was again flamed by Fletcher's combat air patrol. This time, however, the Japanese snooper had begun radio transmission before it kissed the water, and its position was easily calculated by Nagumo's navigation officer.

An hour before Fletcher's strike was launched against the *Ryujo*, the diminutive carrier had sent its own attack group off to bomb Henderson Field. The tiny formation crept onto *Saratoga's* radar scope at 1:30, and the *Sara* quickly passed the word to Henderson. The Cactus Air Force, itself none too large, scrambled in plenty of time to reach twenty thousand feet—"Angels 20"—before the Japanese arrived. When they did, they were jumped from upstairs by fourteen marine Wildcats who flamed all six of the Japanese bombers before tangling with their fighter escorts. Three marine pilots died under the guns of the aerobatic Zeros, but nine of the yellow-winged fighters were sent whirling into the sea by the Cactus Air Force before the Japanese broke off the action[3] and streaked homeward to a mother ship that would be aflame and sinking when they arrived. The sacrificial *Ryujo*, her nest now empty and her mission in life fulfilled, could only await her executioners. She had been quickly located by the *Enterprise* strike force, who left her a burning, sinking derelict. Of *Ryujo*'s five-hundred-man crew, half were taken off by her escort vessels.

At 3:37 in the afternoon, Nagumo launched his initial air strike against Fletcher's carriers. It was the first of many Japanese sorties that by day's end would total seventy-two Val dive bombers, "Kate" torpedo planes, and Zero fighters, most of them from the *Shokaku*. An hour later, radar screens on both the *Enterprise* and *Saratoga* picked up their blips approaching at twelve thousand feet. The U.S. carriers scrambled all available Wildcats and vectored them at the oncoming Japanese. To clear the decks for action, Fletcher also ordered every remaining SBD and TBF launched immediately with instructions to fly north for a parting shot at Nagumo.

North of the *Enterprise* the Vals bored in as their Zero escorts squared off with the big carrier's fighter screen. The first kill was made by Wildcat pilot Albert Vorse, who sent a Zero arcing upside-down into the sea below. A moment later Ens. Francis Register found an enemy fighter in his gunsight, fired a mortal burst, and did an astonished double-take when he saw that his spinning adversary was a Messerschmidt 109,[4] a long way from the Fatherland. It was never explained. The U.S. pilots, many of them new to the business and all of them buzzing with adrenaline, kept up a constant radio chatter on the fighter communication frequency:

> "Don't let them get away, Lou."
>
> "Let's go to high blower, here they come, Hank."
>
> "Barney, just above me. Hey, Scope, on our right, get in back of them, let's go get them, get up there."
>
> "Zero right above us, Scope."

"I don't see them."

"Many bogeys approaching west of us."

"I see them, I'm getting altitude."

"Knock off the chatter about the belly tanks and get in there."

"Those squadrons are ready to attack."

"Hank, they're attacking Enterprise!"

The chatter helped to relieve the terrible loneliness of the Wildcat pilots as they diced across the sky with death. But it also cluttered the radio frequency, making it impossible for the fighter director officer on the Enterprise to picture the scene and communicate with the squadron leaders. As a result, opportunities were missed and holes appeared in the fighter screen through which Vals and Zeros filtered to their advantage. Nevertheless, Enterprise's combat air patrol flamed half of the Vals before they could set up their dives. In the gun galleries that lined both sides of Enterprise's flight deck, the antiaircraft gunners, heads craned far back, squinted into the turquoise, cloud-flecked heavens for the first sign of a tiny, downward-plunging Val with a thousand pounds of high explosive tucked under its belly. Belowdecks, the damage-control parties stood at their battle stations with fire hoses and extinguishers at the ready, following the action with their ears. In the approaching Vals, still at altitude, the Japanese pilots and gunners felt the same straining tension as the first oily gray blossoms from Enterprise's 5-inch flak blotched the sky around them and rocked their aircraft. Moments later their flight leader, with a last glance around for Wildcats, pushed over into his dive, pulled back his stick, and lined up his bomb sight on Enterprise's deck, trying to second guess what evasive action she would take. The rest of his flight followed one by one like barrels over the falls, rear gunners cleared, cocked, and ready for the inevitable plunging onrush of U.S. fighters.

In the antiaircraft galleries the gunners at the pom-poms now opened up, leading the diving Vals like streaking mallards. The thousands of men on battle station in the multistoried city belowdecks, dogged into their water-tight compartments, heard them, and knowing that the Vals were in mid-dive, their hearts pounded with the pom-poms. As each of the diving Vals, fewer now, neared their bomb release point, the staccato 20-millimeters with their big spider web sights, mounted in the galleries that fringed both sides of the flight deck, picked them up with their fire hose streams (sequence: five explosive rounds and one smoking tracer), their intricate patterns weaving through the blue Pacific sky. The fierce *pop-pop-popping* of the 20s signaled to every man aboard that the Val was close overhead at the point where its huge bomb would separate from the cradle and begin its drop toward the flight deck. If you were a praying man, now was the time. When the ship-shaking, whiplashing, steel-sundering detonation of the bomb failed to follow, each man aboard would relax his jaw muscles and cautiously exhale—until the 5-inchers opened up again. Within minutes, the first half-ton bomb tore through the wooden surface of the flight deck and exploded five decks below in the chief petty officers' quarters, mulching the damage control party stationed there.[5] Two more bombs swiftly followed, one of which struck deep into *Enterprise's* vitals and disabled the steering engine. It also penetrated an ammunition locker and touched off forty rounds of gunpowder, killing thirty-eight of the gun crew and combat photographer Robert Read. The last bomb exploded on the flight deck, just forward of the gun tub, where Read and the gunners had perished. Another photographer captured it at the instant of detonation. All told, 169 men were killed or wounded at their battle stations,[6] but none of the hits threatened the life of the ship itself, and the steering engine was repaired in suffocating heat under heroic circumstances. After the third bomb, the battle lost impetus and the surviving Japanese airmen headed north to find their carriers. All this while, the *Saratoga* never came under attack.

Fletcher had directed his first air strike to find and sink the *Ryujo*, but his orders said nothing about Nagumo's two heavyweight carriers, the *Shokaku* and *Zuikaku*. However, not all of the SBDs had been in at the kill of the mini-carrier. Lt. Ray Davis and his wingman, Ens. R. C. Shaw, had missed the show and were still looking for something to bomb when through a rift in the clouds Davis spotted *Shokaku*, unmistakable with her narrow yellow flight deck. In the distance he could also make out *Zuikaku*. From the decks of these two carriers had risen the Zeros, Vals, and Kates that had emasculated the U.S. fleet at Pearl Harbor. As the SBDs climbed to diving altitude, Davis reported the sighting: "Two large carriers, decks full, four heavy cruisers, six light cruisers, eight destroyers, latitude 05-45 south, longitude 162-10 east, course 120, speed 25."

Both men performed their owl-neck exercise, but they saw no Zeros. Usually at the first sight of an enemy aircraft they arrived in force to terminate the intruder, which had inspired a standing joke among navy pilots. "If you spot a Jap carrier," went the joke, "your radio report should read, 'Enemy carrier sighted, position, course and speed so-and-so. Please notify next of kin.'" Both SBD pilots dived with a will, aiming at the large red circle conveniently painted on Shokaku's flight deck, but lookouts with sharp eyes and binoculars signaled the instant the bombs left their cradles, Shokaku's helmsman spun the wheel, and the giant carrier swiveled out of harm's way both times. The bombs exploded in the sea, close enough to do minor damage and injure several seamen. Having shot their bolts, Davis and Shaw pushed their throttles to the stops and headed home. No Zeros pursued them, nor was it necessary to notify their next of kin.

Fletcher's final thrust at Nagumo's carriers had missed its mark as well. Pilots of the SBDs and TBFs, launched from the Enterprise and Saratoga minutes before the Japanese dive bombers arrived, were scantily briefed and otherwise unprepared to fly into the twilight in search of Nagumo's carriers. So hectic was the scramble to clear the decks that some of Saratoga's pilots, through no fault of their own, found themselves airborne with neither flight gear nor charts, so had no way to navigate to or from their target. Others, groping their way through the gathering darkness, were slow to form up, and when they did, had difficulty staying together. Cdr. Max Leslie, the air group commander in charge of the Enterprise strike, was unable to locate any of his squadrons in the inky sky. As if this weren't trouble enough, Leslie, like the commander of the Light Brigade, had been issued orders to attack the wrong target—not Nagumo's two pristine carriers, Shokaku and Zuikaku, but the already burning and sinking Ryujo. Fortunately, Leslie was unable to pass the order on, as his radio wasn't working.[7] Part of the strike group had come upon the battleship force of Admiral Kondo and attacked with marginal success. Another TBF group sighted through the clouds what appeared to be the wakes of a fast-moving naval force and homed in for the kill; but to their mortification the wakes were counterfeit, the work of a swift ocean current foaming over a reef. At the extreme of their range and feeling idiotic, the TBF pilots jettisoned their torpedoes and made for their carrier. A third group of SBDs, Flight 300 from the Enterprise led by Lt. Turner Caldwell, had flown many miles beyond the point where they had hoped to find the Japanese, and their fuel gauges were shivering on empty. Like Lieutenant Commander Felt's flight of the previous day, they headed for Guadalcanal. Again, the marines rigged lanterns and jeep headlights to outline the airstrip, and Flight 300, flaps down and fingers crossed, queued up to land.

For flyers trained to set their aircraft down on a visible carrier deck with arresting cables, which is decidedly challenge enough, landing in the dark on a dirt runway at Henderson Field was an act of pure faith. The pilot whose turn it was lowered himself into the blackness, feeling gingerly for the dirt runway that he assumed was there. When his calibrated intestine told him that he was a few feet above the ground, he quit flying and hoped for the best. All of the SBDs came safely to earth in spite of two down-wind landings. Their pilots and crews were cordially welcomed by the Cactus Air Force, fed marine chow, and put to bed under canvas on medical stretchers to the lullaby of sporadic nearby rifle fire. The next morning they discovered that the Enterprise had sailed away to Pearl Harbor for repairs, and that Flight 300 was until further notice on loan to the Cactus Air Force. In the trying days ahead, the navy carrier pilots and their gunners would fly and fight alongside the likes of marine pilots Carl Mangrum and John Smith, winning high praise from their hosts as the "Bell Bottom Marines."

As far as the two warring carrier skippers were concerned, their part in the Naval Battle of the Eastern Solomons had been played. Both now withdrew, Fletcher southward to refuel, Nagumo and Kondo northward to Japanese waters. But the stoic Tanaka, still under orders to land the reinforcements, pressed on regardless with his loaded transports and their escorts. By the next morning he was only one hundred miles north of Guadalcanal.[8] There the SBDs of the Cactus Air Force, including Flight 300, sniffed him out and plastered the long-suffering admiral's convoy with high explosives, badly damaging Tanaka's flagship and knocking him unconscious. When he revived, he hurriedly transferred his command to a destroyer, arriving on board just as Ens. Chris "Never miss 'em" Fink of Flight 300 delivered a 500-pounder to the deck of one of the crowded transports. The SBDs, their bombs expended, surveyed the damage and headed for Henderson. But it wasn't over. A flight of U.S. Army Air Corps B-17s from the New Hebrides arrived unexpectedly and dropped several sticks of bombs that sank one destroyer and battered a second. Tanaka, by now at the limit of his self-control, reported the situation to Rabaul and once again was told to reverse his course and run for cover. With Tanaka's withdrawal, the invasion threat had lifted for the moment. Lifting it had cost the U.S. Navy and Marine Corps the loss of six pilots and twenty-five aircraft, as well as death and destruction aboard the *Enterprise* that would take her out of play for two months at a critical time. The Japanese lost the aircraft carrier *Ryujo* and half of her crew, as well as the lives and planes of many skilled pilots, and suffered the repulse of Tanaka's convoy with its loss of ships and lives. But of far greater consequence, the Japanese had been confronted at sea and turned away. Their first serious attempt to retake Guadalcanal had failed.

The Tokyo Express

What at first had seemed a gnat bite and then a second-class problem was now viewed by the men who steered Japan's war machine as a menace to their grand strategy. Accordingly, on 31 August 1942, Imperial General Headquarters put the Port Moresby invasion on hold and resolved to spare no effort in retaking Guadalcanal and ridding the island of Vandegrift and his pestilential marines. Spearheading the new campaign would be a brigade-strength unit built around the 124th Infantry Regiment and commanded by Maj. Gen. Kiyotake Kawaguchi. The general was ordered to proceed directly to Guadalcanal via Admiral Tanaka's destroyer transports. There were, he was told, no more than two thousand Americans on the island.

Kawaguchi, a seasoned campaigner with a fierce moustache, began the assignment by banging heads with Tanaka. He disputed Tanaka's recommendation that his brigade be ferried to Guadalcanal by destroyer transport. Rather, Kawaguchi insisted, they must go in stages by motor-driven barge, a method he had used with success in his previous campaign. Tanaka pointed out the many drawbacks of barge transport—their snail-like pace, unseaworthiness, and lack of antiaircraft weapons. In the end, the two men compromised. Barges and destroyers both would be employed,[9] and with this the Tokyo Express was born. In the next three months it would ship fourteen thousand Japanese soldiers down the Slot to Guadalcanal. By 4 September the Tokyo Express had delivered two-thirds of Kawaguchi's troops by destroyer transport to Taivu Point, sixteen miles east of the marine perimeter (these destroyer runs were coded "rat transport"). The remaining third of Kawaguchi's brigade, commanded by Col. Akinosuka Oka, were loaded into forty-eight large and small barges ("ant transport") and sent off down the Slot. Oka's detachment, bobbing along in their lubberly craft, was spotted en route and repeatedly attacked by the Cactus Air Force. Many of the barges were holed and sunk, four hundred officers and men perished at sea, and the survivors were delivered in confusion to the wrong end of Guadalcanal.

Kawaguchi and his staff arrived via rat transport without incident at Taivu on 1 September, where the rash Colonel Ichiki had begun his march. There Kawaguchi's numbers were increased by the survivors of Ichiki's disaster and stragglers from the earlier August skirmishes, about sixteen hundred in all. The general immediately set about executing his plans for the capture of Henderson Field and the defeat of Vandegrift's low-rated marines. His strategy called for a long approach march through the jungle, followed by three closely coordinated night attacks against marine positions thought to be vulnerable. So detailed were Kawaguchi's plans that they included the protocol for Vandegrift's surrender. Following the battle, the U.S. Marine general and his staff were to present themselves at the mouth of the Lunga River, where Kawaguchi, wearing a white uniform tailored for the occasion, would accept Vandegrift's sword. The U.S. surrender party would then be marched to Henderson Field, flown to Tokyo, and paraded through the streets.

Kawaguchi's engineers immediately began hacking a narrow footpath through the rain forest toward a point south of the airfield. Had Kawaguchi first reconnoitered the terrain, he might have had second thoughts about the route. It would confront his marchers with everything the jungle had to offer: steep ravines choked with fallen trees, chest-deep swamps, stupefying heat, and a perpetual fog of mosquitoes. Nevertheless, on 6 September Kawaguchi left behind him at Tasimboko a base camp detachment of three hundred men, and led his brigade of thirty-one hundred veteran infantrymen into the jungle on a march that he firmly believed would conclude with the recapture of Henderson Field and the surrender of U.S. forces on Guadalcanal.

The Loss of So Many Carriers

While the Tokyo Express was busy ferrying Kawaguchi's brigade to Guadalcanal, Fletcher's flagship, *Saratoga*, had been jogging along at thirteen knots on a rectangular patrol course southeast of Guadalcanal. In the post-midnight hours of 31 August, one of her radar operators saw a tiny blip on his screen. As he looked, the blip disappeared. Diving submarines sometimes read this way on a radar scope. The seaman reported the blip and a destroyer was sent to check out the area, but nothing came of it. Several hours passed. Aboard the *Sara*, the crew sat down to breakfast. Meanwhile, the big carrier completed another leg of her rectangular course, turned 90 degrees, and proceeded to make thirteen knots back into the area where the predawn sighting had occurred.

On the Japanese submarine I-26, running just beneath the surface, Commander Yokota ran up his periscope for a look around. What he saw made his heart leap. Into his field of vision swam a battleship, several cruisers and destroyers, and a large aircraft carrier. The silhouette of the carrier was unmistakable: it was the *Saratoga*.

At 7:48 A.M. one of *Sara's* escorting destroyers reported a submarine sighting. At the same moment a lookout on *Sara's* bridge wing spotted a porpoising torpedo and sounded the alarm. Capt. DeWitt Ramsey ordered full right rudder and rang the engine room for full speed, but it was too late. The Long Lance torpedo bored into the carrier just below the island and exploded with shuddering impact. Twelve men were wounded.[10] One of them was Fletcher, who received a gash on his forehead. An engine room was flooded, the ship's twin generators shorted out, and the carrier developed a list, which was soon corrected. The generators were another matter, however. The *Sara* headed southeast for Tongatabu, and then for Pearl Harbor, where she would languish in dry dock for three months. The I-26 dove deep, hovered silently, and escaped.

Admiral Nimitz used Fletcher's gashed forehead as reason enough to bring the admiral back to the United States for reassignment and awarded him the Distinguished Service Medal for his brilliant victory at Midway. In the fullness of time, Fletcher would also be awarded the Medal of Honor. With the *Sara* out of the fight, U.S. carrier strength in the South Pacific now consisted solely of the *Wasp*. As far as Nimitz knew, the Japanese had eight operational carriers. Before the *Saratoga* headed for dry dock, her captain ordered all of her planes—twenty Wildcats and nine SBDs— flown off to Espiritu Santo for safekeeping. Soon they would be rerouted to Guadalcanal, where their navy pilots and aircrews would be enlisted in the Cactus Air Force. The windfall prompted a marine general to observe wryly that "it was the loss of so many carriers that saved Guadalcanal."

Good News and Bad

The events of late August and early September were a mixed bag consisting of the daily nitty-gritty of war, some top brass politics, several welcome arrivals, a second airfield, a couple of hostile to-ings and fro-ings, and examples of marine local color. But the undertone was one of concerned expectancy.

The 67th Army Air Corps Pursuit Squadron landed at Henderson with a flight of fourteen new P-400s to help flesh out the Cactus Air Force.

Adm. Kelly Turner sent off a letter to Adm. Robert Ghormley saying that unless directed to the contrary he would organize and train provisional Marine Raider Battalions in the 2d, 7th, and 8th Marines, the first two of which were or soon would be fighting on Guadalcanal. The Raider Battalion concept was a hot potato among Marine Corps brass and in the White House, where President Franklin Roosevelt was determined to create a number of British-style "commando" units within the Marine Corps. The potato would get even hotter with the creation of the 2d Raider Battalion, whose executive officer was Maj. Jimmy Roosevelt, FDR's son.

Nineteen marine Wildcats, commanded by Maj. Robert Galer, arrived at Henderson Field. With them were the twelve SBDs of VMSB-231, led by Maj. Leo R. Smith.

A few blockade running ships were now slipping in from Noumea and Espiritu Santo bearing food as well as ammunition. When word of this reached the rank and file, many were optimistic that they soon might be eating not two, but three meals a day. The optimism was unfounded.[11]

The 6th Seabees (a naval construction battalion, newly arrived and greatly admired by the marines) completed work on Fighter One, a second and shorter air strip a mile east of Henderson and designed primarily for Wildcat operations.

The refurbished aircraft carrier *Hornet* arrived back in the Coral Sea from its berth at Pearl Harbor.

A meeting of generals and admirals was held aboard Admiral Ghormley's flagship in Noumea Harbor. Ghormley's prognosis for the survival of Vandegrift's beachhead perimeter was dubious. General MacArthur's aide proposed that Guadalcanal be abandoned to the Japanese, and that MacArthur should retrieve the initiative by launching a thrust northward from Australia through New Guinea.[12]

Marine brigadier general Roy Geiger arrived to take charge of the Cactus Air Force. One of the white-haired, fifty-seven-year-old general's first acts was to climb into an SBD and dive bomb a Japanese position west of the perimeter—after which Geiger's credentials were never in doubt.

Red Mike Edson and his 1st Raider Battalion embarked from the perimeter via landing craft and churned east to a position near Taivu, where they slipped ashore at dawn, found no Japanese, and began working their way east along the coast. After meeting light resistance, they summoned the Cactus Air Force, who arrived in short order to bomb and strafe just ahead of Edson's skirmish line. By early afternoon, the Raiders had fought their way to Kawaguchi's supply base at Tasimboko and found it stocked with rice, clothing, canned goods, ammunition, and artillery pieces. As there was no way to carry the loot back, Edson and his men set about ruining it for Kawaguchi. The artillery pieces were spiked with grenades. The canned goods were punctured with bayonets and the bags of rice thrown into the surf or rendered unpalatable, the latter employing the Raiders' own imaginative technique. The battalion then returned by boat to the perimeter.

The first air-search radar set arrived at Guadalcanal.

A thrust west of the Matanikau to stir up the Japanese was badly muddled, arguably because the orders given its commanding officer were ambiguous. The battalion commander was relieved in the field by his superior, and his career in the Marine Corps would suffer.

An oven for baking bread was made from a Japanese safe. Archer

Vandegrift sent a message to Nimitz's headquarters in Hawaii requesting a hundred gross of condoms. It arrived in the middle of the night. The admiral's aide, thinking perhaps that the message was in code, decided to wake the commander in chief, Pacific. Nimitz read the message, smiled, and said, "General Vandegrift is probably going to use them on the rifles of his marines to keep out the rain."[13]

The Cactus Air Force's highest scoring ace with twelve confirmed kills, marine captain Marion Carl, failed to return from a sortie against the Tokyo Express. Five days later he walked out of the jungle, escorted by friendly natives. When informed that in his absence Capt. John Smith, Carl's rival ace, had shot down several Japanese planes, thus raising his score to sixteen, Carl was miffed. "Well," demanded Roy Geiger, "what are you going to do about it?" "Goddammit, General," Carl snapped, "ground Smith for five days!"

The first latrines on Guadalcanal were constructed, using captured Japanese housing sections. But there was no toilet paper.

Kawaguchi, floundering through the jungle on his way to seize Henderson Field, was ordered by Rabaul to advance the date of his attack to the night of 12 September. This would allow him barely enough time to reach his jump-off point and deploy his troops for the assault.

Living Rough on the 'Canal

More than a month had passed since the men of the 1st Marine Division had set foot on Guadalcanal, and the figurative term "Raggedy-Ass Marines" had become a fact. Their weapons were clean, but the men who cleaned them were ragged, filthy, and malodorous. There had been no clothing resupply since Turner was forced to pull out on 9 August. As a result, most marines still wore the same government issue in which they had waded ashore. Dungarees were caked with dirt and sweat, and in the rifle companies were worn through at the knees and elbows from crawling. Skivvies were gray and tattered, or had been converted to weapon cleaning rags. Socks were history. Boondockers had begun to molder and separate at the toes like clown shoes. Lee's Confederate army had looked more presentable at Appomattox. Hearing of the boondocker crisis, the commanding general of the army's Americal Division in New Caledonia,

Maj. Gen. Alexander Patch, rounded up twenty thousand pairs of new army boots and routed them to Guadalcanal. In the same charitable vein, Maj. Gen. Millard Harmon, U.S. Army commanding officer for the Southwest Pacific Area, having by some mischief been shipped a consignment of cavalry sabers, ordered them cut down to machetes and forwarded to the marines. Occasional bathing and laundering were possible only in the scummy Lunga River, with one eye on the crocodiles and an ear cocked for the air-raid alarm.

There were other aggravations as well, some of them life threatening. Among the milder evils were skin problems that itched, smarted, and oozed. The slightest thorn prick that back home in Iowa would have healed overnight, on Guadalcanal began to redden, then spread, then erupt into a crater of pus the size of a quarter. Sulfa powder wouldn't dent it. Scuttlebutt had it, however, that if you could get a dog to lick the sore, it would heal. In time the repulsive eruption would scab over and grudgingly disappear. Prickly heat was epidemic, as was jock itch, known to marines as crotch rot and difficult to treat in the sweaty, unwashed environment. Boils came up on the bottoms of feet and on the buttocks, which made walking and sitting a heroic business. But these were insignificant compared with dysentery and malaria, both of which had begun to stalk the perimeter in late August. Dysentery was the result of poor field sanitation. Until latrines were built, the thousands of men living rough on the jungle's edge had no choice but to visit a bush when the need arose, and the perimeter quickly became an open sewer. Soon long lines were forming at the medical tents. The grinding, scalding diarrhea threatened to debilitate the entire 1st Division. One man in five was so weak that he needed help to get his pants down and up.[14] Some made the trip to the reeking slit trenches twenty or thirty times a day. Correspondent Richard Tregaskis wrote of jumping into a dugout during an air raid and finding it "crammed with sick people. The feverish, emaciated wrecks . . . were a pitiful sight." Between dysentery and the acute food shortage, the average marine lost thirty-five pounds on Guadalcanal. Vandegrift recorded sorrowfully that "day by day I watched my marines deteriorate in the flesh."

The epidemic was slowly brought under control, only to be replaced by malaria. This disease, endemic to the Solomon Islands, was spread by the bite of the female anopheles mosquito. One sufferer described its effects thus: "Even while I was shaking with cold, my nose was hot . . . my eyeballs must have been on rubber bands hitched to sore places in the back of my brain, for every time I moved my eyes I could feel the stretch clear to the back of my skull, and my skin felt raw and dry even while cold and wet."[15] Once contracted, the disease could recur and recur. Malaria and dysentery would account for five times more marine casualties than enemy action. The only comforting thought was that the Japanese were shaking and sweating as badly as the Americans. There was a preventative for malaria—atabrine. One pill daily suppressed the parasite. But around the tents and dugouts of the perimeter it was rumored that atabrine ruined your sex life. This was reason enough for many marines to avoid the pill. Finally, the navy medical corpsmen got tough. The men were lined up every day, an atabrine pill was popped into each mouth, the man was told to swallow—and to make sure the corpsman had a look inside. Since 1798, marine medical needs had always been attended to by navy medical corpsmen, and the relationship had been a tight one. Every combat platoon had a corpsman permanently attached, traditionally called "Doc." For lesser ills, Doc usually issued an "APC" pill. Only the navy pharmacists knew what "APC" stood for, but marines claimed it meant "all purpose cure." If a marine got too obstreperous, Doc might threaten him with a shot in the arm, which all marines loathed and feared. In difficult cases, it might even be hinted that he was about to get "the bicycle pump," a gigantic but wholly mythical hypodermic syringe that was never actually produced. Navy corpsmen shared the terrors of combat with their marine platoon mates. Their job was to creep up under fire and save marine lives, doing what they could to keep their charges breathing until they could be evacuated to the battalion aid station. Many corpsmen died doing so.

Disease was only one of the harassments attending the Guadalcanal campaign. Another was flying metal in the form of bombing, shelling, and small arms fire. At least one of the three was going on somewhere in the perimeter most hours of the day and night. The almost daily bombing raids could be expected any time between 11:00 in the morning and 2:00 in the afternoon, announced by the bonging of the dinner bell and, as Guadal technology evolved, the hoisting of a black flag up the Henderson flagpole. The coastwatchers stationed up the Slot were quick to warn of approaching Vals and Bettys, so that marines and seabees working at Henderson Field, the usual target, could trot to their dugouts and foxholes in plenty of time. But there was always a tardy someone above ground who was wounded or killed. The worst moment was listening to the wish-wish-wish of the falling bombs while reflecting on your mortality. The sensation was one of utter helplessness. Each of the bombs had to fall to earth somewhere, right? So why not a foot away? Meanwhile the air fluttered with shock waves, you raised yourself on your elbows to minimize ground concussion, and your mind snatched at silly distractions, wondering suddenly what time it was or repeating over and over, "Mary had a little lamb, its fleece was white as snow." The close ones left your ears singing as if full of gnats. After the "all clear," off-duty marines could walk over to the Tojo Ice Factory and check the "score," which was posted on a blackboard together with yesterday's American and National League baseball standings. The "score" was the tally of enemy planes downed versus Cactus Air Force losses. The marines and seabees identified wholly with their flyers in the way that Chicago fans identify with the Chicago Bulls, and a winning score was greeted with rebel yells, grins, and exclamations of "Hey, we really nailed 'em," while bad news was mirrored in grim faces.

A variation on daylight bombing was after-dark shelling, which could take place any time between dusk and dawn. The Tokyo Express, having made its nightly troop delivery, usually saluted the marines before leaving. This meant anywhere from a dozen to fifty shells crashing into the perimeter with no object but to get the 1st Marine Division up and running for dugouts in the dark. Because of this everyone slept fitfully, and the prudent man slept with his pants and boondockers on. The nightly experience of leaping from a canvas cot into a hole in the ground with six inches of water at its bottom gnawed away at one's sense of well-being. Nor was there the satisfaction of drawing enemy blood, as the Japanese warships outranged the few marine coastal guns. The shelling had its lighter moments, however. Civilian correspondent Richard Tregaskis reported that on 26 August he was summoned before a solemnly convened court martial, Col. LeRoy P. Hunt presiding, and awarded membership in the "Lunga Point Shell-dodging Marines." In between these midnight shellings, Louey the Louse or Washing Machine Charley buzzed over the perimeter, scattering green flares and small bombs. One moonless night, Colonel Pepper's 3d Defense Battalion tried for an hour to bring down Louey, or maybe it was Charley, with antiaircraft fire, but no cigar.

Bombing and shelling had an impartial quality, but a rifle bullet was intensely personal. You felt that you had been singled out by some egregious Japanese bastard who could see you over his rifle sights and was intent on killing you. The nasty sound of his inches-away bullet provoked your resentment and hardened your heart against that particular individual. Contrary to popular belief among U.S. troops who had yet to tangle with Japanese infantry, many were expert rifle shots, and almost every sector of the perimeter had its pet sniper. You could picture him as a patient and businesslike, perhaps bespectacled young man with a good optical scope who had carefully memorized the marine position on his front and would wait all day for someone to grow careless and show himself. Marines quickly learned not to duck at the sound of his bullet because, once heard, it had missed. But then you had better get your ass down before he could shove another round up the chamber. If the sniper was not well camouflaged, he could eventually be spotted and flushed with mortar or machine-gun fire. If not, he might claim two or three victims a day. Even his misses were effective, as they contributed to the abrasiveness of life at the front.

Japanese rifle bullets made a variety of sounds. In the open they went hissing and buzzing off through the bush, but when you were lying in a foxhole they snapped wickedly overhead like a whip. If a bullet glanced off of metal—a strand of barbed wire or piece of equipment—it went spinning away head over heels with a ricocheting whine like the shots fired in Hollywood westerns. If the lead slug struck a man, the impact would make a sound ranging anywhere from a soft thud to a loud wallop, depending on the bullet's caliber, where it struck, or if the slug was tumbling when it hit.

Once a marine had become combat savvy, he could pick out every weapon in the enemy arsenal by its sound. The Japanese knee mortar emitted a brassy, metallic twang when fired. Their Arisaka rifles had a higher, flatter crack than marine Springfields, and their Nambu machines guns fired at a much faster rate than ours, so fast they often sounded like gargling. Japanese hand grenades were primed by knocking them against a helmet or rifle butt, and the click, coming from behind a bush, tipped off the imminent arrival of the grenade. The larger Japanese mortar shells went thwung as they left their tubes, took anywhere from eight to fifteen seconds to complete their flight parabola, then fell to earth with a low, feathery rustle followed by a godawful clang. The high-velocity Japanese antitank gun fired a shell that was on you almost before you could hear it coming. Japanese artillery shells in flight sounded wobblier than the marine variety and made a shrill, screechy sound that set your teeth on edge like chalk scraping on a blackboard. In these dicey circumstances, it was inevitable that the 1st Division's crap shooters would evolve a table of calculated risks for combat. To save a buddy's life, the average marine would take any amount of risk, including the prospect of death. To reveal himself long enough to kill a Japanese, a three-to-one risk. To save a wounded Japanese, zero risk. If he were dead tired, and who wasn't in combat, he might take a short cut that would expose him to enemy fire, a thirty-to-one risk. But if he were in a great hurry, he would chance as much as a ten-to-one risk.

In the face of these grim actuarial tables the embattled marines not only kept their cool but also set up a funky sort of housekeeping, found things to feel good about, and had a few laughs in the process. One of the signs that the 1st Division was settling in for a long campaign was the "Great Guadalcanal Housing Boom." Where an array of leaky, muddy tents had stood, there mushroomed a shantytown of lean-tos and huts knocked together from packing crates, palm fronds, and Japanese rice bags. The 6th Seabees, noted for their improvisational skills, rigged a moonshine distillery and were soon turning out a savage brew known as "Jungle Juice" which they shared with marines on a barter basis—a gallon of white lightning for, say, a samurai sword. The Cactus Air Force, which reputedly had access to the stocks of alcohol used in aerial torpedoes, mixed fruit juice with the throat-scorching stuff and relaxed after a tough mission with a sociable glass of "Torpedo Juice."[16] Crap shoots and card games flourished, poker and "Red Dog" being the traditional favorites.

Early in September the first mail arrived since the division's departure from New Zealand. An intensely private matter to each marine, the letters were read and reread until they came apart at the folds. Souvenir hunting and swapping thrived. The hottest items were samurai swords, Arisaka rifles and Nambu pistols, Japanese battle flags (an orange-red "meatball" on a white field), binoculars, and, highly prized, the "belt of a thousand stitches," a white cummerbund in which a thousand well wishers had each taken a stitch. Another lucky find was the rubber waterproof pouch in which Japanese soldiers kept photos of their family, letters, and sometimes a diary. Marines put it to the same use. One of the few perks of being in a line company was speedy access to the goods. It was said that certain marines could shoot a "Nip" at twenty paces and field strip him for souvenirs before he hit the ground. This was hyperbole, of course, but it illustrated the moral concession that the nineteen-year-old marine rifleman had made to combat. Moreover, frisking Japanese corpses for personal effects was more than just souvenir hunting; it was one of war's oldest ceremonies, the taking of enemy scalps.

Ernie Pyle, the World War II correspondent, noted that "the rougher men live, the rougher they talk." This was conspicuously true on Guadalcanal. The Marine Corps has never been known to talk pretty, but rough life and times on the 'Canal catapulted swearing to new heights of fluency. Swearing became an art form, and the F-word its quintessence. The challenge was to use the word as extravagantly as possible. For example: an SBD has just flown over Henderson with one wheel down. A civilian, an army engineer, and a marine rifleman all point this out to their chums:

> Civilian: "Hey, look at that SBD!"
> Army engineer: "Hey, look at that fucking SBD!"
> Marine rifleman: "Hey, look at that fucking SB-fucking-D!"

The other often-heard expression was "Jesus Christ!"—usually uttered at times of stress. For example: a marine cowering in his foxhole during a Japanese mortar attack sees the shellbursts "walking" in his direction. The next one could be a direct hit. He clenches his fists, squeezes his eyes shut in terror, and says, "Jesus Christ!" At such moments, profanity and prayer are indistinguishable.

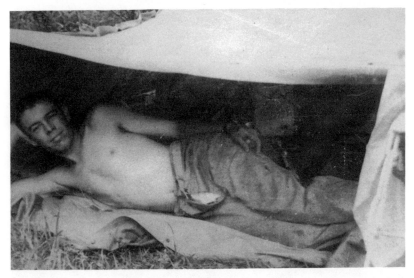

Deep behind Japanese lines, 1st Lt. Cleland Early takes a jungle break with
the 2d Marine Raider Battalion.
Courtesy Col. Cleland Early, USMC (Ret.)

Lt. Col. Evans F. Carlson, *center*, U.S. Marines, conducts a jungle conference
during his battalion's historic thirty-day patrol through Guadalcanal's
tangled rain forest in pursuit of fleeing Japanese.
U.S. Marine Corps photo

Edson's Ridge looking south toward Mount Austen.
Australian Army Cinemagraphic Section photo

Regimental officers of the 1st Marines.
Australian Army Cinemagraphic Section photo

Col. Clifton B. Cates, commanding officer, 1st Marines, looking spit and polish despite the appalling conditions on Guadalcanal, gazes seaward toward Iron Bottom Sound.

U.S. Marine Corps photo

Marine patrol returning over Edson's Ridge from the jungle.
Australian Army Cinemagraphic Section photo

Japanese dog tag.
Courtesy Guadalcanal Museum,
Kalamazoo, Michigan

An SBD dive bomber taking off from a carrier for a Solomon Islands raid,
7 August 1942.
U.S. Navy photo

Formal portrait of a Japanese couple, from a captured photograph,
original source unknown.

Courtesy Guadalcanal Museum, Kalamazoo, Michigan, and Ken Russeau, contributor

Japanese officer with Hitler moustache, from a captured photograph, original source unknown.

Courtesy Guadalcanal Museum, Kalamazoo, Michigan, and Ken Russeau, contributor

Coast Guardsman and Medal of Honor winner Doug Monro.
U.S. Coast Guard photo

M.Sgt. Jacob Vouza, U.S. Marines (Ret.).
U.S. Marine Corps photo

The USS *McCawley* (famous as the "Wacky Mac"), Rear Adm. R. K. "Kelly" Turner's flagship in which he made his "hallelujah" sorties through Japanese-controlled waters to supply Guadalcanal.
U.S. Navy photo

Group of GI buddies, Easy Company, 161st Infantry, 25th Division, U.S. Army.
Courtesy Guadalcanal Echoes and Ted Blahnik, editor, and C. E. Razzdale, contributor

The 2d Marine Raider Battalion moving out over steep terrain.
U.S. Marine Corps photo

Sympathy chit.
Courtesy Guadalcanal Echoes *and* Ted Blahnik, *editor. Original source, U.S. Navy; artist unknown*

Lt. Col. John Mather, U.S. Marines, and Jacob Vouza paying a native labor
party.
U.S. Marine Corps photo

PFC Howard B. Trimble, U.S. Marines, *second from left*, with three tent mates
in front of their Guadalcanal "condo."
Courtesy Howard B. Trimble

Face of the George Medal:
The hand of a navy admiral
drops a hot potato into the
palm of a marine in a foxhole.
Photographed by permission of the
Guadalcanal Museum, Kalamazoo,
Michigan

Back of the George Medal: A
cow backs up to an electric fan.
Photographed by permission of the
Guadalcanal Museum, Kalamazoo,
Michigan

Grumman Wildcats on patrol, looking for a fight.
U.S. Navy photo

Antiaircraft emplacement.
U.S. Marine Corps photo

Marines on shaky bridge over impassable jungle terrain.
U.S. Marine Corps photo

CHAPTER SIX

Something Sobbed
Like a Child

THE ROUTE OF MARCH chosen by Maj. Gen. Kiyotake Kawaguchi had proven to be the obstacle course from hell. In the spectral green twilight of the jungle his veterans slithered up and down the oozing ravines, covered with slimy muck and clutching at the interwoven tendrils for handholds. The dead air was heavy with moisture and stank of rot. No wind blew to evaporate their cooling sweat. Great hairy leaves as big as umbrellas sheltered an army of insects—praying mantises the length of a man's hand, ants that bit like rottweilers, spiders that spun their shimmering nets over the foliage like angel hair on a Christmas tree. Just out of sight, something sobbed like a child.

Kawaguchi's plan called for a three-pronged attack, directed against what were thought to be vulnerable points on the marine perimeter. As his brigade neared the airfield, one battalion, commanded by Maj. Eishi Mizuno, would slant off and position itself along the Tenaru. The other three battalions would press on through the jungle to a long and grassy hog-backed ridge identified on Kawaguchi's map as "the Centipede," which rose out of the jungle and meandered toward the airfield. Once in place, they would launch a coordinated attack along the top and flanks of the Centipede until they broke into the perimeter. They would then seize Henderson Field and attack the marine lines from within until all enemy resistance had ceased. Meanwhile, the truant Colonel Oka would attack from the west across the Matanikau, and Major Mizuno's battalion would jump off from the east, across the Tenaru. The attack would be launched at night to thwart the Cactus Air Force and capitalize on the heavy bombardment of the ridge and airfield scheduled by the Imperial Navy.

Whatever Happens, I'm Staying Here with You

Back in the perimeter after his successful raid on Tasimboko, Red Mike Edson checked in with Col. Gerald Thomas, the 1st Division operations officer. "This is no motley of Japs," Edson said, setting down the half-gallon of sake he had liberated from Kawaguchi's supply depot. In the division intelligence shack, Capt. "Pappy" Moran sifted through the maps and documents that Edson had brought him. Factoring in the reports of Martin Clemens's native irregulars and the troop movements glimpsed by the Cactus Air Force, Moran concluded that the approaching enemy were, indeed, "no motley of Japs." They were instead three thousand freshly landed Japanese infantry. Poring over maps and aerial photos the next morning with Edson, Gerry Thomas agreed. "Yes," he said, "they're coming, but which way?" Edson put his finger on a photo of the ridge that lay a mile southeast of Henderson. "This looks like a good approach,"[1] he said in his grating whisper. The ridge, like a long, Kunai grass–covered gangplank, connected the jungle with the southern approaches to Henderson Field. For lack of manpower Major General Vandegrift had left it undefended.

On 10 September, two days before Kawaguchi's scheduled attack, Edson moved his Raider Battalion and the remnants of the Parachute Battalion up onto the ridge, explaining with fingers crossed that there was "too much shelling and bombing here close to the beach, we're moving to a

quiet spot." He ordered his eight hundred men to dig in along the southern knob of the ridge, and fanned two companies of Raiders out toward
the Lunga River bank. The Paratroop Battalion he extended in the opposite direction. The following day, as Edson's marines were wiring in their
front, the air-raid warning sounded. Well, no worries, chum, the Nips
always targeted the airfield, right? Wrong! Twenty-six Bettys dropped their
lethal ordnance the length and breadth of the ridge, including "daisy
cutters" fused for instantaneous detonation and hip-high shrapnel effect.
Most of Edson's men dived into their foxholes and emerged with whole
skins, but twenty-five marines tried to outrun the vicious orange and black
flashes and were killed or wounded in midstride. "Some goddam rest
area," yelled a corporal in Edson's direction.

That same day, 11 September, Kelly Turner flew in from Noumea with
Rear Adm. John "Slew" McCain, the man in charge of all land-based
aircraft in the Southwest Pacific. They were fresh from a meeting with
Ghormley. Vandegrift met them and thought that Turner looked tense.
After dodging a second air raid, they proceeded with Gerry Thomas to the
1st Division command post. There Turner reached into his shirt pocket,
pulled out a navy communications form, and handed it silently to Vandegrift. As the general read it his face went white.[2] The message was a situation appraisal drawn up by Ghormley's staff with his endorsement. It
reported that the Japanese fleet was now concentrated at Truk, their principal mid-Pacific naval base; that enemy air strength at Rabaul and Kavieng
was increasing; and that a major Japanese effort to retake Guadalcanal
within ten days was probable. It went on to detail U.S. Navy and Marine
Corps weaknesses and concluded by stating that, as commander of U.S.
naval forces in the South Pacific, Ghormley could no longer support the
marines on Guadalcanal. In effect, Ghormley had abdicated. As Vandegrift
handed the message to his operations officer, Turner reached into his travel
bag, produced a bottle of scotch, and poured four drinks. Hoisting one
of them, he said, "Vandegrift, I'm not inclined to take so pessimistic a
view of the situation as Ghormley does. He doesn't believe I can get the
7th Marines in here [from Samoa], but I think I have a scheme that will
fool the Japs." He went on to spell out his plan. When he had finished,

Vandegrift told Thomas, "Put that message in your pocket. I don't want anyone to know about it." The four men then sat down to compose a message to Ghormley, urging him in the strongest terms to authorize Turner's plan (which, to Ghormley's credit, he would do). Afterward, Vandegrift elicited a few chuckles by producing Major General Kawaguchi's white dress uniform, part of the loot from Edson's raid on Tasimboko. Unknown to those present it was the tailor-made finery in which Kawaguchi, who was something of a dandy, planned to accept Vandegrift's surrender. Had Vandegrift known this, he might have uttered something historic. As it was, Turner broke out another bottle of scotch.

The next morning, 12 September, Archer Vandegrift said to his operations officer, "Gerry, we're going to defend this airfield until we no longer can. If that happens, we'll take to the hills and fight guerrilla warfare. I want you to go see Bill Twining [Vandegrift's executive officer], swear him to secrecy and have him draw up a plan." Vandegrift then went looking for Roy Geiger to fill him in. "When the time comes that we can no longer hold the perimeter," Vandegrift told him, "I expect you to fly out your planes." The white-haired commander of the Cactus Air Force nodded. "Archer," he said, "if we can't use the planes back in the hills, we'll fly them out. But whatever happens, I'm staying here with you."[3]

Raiders, Rally to Me

There were plenty of clues. The information contained in Ghormley's abdication letter was one, yesterday's bombing of the ridge another. Clemens's scouts continued to report troop movements in force to the south and east. SBDs of the Cactus Air Force on their afternoon patrol found the northern waters of the Slot speckled with Japanese warships racing southeast. Hearing this, the ground crews at Henderson Field hurriedly dispersed the bombers and fighters to minimize bombardment damage. The air crackled with tension. Lt. Herb Merillat, marine combat correspondent attached to 1st Division HQ, wrote in his diary that for the first time after an air raid he noticed that he was trembling. The Raiders and Paratroopers manning the ridge—their "rest" area—needed no prodding from Edson to dig deeper. When they did, they found rock.[4] Darkness fell and the smoking lamp was declared out. The perimeter was on full alert. At 9:30 Louey the Louse droned overhead, a green flare blossomed in the night sky and shed its Halloween light on the ridge. A moment later the horizon north of the beachhead was lit by vivid yellow flashes, and a salvo of 8-inch naval shells trundled noisily over the perimeter to geyser among the foxholes of the Raiders and the Paratroopers. There were shouts of "Corpsman!" Vandegrift and Turner crouched behind a wall of sandbags as the 8-inchers plowed the air above them and the earth shook. For twenty minutes the bombardment battered the marine positions, then abruptly it stopped. The defenders braced themselves. From the jungle at the foot of the ridge a red rocket arced skyward to the hackle-raising war chant of Kawaguchi's 3d Infantry Battalion.

"Banzai! Banzai! Banzai!"

"Kiss my coon dog ass!" bellowed a marine through cupped hands.

"Drink marine blood!" promised a Japanese voice.

From the 1st Division command post Vandegrift and Turner heard the rifle fire swell into a chorus of machine guns and mortars, then the thud of hand grenades that meant a fight at nearly bayonet point. A flying wedge of Japanese had flung itself at the vulnerable juncture between the two Raider companies anchoring the flank of the ridge to the Lunga River. The charge was blunted, but in the furious night action seven marines went missing. A second thrust momentarily isolated a platoon of C Company, and a third Japanese phalanx grenaded and bayoneted its way between C Company's right flank and the river. In the darkness and confusion, lit only by grenade flashes, captains lost touch with their companies, lieutenants with their platoons, and the struggle became a midnight alley fight, with Japanese in among the marines, and bypassed marines firing into the backs of the Japanese. Between bursts of fire, the sergeants could be heard shouting, "Raiders, rally to me! Raiders, rally to me!" PFC Ray Herndon and his squad stood off charge after charge until only four men were left standing. Then a bullet whacked into Herndon's abdomen. Knowing that he was a dead man, Herndon, armed with a Colt 45, yelled at the others to pull back while he stood off the next rush.[5] His body was later recovered. The thin green line of Raiders held, but bent back under the hammer blows until the last marine on the right had the ridge to his rear and was facing the Lunga River. Then, as quickly as they had appeared, the Japanese dissolved into the jungle and the firing sputtered out.

When the attack on the ridge had begun, the Japanese naval bombardment had lifted, then readjusted its fire to fall on Henderson Field.[6] The bell-bottomed Marines of Flight 300, all of whom tented together, dived into their L-shaped slit trench, flattening against its wall as the 8-inch shells clipped palm tree fronds over their heads and spewed hot metal in all directions. No one in their trench was wounded, but a few yards away the marine pilots caught hell. The top of their dugout took a direct hit, killing Lieutenants Rose and Baldinus and wounding two others. At first light, when Ens. Harold Buell, one of the Bell Bottomed pilots, walked up to his SBD to fly the dawn patrol, he almost fell over a body lying beside the wing. It was a dead Japanese. Sitting in the SBD's cockpit was a skinny young Raider in filthy dungarees. "Howdy," he said to the astonished Buell. He then explained. Edson had predicted that any Japanese infiltrating as far as Henderson Field would try to destroy parked aircraft by putting a hand grenade in the cockpit. So, drawled the Raider, Edson had assigned each plane an armed guard. When the infiltrator stepped out of the darkness and mounted the SBD's wing, the skinny young Raider had shoved his BAR against the man's chest and squeezed off a burst.

The Devilish Jungle

Kawaguchi's intent had been to jump off with his attack at 8:00 the night of 12 September, but only one battalion had arrived at the staging area on time. The other two, disoriented in the jungly maze, straggled in three hours later. The march to the jump-off point presented further difficulties. With visibility limited to a few feet in the blackness of the rain forest, Kawaguchi's battalions might as well have been blindfolded. They drifted west, holding onto one another's packs and intermingling until they lost all unit integrity. Kawaguchi himself went astray and stumbled into the Lunga River with his entire staff, wading downstream until the strong current and the depth forced him onto the east bank. Then entirely by chance his 3d Battalion had bumped the Raider lines and, like a hor-

net brushing a bare arm, reflexively attacked, were fought off, and withdrew. Meanwhile, the 11th Marines, furiously serving their guns, combed
the jungle south of the ridge with 75- and 105-millimeter shells, many
of which fell on Japanese concentrations and did great execution. Neither
of Kawaguchi's wing detachments, Mizuno on the Tenaru and Oka on
the Matanikau, fired a shot. The jungle had defeated them. Shortly before
dawn, Kawaguchi, soaked and infuriated, sent runners with orders to call
off the attack and reassemble that coming night for a second effort. He
later wrote, "Because of the devilish jungle, the brigade was scattered all
over and completely beyond control. In my whole life, I have never felt
so helpless."

Hopes had run high at Japanese 17th Army Headquarters on Rabaul.
There had been no radio communication from Kawaguchi the night of
the twelfth, but American radio intercepts, optimistically interpreted,
reinforced Japanese feelings of confidence. Then a message was received
early on the morning of the thirteenth from a reconnaissance flight over
Guadalcanal. The message read "Success"—meaning that Henderson Field
was in Japanese hands. The agreed "Success" signal, two torch fires dis-
played fifty meters apart, had been clearly visible from the air. A 17th Army
staff officer was dispatched in a second reconnaissance plane with a Zero
escort to confirm the news. On arrival, two dozen Cactus Air Force Wildcats rose from Henderson Field to see them off. Unimpressed, the staff
officer returned to Rabaul with the confirmation.

The Spooky Stare of Exhaustion

As the sun rose on the morning of 13 September, Red Mike Edson sat on
his ridge, thoughtfully spooning up a breakfast of cold C-rations. "They
were testing, just testing," he told his officers. "They'll be back tonight."
He gave orders for the line to be pulled back two hundred yards to more
defensible ground. The move would also present the oncoming Japanese
with an unfamiliar front and force them to charge across two hundred
yards of grassy ridgetop, where the grazing fire of marine machine guns
could chew them up. The Raiders and the Paratroopers were woefully

lacking in numbers for the job at hand. Both battalions had been badly shot up in the Tulagi-Gavutu-Tanambogo assaults, then drained by dysentery and malaria, and last night's action had further whittled them down. D Company Raiders, whose table of organization called for 250 riflemen, could muster only twenty, most of them feverish and starved of sleep. But there were no replacements. Every other marine rifleman on Guadalcanal was holding down his own bit of the perimeter. Edson himself looked like a scarecrow, with holes in his dungaree jacket where two bullets had scorched through without touching him.[7] The manpower shortage had made it impossible for him to set up a continuous defense. Instead, Edson plugged the gaps in his line with strongholds situated a football field apart—a leaky arrangement. Later in the day Lt. Col. Merrill Twining, one of Vandegrift's staff officers, visited the ridge and found Edson's men bone weary, with the spooky stare of exhaustion.

Closer, Closer

At 9:00 P.M. Louey the Louse closed his throttle, glided silently in over the Lunga River delta, and released a dripping parachute flare that etched the ridge and its defenders in stark green relief.[8] As it descended, a second flare, bright red, rose from the jungle, and two thousand shrieking Japanese infantry, bayonets glinting in the ghastly light, broke from cover and advanced at a trot. "Gas attack, gas attack," they shouted, hurling grenades that burst into clouds of red smoke. Their forward element, led by the sword-swinging Major Kokusho, powered its way into the marine right flank, hurling one Raider company back, cutting off one of its platoons, and drawing marine blood. But cued by the red rockets, the 105s of the 11th Marines, bucking and roaring, laid down so killing a barrage on the jungle fringe that the following Japanese ranks were scattered and the momentum of their charge blunted. Seeing this, the 11th Marine gunners fired whenever a red rocket went up to signal another charge.[9] Without their accuracy and speed of delivery it is unlikely that the line would have held. Even so, the battle was touch and go far into the night. Time after time, the forest of bayonets—two full battalions—surged up the south face of the ridge, or in the darkness and confusion slipped along its flanks. With each new charge, Edson shouted, "Closer, closer!" to the forward artillery observers who were directing the fire, and the next rounds would spin in so closely that the panting marines could feel the hot breath of every shell burst. Confronting the human wave at the south face of the ridge were just three hundred battered, punch-drunk Raiders, pulling triggers and flinging hand grenades with their last drops of adrenalin.

Suddenly, as the focus of the battle shifted from one critical point to another, Edson found his east flank exposed. The Paratroopers manning it had been evicted from their foxholes by sheer press of enemy numbers and had fallen back in disarray to a high knoll at the ridge's center. It was the crisis. Reacting instantly, Edson ran forward under fire to the high knoll and, encouraging this man and blistering that man, he rallied the rest of his command around him and organized a new line of defense. At one point, a file of battle-dazed marines stumbling back down the spine of the ridge to the new position thought they heard an order to "Withdraw!" and kept going. Other marines looked at them, then at one another, wondering if they were meant to pull back as well. Fortunately, what could have been an epidemic was stopped in its tracks by Maj. Ken Bailey, who confronted the wavering men and in his best parade-ground roar ordered them to about-face and get their asses back on the line. They did and the line held.

Now Edson's new stronghold was the only thing that stood between the Japanese and Henderson Field. The Japanese stormed it with charge after charge, and in the lulls flailed it with machine guns and mortars, but still the Raiders clung to the knoll. The telephone line to division was cut by mortar fire, and for a while it was impossible to pass the word that the ridge's defenders were running out of ammunition and grenades. When the line was mended and supplies were brought up, Ken Bailey spent the next hour crawling from foxhole to foxhole handing out 30.06 Springfield clips and hand grenades. He would be awarded the Medal of Honor for his night's work but would die in a later action before he could collect it.

Still the waves of resolute Japanese, fewer of them now, continued to crash and break against the knoll and its flanks, while Merritt Edson, silhouetted by the yellow grenade flashes and shellbursts, presided over the scene like some Wagnerian war god, his hoarse voice cutting through the chaos between outbursts of firing. Where the action was hottest, there he was, shouting encouragement to his men, and if a glassy-eyed marine should stumble away from the fight, Edson would shame him, pointing toward the Japanese and shouting, "Get back where you came from—the only thing they've got that you haven't got is guts." There was one serious breakthrough. Fifty Japanese, survivors of a heavily shelled company, found a gap in marine lines and made their way to Fighter One, the recently completed fighter strip. There they tangled with C Company, 1st Engineer Battalion, capturing two machine guns. The engineers fought them off with the help of hastily mobilized rear echelon personnel from Headquarters Company.

At 4:00 A.M. Vandegrift began feeding the division reserves into Edson's ragged line, where they helped throw back two last convulsive Japanese thrusts. When the remnants of these attackers fell back into the jungle, Edson rasped into the field telephone to Gerry Thomas, "We can hold now." With the dawn came the shark-toothed P-400s of the army's 67th Pursuit Squadron to skim the treetops and pump their 20-millimeter cannon shells into the survivors of Kawaguchi's brigade huddled in clearings near the ridge. Two of the P-400s were struck by ground fire and their engines seized. Both pilots, holding their breaths, managed to stretch their glides to Henderson's runway. Meanwhile, the 11th Marines' artillery fire walked back and forth through the jungle probing for any Japanese the P-400s had missed.

There were sideshows and echoes of the battle:

At 10:00 P.M. the previous night Kawaguchi's right wing battalion, commanded by Major Mizuno, had crossed the Tenaru upstream of the perimeter and, thoroughly lost, had blundered into the machine guns of 3d Battalion, 1st Marines. The Japanese immediately attacked, were repulsed, and left twenty-seven of their number hanging on the marine wire, including Major Mizuno. Ineffectual attacks were made the following two nights to no purpose.

The truant Colonel Oka with his small detachment of barge-voyaging survivors skirmished on the Matanikau flank with 3d Battalion, 5th Marines the night of the thirteenth but was seen off by the pinpoint accuracy of Marine artillery shells. Two half-hearted attacks were attempted the following day, both futile.

On 15 September, the day following his defeat, Kawaguchi radioed the humiliating news to his superiors at Rabaul. It was received with shock and disbelief. One of Yamamoto's staff officers observed that the army had been accustomed to fighting the Chinese.

Even in its death throes, Kawaguchi's brigade fought on. The morning after the all-night battle, the fire of Japanese snipers made Edson's ridge and its surrounds hazardous. A jeep load of marine casualties on its way to the battalion aid station was machine-gunned by a solitary Japanese who had slipped through Edson's lines. Several of the wounded marines were killed.

Two marine companies sent into the jungle to speed Kawaguchi on his way got into serious trouble. One was forced to break off action and withdraw in the face of heavy fire. A platoon of the second company was ambushed and all but wiped out. The bill for this postvictory skirmish came to eighteen dead marines.

At Vandegrift's command post between the ridge and the airfield, Marine Gunner (Warrant Officer) Sheffield Banta was seated at his work table, typing a report. His train of thought was interrupted by a loud shout of "Banzai!" Grabbing his 45, Banta stepped out of the tent just in time to see a Japanese withdrawing his bayonet from the body of a marine. Banta flipped off the safety of his pistol and matter-of-factly dropped the bayonet wielder with one shot. As he fired, a second infiltrating Japanese was tackled by another marine, then shot, while a third Japanese legged it back into the bush and disappeared. Holstering his 45, Gunner Banta returned to his tent and his typing.

Edson was recommended by Vandegrift for the Medal of Honor. Unlike Ken Bailey, Edson would live to collect his.

Kawaguchi gathered together what men he could find and retreated to the west, away from his ruined food and ammunition depot at Tasimboko. His men had carried rations for three days only, expecting to eat marine food once they had overrun the perimeter. Now they straggled westward across some of the most punishing terrain on Guadalcanal, their bellies cramped with unrequited hunger. They ate what they could find along the hacked-out jungle trail—betel nuts, weeds, bamboo shoots, fish stunned with hand grenades, roots, and insects. When none of these were at hand, they gnawed tree bark and chewed their leather rifle slings. Many of the stretcher-borne wounded died along the way. Their bones define the trail to this day, together with their rusted weapons and equipment. The terrible ordeal is preserved in this portion of a poem by Guadalcanal veteran Sgt. Kashichi Yoshida:

> No matter how far we walk
> We don't know where we're going
> Trudging along under dark jungle growth.
>
> Our rice is gone
> Eating roots and grass
> Along the ridges and cliffs
> Leaves hide the trail. We lose our way
> Stumble and get up, fall and get up.
>
> Flies swarm to the scabs
> No strength to brush them away
> Fall down and cannot move
> How many times I've thought of suicide.[10]

On 19 September the sad procession finally reached Kokumbona, where Kawaguchi discovered that one of his battalions had retreated in the opposite direction, east to Koli Point, hoping perhaps to find the food which Edson's Raiders had punctured, peed on, or dumped into the sea. A month would elapse before Kawaguchi could return to the offensive.

Marine casualties for the Battle of Edson's Ridge came to 96 killed and missing and 222 wounded. The Parachute Battalion was finished as a fighting unit. Of the 397 men who had stormed Gavutu on 7 August, then fought on Edson's Ridge, only 86 answered roll call the morning after the battle. The 1st Raider Battalion was scarcely better off.

Japanese losses, counting the barging casualties, were estimated at eight hundred killed and missing and five hundred wounded.

Little Boys with Dirty Faces

As the sun rose on the morning of 14 September, it shone upon a surreal scene. Edson's ridge looked as if some colossal dump truck had crawled the length of its quarter-mile spine, spilling bodies as it went. More than five hundred of them were Japanese. Here and there sprawled a marine, sometimes locked in a death embrace with a Japanese. "The Jap dead don't bother me," a marine officer said, "but it's hard for me to look at the marines. They seem like little boys with dirty faces who have just fallen asleep." The marine dead were quickly recovered, identified, and covered with ponchos. They were then taken by truck to the marine burial grounds, known as "Flanders Field," prayed over according to their faith, and solemnly buried alongside other fallen marines. Their funeral services were attended by their off-duty chums. Later the wooden crosses or Stars of David on their graves would be decorated and inscribed by their buddies. A favorite inscription was a fragment of oft-quoted Marine Corps doggerel:

And when I get to heaven,
To Saint Peter I will tell,
Another marine reporting, sir,
I've served my time in hell.

One marine's grave especially touched war correspondent Ira Wolfert, who wrote, "His friends trimmed its mound pathetically with coconuts and fashioned a rude wooden cross for a headstone. A helmet with three holes in it, the holes as blank as dead eyes, tops the cross and is penciled, 'A Real Guy.' Against the cross stands a photograph of a very pretty girl, staring silently."

The five hundred Japanese corpses took longer to bury, and by noon the equatorial sun beating on the unshaded ridge was hastening the process of decay. Unless punctured, the dead bellies began to bloat with gas, which found its way out through the body's natural vents, making at times startling, lifelike sounds. The dead faces, already yellow-gray, would soon turn red. If the body was not quickly buried, the face would turn from red, to purple, to green, to black, and finally to slimy. Meanwhile, the voracious land crabs and whirling funnel clouds of loudly buzzing flies sped the work of corruption. Many of the corpses grinned, as if death were a joke. But far worse than the sight of death was the smell of death —sweet-sour and heavy. It stank worse than the jungle, worse than vomit, worse than a ripe latrine. If you were downwind, there was no escaping it. With every breath, you sucked death up your nose where its ghoulish stench confronted you with the unsavory fact that one fine day you too would smell like that.

To the young marines on Guadalcanal the fear of death was ever present, but most had learned to live with it. Having by now experienced fear many times, they were wise to its ways—the dry mouth, thumping heart, hyperventilation, and near-panic; the compulsion in combat to move at a crouch, hunch your shoulders, and pull in your neck; and a feeling that at any moment you could lose control of your bowels. They had also learned that none of these symptoms could kill them, and that fear, in fact, could be an ally of sorts. The adrenaline rush that comes with fear greatly sharpens the senses, concentrates the mind, and does wonders for your speed over the ground when crossing a Nambu fire lane. They also found ways to suppress their fear. One way was to joke about it. By conjuring up their fear, then mocking it with the sardonic humor that has always run in the veins of the Marine Corps, they took some of the ache out of it. Nowhere was this more apparent than in the songs they caterwauled:

> Take down your service flag, Mother,
> > Put up that star of gold,
> Your boy was an aerial gunner,
> > And died only nineteen years old!

> When the war is over we will all enlist again,
> > When the war is over we will all enlist again,
> When the war is over we will all enlist again,
> > In a pig's asshole we will!

> Oh, the rifles bang and the mortars clang,
> > and the Nips they blaze away . . .

Ship me over, Sergeant Major,
　　　Ship me over, I'm a fightin' sonofabitch!

The Cactus Air Force had its own interpretation:

I wanted wings 'til I got the goddamn things,
　　　Now I don't want them anymore,
They taught me how to fly, then sent me here to die,
　　　Now I've got a bellyful of war.
You can give all the Zeros to the dashing young heroes,
　　　Distinguished Flying Crosses
Do not compensate for losses, Buster,
　　　I wanted wings 'til I got the goddamn things,
Now I don't want them any more.[11]

The privates and PFCs also sang songs that needled their noncoms, usually out of earshot:

Fuck 'em all, fuck 'em all,
　　　The long and the short and the tall,
Fuck all the sergeants, the sour-faced ones,
　　　Fuck all the corporals and their bastard sons,
So we're saying goodbye to them all,
　　　As over the gangway we crawl,
There'll be no promotion this side of the ocean,
　　　So cheer up my lads, fuck 'em all.

There was one quintessentially marine song that thumbed its nose at rank, while spelling out, in the Corps' own sardonic, irreverent fashion, the pride taken by the lowly private in his Marine Corps:

I'd like to see the majors in the grave yard,
　　　The captains and lieutenants by their side,
The sergeants and the corporals in the guard house,
　　　The privates and the musics running wild—
As we go marching,
　　　And the band begins to P-L-A-Y,

You can hear them shouting,
> The Raggedy-Ass Marines are on parade!

With receipt of the dismaying news from Kawaguchi on 15 September, Imperial General Headquarters immediately convened to think the Guadalcanal problem through again. By the end of the day they emerged from their deliberations with an entirely new perspective. The island of Guadalcanal, the IGHQ now believed, was the United States' choice of location for the decisive battle of the Pacific war, the outcome of which could determine Japan's world status for years to come. Therefore, New Guinea was struck off of the priority list, and it was resolved that all of Japan's military might would now be committed to recapturing Guadalcanal and denying the United States this victory.

CHAPTER SEVEN

The Cactus Air Force

1 SEPTEMBER 1942, 9:00 P.M.: The Guadalcanal sky was moonless and blanketed with cloud. Navy lieutenant Hal Buell of Flight 300 sat in the darkened cockpit of his SBD at one end of Henderson Field and peered down the V of faint and far-between lights that defined the single runway. In the rear-facing gunner's seat, Airman 3d Class Johnny Villarreal could see nothing. Their orders were to take off into the night and dive-bomb the Japanese warships in Iron Bottom Sound that were casually lobbing shells into the perimeter. Several had fallen with a *crash* near the dirt airstrip in the minute or so that Buell had sat there, running up his engine. Now he eased the SBD's throttle forward, the engine surged mightily, and the slate-blue dive bomber began to rumble down the rutted, potholed runway, quickly gathering speed. Suddenly an explosion rocked Buell's aircraft. The SBD veered sharply left toward two other SBDs taxiing down the edge of the strip. Buell hauled back on the stick and his aircraft ballooned into the air, shuddered, and stalled. A crash was inevitable. Hands

moving like rattlesnakes, Buell closed the throttle and switched off the magnetos. Dead ahead loomed an immovable object—a steamroller parked by the taxiway. Buell's SBD caromed off the steamroller and plowed on down the runway, shedding parts as it went. Fifty yards later it ground to a halt. Buell was out in an instant. The danger now was fire and the plane's five-hundred-pound bomb. Luckily the big bomb had torn free and lay behind him near the steamroller. The plane's engine had also parted company and come to rest some distance away, a ball of metallic junk. Of the wings, only stubs remained. Gasoline from the gashed fuel tanks soaked much of the wreckage.

Rear gunner Villarreal was groggy and still hanging by his harness. Working frantically, Buell unbuckled him, and the two men reeled away from the remains of their SBD. Buell could scarcely walk: his inside thigh muscles had been battered by the flailing control stick. A jeep careened up and three marines jumped out. One of them shined a flashlight on Buell's face and exclaimed, "My God, lieutenant, you've gouged your eye out, Sir!" Buell, who had been wondering why he couldn't see out of his left eye, explored it cautiously and found a half-inch shard of glass protruding from his eyeball. He pulled it out. At the medical tent the doctors diagnosed the injuries of both men as painful but superficial, including Buell's punctured eyeball. They were patched up and two days later were back in the air, bombing and strafing a Tokyo Express run. Their SBD was pronounced "totaled" and hauled off to the "bone yard," where, as an organ donor, it would help to keep other SBDs flying.[1]

The original Cactus Air Force had consisted entirely of Marine Air Group 23 (MAG-23), which arrived at Guadalcanal on 20 August to the cheers of the marines. It was soon augmented by the U.S. Army Air Force's 67th Pursuit Squadron, and by the navy's Flight 300, on loan from the stricken *Enterprise*. Three weeks after its debut, it was in crisis. Its Wildcat fighters were being shot down, crash landed, or wrecked on takeoff at a rate of 26 percent per week.[2] Its SBDs had fared little better. Of the fourteen original army air force P-400s, only three were still flying. And every day there were more empty cots in the tents of the embattled pilots and aircrew who flew them.

To Rear Adm. John S. McCain on Noumea, the officer in charge of all shore-based aircraft in the U.S. Navy's patch of the South Pacific, this rate of attrition was a make-or-break issue. A feisty, pint-sized Alabamian with false teeth and a lobster claw profile, he saw the Battle of Guadalcanal as a mutual assistance pact between the Cactus Air Force and the "ground-pounders"—the foxhole marines. The Cactus Air Force defended the ground-pounders by bombing Japanese reinforcement convoys at sea, and the ground-pounders defended the Cactus Air Force by fighting off Japanese thrusts at Henderson Field. If either defaulted, Guadalcanal was lost. From his HQ on Admiral Ghormley's flagship, McCain radioed Adm. Chester Nimitz, commander in chief, Pacific, in Hawaii, insisting that the problem was acute: Cactus Air Force pilots were stumbling with exhaustion, their ranks were thinning rapidly and their planes were catching hell. They must have reinforcements immediately, he urged, declaring that "the situation admits of no delay whatever . . . if the reinforcement requested is not made available, Guadalcanal cannot be supplied and hence cannot be held." But with timely reinforcement, McCain predicted, "Guadalcanal can be a sinkhole for enemy air power and can be consolidated, expanded and exploited to the enemy's mortal hurt. The reverse is true if we lose Guadalcanal."[3]

McCain's alarm was justified. The men and machines of the Cactus Air Force were perilously near crackup. Ground crews were short of everything needed to keep the planes in the air—gasoline, hand-pumped refueling equipment, spare parts, tools, starter cartridges, experienced ground crews, or enough hours in the day and night in which to do the job. Mechanics often had to borrow starter cartridges from the marine tank battalion before engines could be turned over. Also lacking were hoists for slinging the half-ton bombs under the SBDs, spare propellers, wheels and tires, and machines for belting 50-caliber ammunition. The planes themselves were plastered with bullet-hole patches, and too many of their vital parts were secondhand transplants from the bone yard. Nor was the original equipment always reliable: three Wildcat pilots had died when their oxygen systems failed; they had drifted into unconsciousness and fallen four miles into the sea. Henderson Field itself was a menace to users. There was only enough steel matting to cover one thousand yards of the runway. When it rained, as it did every day, the remaining dirt surface became a sea of slick, ankle-deep mud, hiding submerged pot holes and ruts in which landing gear collapsed and speeding aircraft slewed, ground-looped, or somersaulted. Fortunately, the runway dried quickly in the equatorial sun, but then became a dust bowl. The continual naval bombardments and air raids had destroyed many sitting aircraft and damaged others. To counter this, SBD pilots jumped in their planes and flew them out of harm's way whenever the air-raid warning sounded. Even the "scrambles" sometimes took off half an hour late, as jeeps were often unavailable to ferry pilots to their distant revetments, and the phone line to the motor pool was frequently down.

For the pilots and air crewmen of the Cactus Air Force, time spent on the ground between sorties was only slightly less abrasive than time spent aloft in combat. They shared Guadalcanal's squalor with the foxhole marines, taking their turns at malaria, dysentery, jungle rot, and boils; leaping from their cots at 2:00 A.M. into watery slit trenches when Washing Machine Charley chugged overhead or shells began dropping into the perimeter; losing close friends as the air war of attrition bit into their ranks. The grubby clothing they wore was that in which they had stepped off the boat or plane, except for the baseball caps issued on arrival by the Cactus Air Force—pilots, blue; mechanics, red. Their tents were pitched on a few acres of real estate between Henderson Field and the beach, known as "Mosquito Gulch."[4] The tents had dirt floors, and seepage from the daily cloudburst soaked the mats on which the newest arrivals slept. Sporadic firefights with enemy patrols broke out just a rifle shot from their bivouac, while infiltrating Japanese sniped at pilots and ground crews as they went about their business.

The cooks did their best, but the food was dismal—wormy Japanese rice, Spam, dehydrated potatoes, hash, and powdered eggs, to which, went the joke, the cooks added bits of Ping-Pong balls to simulate the real thing. This flavorless and tiresome diet not only melted flesh from the pilots' bones but also generated gas that expanded as a pilot took off and climbed. The result might have been entertaining, had it not been painful. The oxygen they breathed at altitudes above fifteen thousand feet raised their metabolic rate, leaving them woozy. Worried about the pilots' deteriorating health, the doctors prescribed vitamins and fresh fruit, all in scant supply. Now and then in the midst of this relentless angst there were moments of comic relief. During an air raid two pilots were seen running frantically from falling bombs that seemed to pursue them. The hindmost, red-haired Bill Pittman, yelled to his fellow sprinter, "Hey, Ritchie, wait for me—I don't want to get killed and not have anyone *see* it!" On another day Pittman's rear gunner suffered burst eardrums when their SBD, trying to lose a Zero, plummeted thousands of feet without dive brakes. Pittman then recruited a large marine baker to sit in the gunner's seat and cover the SBD's rear with the twin 30-calibers. All went well until the baker accidentally popped his parachute and for the rest of the flight was engulfed in billows of white nylon.[5]

The endless round of sleep deprivation, disease, poor nutrition, and daily confrontation with death in the sky gnawed at even a strong man's psyche until he no longer recognized himself. Some pilots—iron men like Maj. Dick Mangrum, Capt. Bob Galer, and Capt. John Smith—seemed to thrive on the diet, but most others found the punishing routine increasingly hard to take. It was said by carrier-based pilots who had dropped in at Henderson for a tour with the Cactus Air Force that one month on Guadalcanal was the equivalent of six months of carrier duty. Even marine riflemen who spent time at Mosquito Gulch were relieved to get back to their foxholes. Combat fatigue soon began to surface among the pilots, taking various forms. One was the well known "bulkhead stare" of the man who had momentarily switched off his mind and defocused his eyes to escape reality. Other symptoms included a higher rate of accidents, a wandering mind while on reconnaissance, blanks in a usually good memory, and a creeping, numbing apathy. In rare cases, a pilot with combat fatigue was unwilling to fight, either refusing combat or not seeking it.[6] He simply had no more to give. Commanding officers soon realized that the average pilot's combat effectiveness fell off abruptly after one month in the Guadalcanal meat grinder. Ordinarily the pilot would be relieved and rested, but the replacement shortage made this virtually impossible.

Nevertheless, in the face of these daily horrors and harassments, the men
of the Cactus Air Force, with red-rimmed eyes and gritted teeth, continued to climb into their planes, take off, and get the job done.

This was the leadership challenge that greeted Brig. Gen. Roy Geiger
when he arrived at Henderson Field the evening of 3 September to take
command of the Cactus Air Force. A burly, white-thatched veteran of
fifty-seven, Geiger was one of the Marine Corps' saltiest pilots, having
won his wings in time to see air combat in World War I and later in the
"Banana Wars" of Haiti and Central America. The general's features were
as sharp as his tongue, his manner was preemptive and demanding, and
no one in his right mind talked back to him. It is worth repeating that
one of Geiger's first acts was to climb into an SBD and dive-bomb a
Japanese position east of the perimeter, after which his credentials were
never in doubt. Geiger's number two, Col. Louis Woods, was of the same
hard-nosed persuasion. Together, they imposed an iron-fisted mandate
on the Cactus Air Force. When medical officers reported that pilots were
too sick or exhausted to fly, Woods snapped, "They've got to! It's better
than getting a Jap bayonet stuck in their ass!" This cold-blooded command ethic was the only option open to Geiger and Woods, short of con-
vening a court martial and trying the offender: without a Cactus Air Force
the Battle of Guadalcanal was lost.

The pair set up their Operations Headquarters near the airstrip in a
picturesque structure dubbed "the Pagoda," which also served as a control
tower. Built by the Japanese, it was carpentered along traditional Japanese
lines with a shrine-like roof, wooden pegs for nails, and beautifully dove-
tailed joins. In the Pagoda, pilots were briefed and debriefed, coastwatcher
sightings were evaluated, orders were issued for Cactus Air Force missions,
and the needle was freely plied by Geiger and Woods. The atmosphere
surrounding the Pagoda was at all times one of extreme urgency. Pilots
and gunners hustled to get into the air without waiting for the rest of their
unit; Cactus dive bombers and fighters arrived and departed at all hours
with little regard for weather or runway conditions; and returning planes
were gassed and rearmed at pit-stop speed to get them back in the fight,
because invariably, it seemed, the Tokyo Express was headed down the Slot
for Guadalcanal, drawing nearer every hour, its transports loaded with

reinforcements, while twenty-eight Bettys with Zero escorts had been
sighted over Bougainville en route from Rabaul to pound Henderson Field.
And there was always a Japanese installation somewhere that Geiger
wanted bombed, like the seaplane base at Gizo Bay. The Cactus Air Force
even had a song about it ("Come on Charley, give us your number" . . .
"Yeah, let's hear it, Charley"), sung to the tune of "On the Road to
Mandelay":

Charley: (Verse)   In Cactus Operations,
                         Where the needle passes free,
                         There's a hot assignment cookin'
                         For Marine Group twenty-three.
                         As the shells burst in the palm trees,
                         You hear Operations say,
                         "Fill the belly tanks with juice, boys,
                         "Take the Scouts to Gizo Bay,
                         "Take the Scouts to Gizo Bay"—

Everybody: (Chorus)   Oh, pack a load to Gizo Bay,
                       Where the Jap fleet spends the day,
                       You can hear their Bettys chunkin'
                       From Rabaul to Lunga Quay.
                       Hit the road to Gizo Bay,
                       Where the float plane Zeros play,
                       And the bombs roar down like thunder,
                       On the natives 'cross the way![7]

Although it was chronically outnumbered, the Cactus Air Force did enjoy
two tactical advantages. One was the predictability of Japanese air raids.
The 565-mile flight to Guadalcanal forced the Bettys and Zeros of Rabaul's
11th Air Fleet to wait for first light before taking off, or risk the accidents
and other snafus that usually attend the launch of fifty aircraft into predawn darkness within minutes of one another. This meant that the Japanese formations would appear over Henderson no earlier than 11:30 A.M.
and depart no later than 1:30 P.M. in order to arrive back at Rabaul before
dark. Furthermore, their progress toward Guadalcanal could be monitored

to the minute by eagle-eyed coastwatchers. This gave Cactus Operations a forty-five minute jump on their assailants, time enough for the Cactus Air Force's flyable aircraft to get airborne—for the F4Fs to reach the thirty-thousand-foot altitude they needed before diving on the Bettys and for the SBDs to fly clear of the action. The P-400 fighters, lacking high-altitude capability, tagged along with the SBDs.

The other tactical advantage of the Cactus Air Force lay in the fact that it was playing in its own ball park. The Japanese had to fly the equivalent of Chicago to Memphis to attack Henderson Field, but the Cactus Air Force was already there, and it enjoyed the benefits. A crippled Wildcat in the hands of a capable pilot could often get back to Henderson even with a conked-out engine, gliding down from thirty thousand feet to make a dead stick landing. A badly shot-up Zero had a four-hour flight back to Rabaul, and few made it. But a Cactus pilot who ditched in the water or parachuted onto a nearby island was usually followed down by his wingman, his position reported by radio, and his rescue effected by a PBY Dumbo or friendly natives in dugout canoes. A Japanese pilot in the same predicament was unlikely to be rescued at sea by his comrades, who lacked the means. If he fell into the hands of the local natives, he would at worst be hacked to death, or at best delivered to the marines for interrogation and imprisonment. Most Japanese pilots downed at sea refused rescue. Some even fired their pistols at would-be rescuers, who paddled away and left them to the sharks.

Down and Down They Plunged

There were two principal weapons in the Cactus Air Force arsenal: the Douglas Dauntless SBD dive bomber and the Grumman Wildcat F4F fighter. The SBD, or "Slow but Deadly" in pilot idiom, enabled the otherwise stationary marines to reach out to sea and counterpunch at the Imperial Japanese Navy, striking at reinforcement convoys, warships, and seaplane bases. Beefy, reliable, and utilitarian, the aircraft was revered by its pilots because on most days it got them safely to the target, provided them with a rock-steady platform from which to drop their bomb, then brought them home again. Like the Wildcat, the SBD was remarkably lead-resistant. Its least bullet-proof components were its pilot and rear gunner. But mechanically, nothing short of an extensive working over by the dual 20-millimeter cannons of outnumbering Zeros or a chance anti-aircraft burst would bring it down. However, the SBD did have certain liabilities. With a half-ton bomb slung underneath, its top speed was a leisurely 130 knots, obliging its escort of F4Fs to S-turn in order not to leave it behind. The SBD's rate of climb with the bomb aboard was 450 feet per minute, compared with the Zero's twenty-six hundred feet per minute and the Wildcat's twenty-three hundred. But these shortcomings were an acceptable tradeoff for the SBD's many virtues.

An SBD pilot on a dive-bombing mission had three things to worry about: getting to his target, scoring with his bomb, then getting the hell out of there and safely back to Henderson Field. Once the target was located, getting over it was relatively easy, unless the target was protected by Zeros. If so, the Zeros swarmed out like maddened, yellow-winged hornets to greet the oncoming SBDs and their fighter escort. The F4Fs flung themselves at the Zeros, but some of the lithe fighters always slipped through to duel with the SBDs' tail gunners. At this point, the lesson learned at the Coral Sea and again at Midway paid off—which was that a lone SBD was dog meat for the Zeros. But a tight six-plane formation of SBDs, its twin rear-facing 30s all spewing lead at the same point in space, was a formidable object to approach. A twelve-plane SBD section was impenetrable, the collective firepower of its twenty-four machine guns so terrible that it shredded attackers like cabbage. As the SBD formation neared its target—for example, a well-defended Tokyo Express run —clusters of antiaircraft fire burst like greasy, black popcorn in the sky around it. If the shells burst ahead of it, the formation turned toward the cluster, since flak rarely bursts in the same place twice. Over the target, the formation opened up. One after another the pilots of the white-starred dive bombers opened their dive flaps and pushed over, eased back on their throttles, and, like links in a chain, began their 70-degree dives. Down and down they plunged for more than two miles, ears popping, while smoking tracers from the convoy's escorting warships poked up at them like long, spidery fingers. Each pilot, right eye to the bombsight, centered his crosshairs on the target's deck, darted glances at the altimeter, and at two thousand feet reached down and tugged the bomb release. The plane shrugged slightly as the bomb left the cradle. Then it was stick back, flaps closed, and throttle to the stops as the SBD pulled out of its dive and raced across the wave tops, pursued by Zeros and antiaircraft fire. Did the bomb hit? The pilot, his back to the target, would have to get the word on the intercom from his rear gunner. With pluck and luck the fleeing SBD would arrive at its point of rendezvous, join its fellows, and form up for the flight home to Henderson Field. This was how an SBD pilot and his rear gunner earned their daily bread in the Cactus Air Force.

The Ancient Art of Ambush

The other fist of the Cactus Air Force was the Grumman F4F Wildcat fighter. It was in appearance an aircraft only a mother could love. Unlike its opposite number, the elegant and sexy Zero, the F4F was known as the "Knock-kneed Bumble Bee" because of its queerly shaped landing gear and portly fuselage. Its designers had concerned themselves more with durability than speed and nimbleness, and least of all with appearance. As a result, the homely little Wildcat was built like a bank vault, a virtue esteemed by its pilots, who were grateful for the heavy armor plating that shielded their backs, the direction from which most Japanese bullets arrived. It was also fitted with self-sealing gas tanks and six 50-caliber machine guns.

For these amenities the F4F gave away speed, rate of climb, and turning ability to its dangerous adversary, the Mitsubishi Zero. The Zero was one-third lighter than the F4F, could in sixty seconds outclimb it by the length of a football field, and in straight and level flight rocket away from the Wildcat. The Zero could not, however, dive after the F4F, or its wings might come off—a frailty that the U.S. pilots exploited, together with the Zero's other shortcomings, which included no armor protection for the pilot and nonsealing gas tanks. The latter oversight caused the Zero, when struck in its fuel tank by a glowing tracer, to ignite in a ball of orange fire and immolate its pilot. It was thought in Japan's aeronautical circles that the pilot's superior skill and sense of divine mission would make up the difference, which in many cases proved true. In 1942 Japanese fighter pilots were easily the world's finest, having been at it since 1931 when Japan invaded Manchuria. They were the pick of Japan's young manhood and had been schooled like olympic gymnasts in training programs lasting as long as seven years. Their primary mission as Zero fighter pilots was to escort Betty bombers over the target, and to the extent that their fragile aircraft held together they were virtually unbeatable in a one-on-one dogfight. Most F4F pilots who tried it soon found shells from the Zero's two 20-millimeter cannons exploding in their cockpits. This was the daunting problem that faced F4F pilots each time they heard the words "Tally ho!" in their earphones—how not to be shot down by the Zeros!

The man responsible for working out the solution was the cool, poker-faced marine captain, John Lucien Smith. Like Geiger, a relentless taskmaster, Smith headed up Marine Fighter Squadron 223, which rose most mornings from Henderson Field to confront the arriving Japanese. Smith's strategy was to adapt guerrilla tactics to aerial combat. The role of the F4F, he reasoned, was not to shoot down Zeros but to destroy the bombers they protected, the twin-engine Bettys. To this end, Smith designed a hit-and-run technique for his squadron that maximized the strengths of the F4F and exploited the shortcomings of the Zero. It employed the ancient art of ambush, and it worked well against attackers forced to fly a great distance to their target, whose strictly rationed fuel supply kept them at lower altitudes. Early warnings by the coastwatchers usually gave Smith's fighters enough time to climb to their ambush altitude of thirty thousand feet. Then, as the Japanese bombing formation passed beneath them, the F4Fs did what they were best at doing. They rolled over on their backs and dropped like cast iron stoves on the Bettys. Flashing past the Zero escorts at 350 miles per hour, each Wildcat's sextet of 50-caliber machine guns walked up its target's spine, searching out the Betty's fuel tanks. Where the tracers connected, orange flame spurted from the bomber's wing root and it fell out of formation, trailing the long black smudge that, like an exclamation point, marked it for Nirvana. The Zeros, reacting instantly, would quickly close on the F4Fs. But now the audacious Americans executed part two of their hit-and-run tactic. They vanished—leaving the sky to the Zeros. Some ducked into a handy cloud, others plunged toward Henderson Field at top speed, daring the gossamer-winged Zeros to follow.

The American ambush seldom turned back the raid, but it drew blood, broke up the Bettys' formations, bumped them off course, and spoiled their aim. It also took a daily toll of Japanese aircraft and the lives of their experienced pilots and aircrews. As the sky war slogged on, the results became evident. F4F pilots began reporting that the Zero pilots they flew against were less skillful than the veterans of August, poorer shots with fewer tricks in their bag; and examination of shot-down Japanese aircraft revealed that many were fresh from the factory, indicating a fast equipment turnover in Rabaul's 11th Air Fleet.

The Long-Nosed Planes

Due largely to Adm. John McCain's interservice inveigling, the army's 67th Pursuit Squadron had reported to Henderson Field on 22 August for enrollment in the Cactus Air Force. Commanded by Capt. Dale D. Brannon, it consisted of fourteen new fighter planes, their unseasoned pilots, and the squadron's wonder-working mechanics. The mechanics were wonder-working because, when the squadron's fighter planes had arrived by sea at Noumea, they were in crates, knocked down and without assembly instructions. The mechanics got them up and flying. The aircraft also were not what the squadron had been told to expect—P-39 Airacobras, proven in China by the Flying Tigers. The chaos that ruled in the U.S. logistical camp during the early months of the war had forced some desperate stateside supply officer to substitute the only aircraft he could get his hands on, a flying lemon designated the P-400. Originally built to order for export to the British in North Africa, the P-400 lacked most of the requisites necessary to fight the high-altitude air war that raged over the Solomons. It had neither a serviceable oxygen system nor a supercharger. This meant that its pilot would black out at altitudes over fifteen thousand feet, while its engine would gasp and overheat. But the army air force pilots were determined to get at the Japanese in anything that would fly, so up they went every day with the rest of the Cactus Air Force to wring the most out of the weird little fighter plane with shark teeth painted on its nose. The results were disastrous—in six days, eleven of the original fourteen P-400s were shot down or wrecked, and letters of condolence from the 67th Squadron's commanding officer were en route stateside to the parents and wives of several army pilots.

There was, however, a solution. Making up in part for its shortcomings, the P-400 mounted four 30-caliber machine guns and a 37-millimeter nose cannon and could deliver a five-hundred-pound bomb. It was a flying gun platform-cum-bomber, ideal for low-level strafing and bombing of Japanese ground forces, and that is how Major General Vandegrift put it to work—flying close-support missions for the ground-pounders. In addition to regular daylight patrols over Japanese-held positions, striking at anything that moved, the army air force P-400s smoothed the way for Edson's Tasimboko raid and helped 11th Marines artillery chew up enemy concentrations during the Battle of Edson's Ridge. The Japanese, who had dismissed the eccentric little fighter as "the long-nosed plane," now had reason to fear it.

CHAPTER EIGHT

Torpedoes on the Starboard Bow

As soon as the shock of Maj. Gen. Kiyotake Kawaguchi's failure to capture Henderson Field wore off, Japan's Imperial General Headquarters swiftly issued new orders. The Imperial Army and Navy were to combine forces in a new offensive that would once and for all expunge the odious U.S. presence on Guadalcanal. This time there would be no halfway measures: the strategy would be overkill. To guarantee victory on the ground, Japanese strength on Guadalcanal would be brought up to twenty-six thousand men. Two of Admiral Yamamoto's mammoth battleships, firing 14-inch high-explosive shells in a sustained bombardment, would reduce Henderson Field and other strategic areas of the perimeter to a landfill. The admiral presently in charge of the 11th Air Fleet at Rabaul would be replaced with Japan's most aggressive naval air commander for an all-out assault on the Cactus Air Force. The seventeenth of October—one month away—was set as the date for this mother of battles.

While the IGHQ was pledging to Emperor Hirohito a final solution to the rankling problem, Adm. Richmond Kelly Turner was at sea, en route from Espiritu Santo to Guadalcanal. In the holds of Turner's transports were the reinforced 7th Marines, four thousand strong, together with the supplies that Maj. Gen. Archer Vandegrift, the Cactus Air Force, and the Marine Corps ground-pounders had been longing for. There was ammunition for every kind of weapon, the first ashore since the landing. There was food, glorious food, and for the Cactus Air Force, down to its last seven days' supply of fuel, gasoline to top up its reserves. There were new medium tanks to run interference for the rifle companies, another artillery battalion, engineers and motor transport companies, and for every man in the perimeter, a chocolate bar. But Turner and his hallelujah convoy weren't there yet. His bold attempt to sneak a fresh marine regiment through Japanese-controlled waters to Guadalcanal was like trying to steal home in a world series game. A snooping Kawanishi patrol aircraft that would have radioed his position had already been spotted by Turner's lookouts. And U.S. Naval Intelligence had reported considerable Japanese submarine activity in the area. But Turner had no alternative: without reinforcement, it would very likely be sayonara for Vandegrift and his marines.

Zigzagging along at sixteen knots one hundred miles south of Turner, there to keep an aerial eye on his transports, were the U.S. carriers *Wasp* and *Hornet*, each with its escort of warships. When it came *Wasp*'s turn to launch patrol aircraft, the big carrier slowed, put her helm up, and turned into the wind. Lying off her starboard quarter at periscope depth was the Japanese submarine I-19, which had been planted in *Wasp*'s path. Four Long Lance torpedoes shot, bubbling, from I-19's tubes. On *Wasp*'s bridge one of her lookouts stared, then exclaimed into his headset, "Torpedoes off the starboard bow!" "Full right rudder," ordered *Wasp*'s captain. The helmsman spun the big wheel, but there was no side-stepping the Japanese "fish" and three of them struck home—two forward on the bow and a third near the bridge. The big carrier convulsed. An enormous whiplash of energy ran her entire length and back again, buckling plates, bouncing aircraft and men into the air, rupturing gasoline storage lines and starting fires. Soon the *Wasp* was a holocaust, visible for one hundred miles

under a sky-high pillar of boiling black smoke, parts of her metalwork
glowing incandescent. The order was given to abandon ship. Of her 2,250-
man crew, 200 died in the inferno. The rest, including 375 wounded,
were rescued. For hours the *Wasp* refused to sink. Finally, to keep her out
of enemy hands, the destroyer *Landsdowne* put *Wasp* out of her misery with
a fourth torpedo. The U.S. Navy was now down to one operational carrier
in the South Pacific—the *Hornet*.

Kelly Turner ran for cover, heading his convoy with its irreplaceable
cargo away from Guadalcanal and the waters that were called "torpedo
junction." Then at 3:00 P.M. the next afternoon, with the courage of desperation, he once again turned his convoy northwest and set a course for
Lunga Point, Guadalcanal.

At dawn on 18 September, Turner's hallelujah convoy slipped unscathed
into Iron Bottom Sound and dropped anchor. Aboard ship, the four thousand men of the 7th Marines stared at the great green hump of Guadalcanal, the island that had baptized their brother regiments in blood,
and wondered if they would leave their bones there. Ashore, Red Mike
Edson turned to his executive officer and said, "There comes the greatest
fighting man in the Marine Corps—we'll have some competition now."
Edson's competitor was forty-four-year-old Lewis "Chesty" Puller, a short,
rubbery-faced lieutenant colonel with a chest that resembled a powder
keg. Like Popeye, he was seldom without a stumpy pipe at the corner of
his mouth. He had arrived at Guadalcanal with three Navy Crosses already
to his credit, mementos of bandit-chasing days with the Marine Corps in
Haiti between the two World Wars. To this new generation of marines,
Puller's name was synonymous with "action." Once on the beach with
his battalion he held a back-slapping reunion with Edson, then demanded
to know where the Japanese were. He was handed a map, stared at it for
a moment, then handed it back, saying, "Hell, I can't make head nor tail
out of this—don't we have anything better than *National Geographic* maps?
Just show me where they are." Those present all pointed to the hills. "All
right, let's go get 'em," Puller said.[1] All day long the landing boats plied
to and from the six transports that had smuggled the 7th Marines into
Guadalcanal, and by day's end every man was ashore. In the eyes of most
marines, the U.S. Navy had now redeemed itself.

Only one accident, a tragic one, marred the landing. A Cactus Air Force SBD on patrol buzzed over the anchored convoy and a newly arrived ship's gunner let fly at it. Veteran marines watching from the beach shook their fists and shouted "No! No!"—but an instant later the confused gunner was joined by others in the convoy and the SBD, riddled at close range, crashed into Iron Bottom Sound. The wounded gunner crawled out of the sinking aircraft and was rescued, but the pilot went down with his plane. When Turner's convoy sailed away, it carried with it the remnants of the Parachute Battalion, victors of Gavutu, Tanambogo, and Edson's Ridge, and the first marine unit to be evacuated. The battalion's survivors —burning with malaria and sucked dry by too much combat—could no longer function as an effective fighting unit. They had suffered a battle casualty rate of 55 percent.

Hell, Yes, Why Not?

The arrival of Turner's hallelujah convoy at Guadalcanal was celebrated by a proclamation the next morning that all hands would until further notice be issued three meals a day.

Gen. Hap Arnold, one of the Joint Chiefs of Staff, arrived in Noumea from Washington on an inspection tour and met with Admiral Ghormley. He later reported that "the navy had taken one hell of a beating . . . [and] was hanging on by a shoestring." Ghormley, he said, had not left his harbor-fast flagship for a month.

Capt. John Smith of the Cactus Air Force shot down one of three Zeros he happened upon but was himself shot down by the other two. With consummate skill he plopped his F4F down in a jungle glade, began hiking back to the perimeter, then was picked up by a jeep dispatched by Col. Clifton Cates, who had watched the whole affair.

The commanding officer of the 7th Marines had stepped off the landing boat in a spiffy uniform with spit-shined oxfords and silk socks. His entrance was witnessed by several score of grubby, tattered ground-pounders.[2] A month later he would be quietly relieved of command.

Red Mike Edson was promoted to full colonel and given command of the 5th Marines. Lt. Col. Sam Griffith took over the 1st Raider Battalion.

The Cactus Air Force was now outnumbered by the Japanese 11th Air Fleet two to one in fighters and three to one in bombers.

General Vandegrift traded a case of scotch for a case of General Geiger's bourbon. Later, when Vandegrift visited Geiger's shack, the Cactus Air Force commander offered him a drink of bourbon, looked for it, but came up empty handed. Someone had swiped it.[3]

Torpedo squadron VT-8, on loan from the *Saratoga*, arrived at Henderson Field. Commanded by Lt. Cdr. H. H. "Swede" Larsen, the squadron was equipped with the new TBF torpedo plane, also known as the "Pregnant Beast" because of its distended midsection. The torpedoes they carried would round out the Cactus Air Force's arsenal of weapons.

Adm. Ernest King, Chief of Naval Operations, wrote a memo to Gen. George Marshall, head of the Joint Chiefs, stating that if a flow of fighter planes to the Pacific was not given higher priority than any other theater of war, the navy would not be able to withstand its present rate of aircraft attrition. King's memo arrived at Marshall's office and was pigeonholed.

Sherwood F. "Pappy" Moran, the 1st Division's Japanese language expert and a former missionary, grew wearier each day of the obscenity-rich dialogue of his fellow marines until one morning it finally got to him. Rounding on a marine who had just returned from patrol, he snapped, "Yes, I know, you saw the fucking Jap come up the fucking hill and raised your fucking rifle and shot him between the fucking eyes."

President Roosevelt, in an address to the nation, seemed to be preparing the country for bad news. He soft-pedaled the strategic value of the Solomon Islands and touched on the seriousness of the Guadalcanal situation. FDR, of course, knew what the rest of the United States did not—that the U.S. Pacific Fleet had been routed by the Japanese and the marines on Guadalcanal were blockaded.

Hanson Baldwin, military affairs correspondent for the *New York Times*, arrived on the island to do a story. He told Vandegrift that many of Washington's top people were terribly worried by developments at Guadalcanal, and that the atmosphere at Ghormley's HQ at Noumea was profoundly negative. "Are you going to hold this beachhead?" he asked Vandegrift. "Hell yes, why not?" was Vandegrift's answer.

With the arrival of the 7th Marines, Vandegrift for the first time could afford the luxury of an unbroken line of defense around the perimeter. No longer could Japanese infiltrators crawl nightly through the holes between marine strong points and raise hell behind the lines. The new defense cordon stretched from the ridge line west of the Lunga river to the mouth of the Tenaru river on the east, and included all of Edson's ridge. Potential hot spots were beefed up with newly arrived barbed wire, two rows deep. The unbroken line of perimeter would become a base of operations for Vandegrift's new strategy, which he named "active defense." Where formerly the 1st Division had hunkered down behind its weapons, waiting for the Japanese to attack, now marine rifle battalions, eight hundred strong, could push deep into the Guadalcanal jungle on bushwhacking excursions calculated to harass the Japanese and keep them on their back foot. The first of these forays, known as the "Second Matanikau," would jump off on 23 September.

Tales of Chesty Puller

By way of preparing his battalion of totally green youngsters for the Second Matanikau, Chesty Puller marched them out of the perimeter and into the jungle for two days. On 21 September he set off with orders to patrol south along the Lunga River, deal with any Japanese encountered, and return the following day. Before leaving, Puller warned his nineteen year olds, "Keep those canteens out of your mouth. If you don't save water you'll regret it." The battalion, sweating under full field packs, entered the jungle at a point where the trail became a tunnel, overarched by towering rain forest giants whose triple canopies filtered out the sunlight, casting the young marines into perpetual shadow. Like all newcomers to Guadalcanal's jungle, they were spooked by its orchestra of macabre sounds. From one tangle of vines came the gargle of something being strangled, followed by a scream of "I'm all right!" Another unseen creature sounded off with a whack that sounded like two boards being slapped together. The suffocating heat and dripping humidity took hold. Some of the men reached compulsively for their canteens and drank. Then, as the winding column trudged on, those who had broken water discipline began to suffer from dehydration. Tongues swelled, saliva turned to glue, and lips stuck together. But Puller's pace never slackened and his green marines plodded on, lost in a fantasy of cool, clear water. Later, when the battalion reached a river, many broke ranks, plunged in, and gulped. Others flopped down on the bank and lapped it up. Puller let them do it. He had made his point.

Suddenly firing broke out ahead. All around Puller his young marines hit the deck or lunged for cover. Puller stood for a moment, listening, then strolled up the trail. He walked and talked like someone on his way to the Post Exchange, reassuring his men that everything was under control. No big deal, Puller told them, just small stuff. John Wayne could not have done it better.[4] The commotion was caused by three Japanese defending a bridge over the Lunga. They were dealt with, and the long column of marines prepared to resume the march. Puller jogged forward to the head of the column. There he found that A Company, which had deployed to fire on the bridge, had broken contact with the column and disappeared into the cover. Puller pressed on. Presently Capt. Bob Haggerty arrived, could see nothing of the enemy, and ordered his scouts to cross the bridge. Feeling exposed and vulnerable, the scouts crept cautiously onto the bridge, saw the bushes move on the far side and froze, just as Puller materialized from the same bushes. Like the white-haired Geiger in his SBD, Puller led by example.

The next morning, after a sleepless night of false alarms and mosquito slapping, Puller's men shrugged wearily into their equipment and pushed on, up the steep, baking ridges and down the dripping, tree-choked ravines. Again, firing broke out up front—a Japanese ambush party had bushwhacked the point company. One of the wounded was Capt. Jack Stafford. His chest and throat had been torn by an exploding rifle grenade. Puller, who had trotted forward as usual, arrived at Stafford's side just as the corpsman was injecting him with morphine. Kneeling, Puller examined the wounded man. It was obvious that Stafford was dying, choking to death on his tongue. Unsnapping a large safety pin from an ammunition bandolier, Puller reached into Stafford's mouth, pulled out his tongue and pinned it to the collar of his dungaree jacket. He then organized five relay teams of stretcher bearers to carry Stafford back down the punishing trail to the perimeter. Stafford would live to tell the tale.

That night Puller brought his newly baptized nineteen year olds back to the perimeter. He had done all he could for them in the two days available. They were, he reckoned, as ready as they ever would be for the battle that tomorrow would bring.

That Damned Thing Ain't Goin' Off

The Second Matanikau began optimistically as Archer Vandegrift's first major offensive against the Japanese. It was hexed from the start. The battle plan assumed that Edson's victory at the Battle of Edson's Ridge had taken a heavy toll of Japanese manpower, sending the survivors straggling off through the jungle in search of food. This much was true. But unknown to Vandegrift and his staff, the Tokyo Express, commuting nightly from Rabaul to points west of the perimeter, had meanwhile made up the loss. As a result, Vandegrift's three attacking battalions walked into a buzz saw. Waiting for his two thousand marines in the mangroves along the west bank of the Matanikau, and dug in on the upstream ridges, were more than four thousand Japanese infantry with every expectation of success.

Chesty Puller was the first to discover this. On the morning of 23 September he led his men out of the perimeter and south into the jungle with orders to cross the Matanikau up-country and return along the far bank. The egg-crate hills and braided rain forest sapped and slowed his battalion until the trudging column was a piece of cake for the waiting Japanese. Like wolves on the fold, they swept down from the high ground on Puller and his nineteen year olds.[5] In minutes, seven of them were sprawled in death and twenty-five were wounded. When the shooting started, everyone hit the ground except Puller. His first sergeant, Bill Pennington, recalled: "The colonel just stood there in that grazing fire with that little old stump of a pipe in his face, yelling, 'B Company, second platoon, in line here!' Machine-gun fire kicked up dust all around, and I stayed down in that kunai grass like everyone else in the ranks. . . . He was the only marine you could see standing on that hillside."[6] When a hand grenade fell fifteen feet from Puller, everyone near him dove for cover, but Puller stood his ground and yelled, "Hey, that damned thing ain't goin' off." He was right, remembers Capt. Zach Cox—the grenade was a dud, and Puller's nonchalance restored order. B Company, commanded by Capt. Chester Cockrell, was slow to move forward and form a line of resistance. Puller cursed them at the top of his lungs, shouting, "Cockrell, get 'em the bleep up." A few moments later, a runner reported that Cockrell had been killed. Later, Puller confessed to one of his officers, "God, I hated having to curse at Cockrell out there tonight, he was a good, brave marine. It was something that had to be done."[7]

That night Puller bedded his men down behind a ridge. The next morning, thinking that discretion was the better part of valor, he broke off contact with the Japanese and marched west toward the Matanikau. Again, his battalion was humbled by the steaming jungle and corrugated terrain. When they finally reached the Matanikau on the twenty-sixth, it was too late to force a crossing—their orders required them to return to the perimeter by nightfall. Badly used by the enemy, minus thirty-two of its members, tripped up every step of the way by General Jungle, Puller's battalion had been given a lot to think about. They trudged back to the mouth of the Matanikau, sadder but infinitely wiser.

Good Shot

As Puller's battalion was slogging homeward, new plans were hatched. Red Mike Edson was put in charge of the operation. The 1st Raider Battalion, now commanded by Lt. Col. Sam Griffith (like Edson, another redhead), was dispatched upriver to force a crossing of the Matanikau at the "Nippon" bridge, a ramshackle log affair about a mile south of the river mouth, deep in the bush. Once on the opposite bank, the Raiders would turn back north and attack downstream, driving the Japanese toward the sea. To close the trap, a battalion of the 5th Marines would forge across the sandspit at the mouth of the Matanikau and wait for the Raiders to push the retreating Japanese into their rifle sights. The plan was a classic version of what infantry tacticians call the "Hammer and Anvil." It was, however, attempted without first checking out the terrain or the whereabouts of the enemy. Consequently, no one at Division HQ knew that the Japanese had crossed the Matanikau the previous night and were now concealed in force on the near bank, a pistol shot away from "Nippon" bridge.

The Raiders arrived at the approach to the bridge on schedule, having encountered nothing so far but a lone sniper. Maj. Ken Bailey, Griffith's executive officer who had been recommended for the Medal of Honor after the Battle of Edson's Ridge, walked forward for a look. With him was 2d Lt. Richard Sullivan. Seeing nothing suspicious, they walked back to Sullivan's platoon to issue orders to his squad leaders. Suddenly Sullivan saw helmeted men running along the ridge. As he turned to tell Bailey, a concealed Nambu swept them with a burst of fire. Sullivan hit the deck, but Bailey dropped to one knee and remained there, his head in his hands. Sullivan tugged at Bailey's ankle and he fell over. As his face turned toward Sullivan, the lieutenant saw the bullet hole between Bailey's eyes.[8] Griffith, jolted by the death of his exec, shouted orders to return fire and cover their withdrawal. Leaving a rifle company to keep the enemy occupied, he led the rest of his battalion on a long crawl up a steep ridge, from which he planned to attack the Japanese rear. At the crest, Griffith cautiously got to his knees in the kunai grass and raised his binoculars. Across the valley a sniper's Arisaka rifle cracked and its bullet slammed into the Raider commander's shoulder. As he fell backward, Griffith, always the professional marine, exclaimed, "Good shot!" and was dragged to cover. "So much for that baloney about all the Japs having buck teeth and bad eyes," Griffith said later. "I don't know about that Nip's teeth, but there was nothing wrong with his eyesight."[9] After Griffith's wounding, the Raider attack bogged down. Nor could they establish radio contact with Red Mike Edson at the operational HQ. Finally, Gunner Bill Rust jogged back down the jungle trail to report the situation to Edson, who sent him back with orders for the Raiders to return to the beach.

To further complicate matters, several lucky hits on Henderson Field by the noon air raid had scrambled radio communications. This snafu left Edson with the impression that the Raiders were across the Matanikau and headed back on the far side, as per their original orders. Accordingly, he launched the final phase of the operation. The 2d Battalion, 5th Marines would attack across the sand spit at the mouth of the Matanikau. Meanwhile, Puller's foot-sore battalion, minus Puller, would board landing craft and churn up the seacoast for several miles, then land and hook back toward the river mouth, herding any Japanese coastal units into the trap. Puller would stay with Edson as his assistant. Puller's battalion would be commanded by his exec, Maj. Otho "Buck" Rogers. The battalion crowded into boats and shoved off. The 2d Battalion, 5th Marines then attacked across the sand bar, got a scorching reception from numerous Japanese machine guns, and was forced back to its lines. At this point, the first two elements of the plan had fallen through. This left Puller's eight hundred men at sea and headed for a beach miles from home and help, with the Japanese fully in charge.

Fight Your Way Out

Puller's men arrived at what looked like their designated landing beach and headed in. The hex was still working. Just out of sight behind the belt of palm trees that bordered the shoreline was the bivouac of a Japanese infantry battalion. What they saw was easy pickings. As the marines splashed ashore, the invisible Japanese parted like the Red Sea to admit them. Maj. "Buck" Rogers led his men inland a few hundred yards, then up a hill. Rogers was not a professional marine officer. An amiable, quiet-spoken reservist called up for duty with his Washington, D.C., unit, he had been a post office official before the war, responsible for new stamp issues. Now Rogers stood on a hilltop on Guadalcanal, studying the terrain. Hidden in the jungle a short distance away, something went thwung and a mortar shell rose from its tube. Seconds later it fell rustling through the air to land at Roger's feet. The explosion ripped him nearly in half.[10] "There was so little left of him," remembers 1st Sgt. Bill Pennington, "that we rolled the remains in a blanket." The Japanese then struck, pouring a torrent of lead into the shocked marines. Scrambling for whatever cover there was, the battalion formed a hasty perimeter and returned fire. So close had the Japanese crawled to the American position that Puller's mortar men lay on their backs with their legs in the air, cradling the hot mortar tubes between their boondockers to angle the shell's trajectory as finely as possible. Casualties swiftly mounted. Capt. Charlie Kelly of B Company, a cool head in a fight, took command and ordered the radio operator to call for help. But Kelly hadn't reckoned with the hex: incredibly, the radio had been left behind. Then inspiration struck Kelly. Rounding up a platoon, he ordered the men to strip off their white skivvy shirts and lay them out on the beleaguered hilltop to spell "H-E-L-P." That did it. In the first lucky break of the day, a patrolling SBD flown by marine 1st Lt. Dale Leslie spotted the homemade message and radioed the sighting to Henderson Field, who relayed it to Edson.

All morning, Edson's command HQ had been enveloped in the fog of war. Yes, the Raiders had crossed the Matanikau . . . no, belay that, they hadn't . . . yes, the 2d Battalion, 5th Marines are attacking across the sand spit . . . no, they're falling back. About now, Chesty Puller was puffing and snorting like a rhino. "Christ," he exclaimed to Edson, "most of my men will be out there alone, cut off without support. You're not going to throw those men away." Scooping up a signalman, Puller ran down to the beach and flagged a passing destroyer. The *Ballard*, a World War I refit, sent a boat ashore for him. At Puller's urging, *Ballard* charged up the coast at flank speed. In its wake, like baby ducks, swam a procession of landing craft that Puller had also commandeered. Spotting this oncoming flotilla from the embattled hilltop, Capt. Regan Fuller could scarcely believe his eyes: "An old time four-stacker, and was she boiling, with black smoke trailing out behind her . . . it was a lovely sight!" When abeam of the hill on which his men were now fighting for their lives, Puller signaled them by blinker: "Return to beach immediately." Through his binoculars, he could make out a tiny marine on the hilltop waving semaphore flags, who signaled back: "Engaged, cannot return." "Fight your way out, only hope," signaled Puller. There was no reply. Puller sent: "Will use ship's fire." No answer.

The *Ballard* opened up with its 5-inchers. It lay down two parallel lines of fire on the hillside that would serve as a corridor of shellbursts through which the survivors of the battalion could make their way back to the beach. Down they came, clambering and sliding, carrying their dead and wounded. Some dropped off as rear guards, were overrun, and died for their friends. Regan Fuller, a southerner, yipped a rebel yell as he started down with his company. The Japanese swiftly closed in behind them, firing into their backs. An Old Breed platoon sergeant from Philadelphia, Andy Malanowski, picked up a BAR and told Regan to go on down the hill with the wounded, he would cover their rear. For several minutes, Fuller could hear the *tak-tak-tak* of Malanowski's BAR behind them, then it went silent.[11]

Pvt. John Giles, a machine-gunner, refused to join the withdrawal until the rest of the battalion had left the hilltop. He was overrun. A few yards from Fuller a Japanese officer charged out of the bush, his two-handed sword held high, and with one grunting blow struck off the head of a stumbling marine.

As the remnants of the battalion assembled on the beach and formed a small perimeter, the landing craft, manned by Coast Guard coxswains, turned and headed for shore. Halfway there they came under machine-gun fire and many of them sheered off, away from the beach. Seeing this, Lieutenant Leslie, circling the scene in his SBD, repeatedly buzzed the fleeing landing craft as if to shame them and herd them back, then flew over the stranded marines, firing an air burst from his machine guns by way of proclaiming his support. One wounded marine officer tried to swim out to where he could order the fleeing boats to turn around.[12] After a few more minutes of panic, discipline prevailed and all of the landing craft headed for the beach, grounding thirty yards offshore on the coral. Marines who could walk carried their wounded and dead on ponchos through the surf. Those on the beach waiting to board the boats fired back at the Japanese, who were quickly moving in. Now a Nambu opened up from close range on the survivors. One of the Coast Guard coxswains, twenty-one-year-old Signalman 1st Class Doug Monro of Cle Elum, Washington, stood up in full view of the Japanese, manning his landing craft's 30-caliber machine gun. Dueling with the Nambu, he suppressed its fire while the last exhausted marines struggled aboard. A mortar shell exploded in the water next to Monro and he fell back into his boat, dying. In a letter to his parents, Lt. Cdr. D. H. Dexter, Monro's commanding officer, wrote, "By his action . . . he brought back a far greater number of men than had ever been hoped for. Upon regaining consciousness, his only question was, 'Did they get off?' and so died with a smile on his face." Monro was awarded the Medal of Honor, presented to his parents by President Roosevelt. It was the first ever conferred on a U.S. Coast Guardsman. The hexed action had cost Puller's battalion another twenty-four dead and twenty-three wounded, while the Raiders and the 2d Battalion, 5th Marines had suffered 117 casualties—altogether, 221 deaths and woundings.

Back in the perimeter the next morning, Lewis "Chesty" Puller summoned his battalion officers and made them an unsmiling speech. "I don't want you to be mooning over our losses and taking all the blame on your shoulders," he told them. "We've all got to leave this world some day, and there are worse things than dying for your country. But some things about our action in the last four days I want you to remember forever," he said. "And there are some we'd all like to forget, but they'll be in your mind's eye as long as you live. I hope we've all learned something. Now take care of your men and make yourselves ready. We haven't seen anything yet."[13]

CHAPTER NINE

An Old Friend of Chester Nimitz

CHESTER W. NIMITZ was a prudent man. The blond, freckle-faced admiral, commander in chief of the Pacific Ocean Area, appointed his subordinates only after careful study of each man's record and character. After that, apart from some deft needle-plying intended to motivate or extract information, Nimitz let his appointee get on with the job. However, Nimitz's antenna was at all times tuned in to the stream of detail, official and unofficial, including gossip, that flowed from each subordinate's theater of operations to Nimitz's Pacific Fleet HQ in Hawaii. Vice Adm. Robert L. Ghormley, whose job it was to oversee the white-knuckle Guadalcanal operation from his HQ in Noumea, was an old friend. But for over a month, Nimitz's antenna had been telling him that all was not well with Ghormley's command—that Ghormley, perhaps, was not part of the solution, but part of the problem. Nimitz decided to drop in on Ghormley and look under the rug.

The meeting took place on 28 September aboard Ghormley's sweltering flagship *Argonne* in Noumea Harbor. Present were several other high-ranking officers, including MacArthur's chief of staff and Gen. Hap Arnold, U.S. Army Air Force commander in chief. Nimitz asked Ghormley a number of loaded questions. Why wasn't the U.S. Army's American Division, garrisoned on Noumea, being used to reinforce Guadalcanal's struggling marines? Why were fighter aircraft being hoarded in reserve instead of being forwarded immediately to Henderson Field? Why weren't Ghormley's naval forces being used to keep pressure on the nightly Tokyo Express reinforcement runs? Ghormley had no satisfactory answers. Twice during the meeting, Ghormley, when handed urgent dispatches, read them and muttered, "My God, what are we going to do about that?"[1] Even Ghormley's cramped, airless shipboard quarters contributed to the atmosphere of gloom; the local French authorities had refused Ghormley's request for quarters ashore, and Ghormley had never leaned on them. Finally, verifying the scuttlebutt he had already heard, Nimitz established that Ghormley, the admiral responsible for winning the Battle of Guadalcanal, had never set foot on the island. The commander in chief, Pacific, left the meeting knowing what had to be done. If Ghormley didn't want to fight this battle, Nimitz knew an admiral who did.

Do You Think We Can Get Off?

Two days later Nimitz was en route from Noumea to Guadalcanal on an army air force B-17 bomber. Somewhere over the southern Solomons in heavy weather, the young army pilot confessed that he was lost. Undaunted, a member of Nimitz's staff produced a copy of the *National Geographic*'s handy map, and an hour later they touched down in a lashing rainstorm on Henderson Field. At Guadalcanal, by way of getting the straight "skivvy," as marines called it, the admiral spent time with Archer Vandegrift, pledging him all possible aid. He then inspected Cactus Air Force headquarters, Edson's Ridge, and checked out parts of the perimeter, all in the soaking rain. After which he pinned medals on the faded shirtfronts of a number of marines. When the time came for him to leave,

Nimitz was driven with his staff back to Henderson Field, where another
Flying Fortress awaited, one of two scheduled to appear that day. Its pilot
was a large, black-bearded army major, barefoot and wearing only a jump
suit. At the sight of this prototype Hell's Angel, several of Nimitz's staff
declared their preference for the next B-17. The rain was still drumming
down and the field was a marsh. Do you think we can get off, Nimitz
inquired? The pilot assured him that they could. Nimitz climbed aboard
and sat down in the bombardier's seat in the aircraft's greenhouse nose,
where he would have a panoramic view forward. Taxiing to the end of the
sopping runway the pilot spun around, opened his throttles and charged
down the airstrip in a cloud of muddy spray, pulled back on the yoke to
lift off . . . and nothing happened. He then cut his engines and jammed
on the brakes. The big bomber slewed wildly, traded end for end, and slid
off the runway tail first, coming to rest on the lip of a ravine. Nimitz's view
from the bombardier's nose blister can best be imagined. As a stunned
audience looked on, the pilot restarted his engines and taxied back to
the Pagoda. The bomber's hatch opened and an expressionless Nimitz
appeared. "Let's all go to the general's house and have lunch," he suggested. After lunch, Nimitz calmly reboarded the plane and was firmly
seated amidships by his aide. The rain having ceased and a breeze sprung
up, the plane bearing the barefoot, black-bearded pilot and the commander in chief, Pacific Ocean Area, took off uneventfully for the flight back to
Noumea. There Nimitz ordered Ghormley to ready the 164th Infantry Regiment of the Americal Division for immediate shipment to Guadalcanal.

Disregard Politeness and Kill

After seven weeks on the 'Canal, the men of the 1st Marine Division were
now getting the hang of it. One of their toughest instructors had been
Guadalcanal's jungle:

> "We are learning the hard way to move quietly in this jungle." Plt. Sgt.
> C. M. Feagin, I Company, 5th Marines.
>   "I been in the Marine Corps sixteen years, and I been in three
> expeditions to China and five engagements since I have been in the
> Solomons. I will say that this 1942 model recruit we are getting can

drink more water than six old timers. We have to stress water discipline all the time." *Gun. Sgt. H. L. Beardsley, G Company, 5th Marines.*

"Some of my men thought their hand grenades were too heavy. They tossed them aside when no one was looking. Later they would have given six month's pay for one hand grenade." *Plt. Sgt. H. R. Strong, A Company, 5th Marines.*

"Get used to weird noises at night. . . . The land crabs and lizards make a hell of a noise rustling on leaves. There is a bird here that sounds like . . . a dog barking." *Cpl. E. J. Byrne, L Company, 5th Marines.*

"I practice walking quietly over rocks, twigs, grass, leaves, through vines and so forth. I practice this around the bivouac area. . . . Some of the other NCOs laughed at me . . . but they have stopped laughing because I have been on more patrols than any man in the regiment and am still alive." *Plt. Sgt. C. Arndt, Headquarters and Service Company, 5th Marines.*

"In order to get a true picture of what is going on in this heavy country, I make my staff go up where the fighting is." *Lt. Col. Lewis B. Puller, 1st Battalion, 7th Marines.*

The Japanese also were excellent teachers:

"We learned from the Nips to make the stand-up, covered 'spider hole.'" *2d Lt. H. M. Davis, 5th Marines, promoted on the field of battle.*

"I have observed the Japs often get short of ammunition. They cut bamboo and crack it together to simulate rifle fire to draw our fire. They ain't supermen, they're just tricky bastards." *Cpl. J. S. Stankus, E Company, 5th Marines.*

"In the Raiders, we adopted the custom of dropping all ranks and titles. We used nicknames for the officers. We did this because the Nips caught onto the names of the officers and would yell during the night, 'This is Captain Joe Smith talking. A Company withdraw to the next hill.' My nickname was 'Red Mike.'" *Col. Merritt Edson, commanding officer, 5th Marines.*

"A Japanese trick to draw our fire was for the hidden Jap to work his [rifle] bolt back and forth. Men who got sucked in on this and fired without seeing what they were firing at generally drew automatic fire from another direction." *Cpl. Fred Carter, I Company, 5th Marines.*

"The Japanese do a lot of yelling at times, and at other times are deadly silent. The Japs don't like our men yelling back at them. One night some Japanese got in our marching column. We discovered them and bayoneted them." *Lieutenant Sheppard, 7th Marines, promoted on the field of battle.*

"I was on my first patrol here, and we were moving up a dry stream bed. We saw three Japs come down the river bed out of the jungle. The one in front was carrying a white flag. When they got up to us, they dropped the white flag and then all three threw hand grenades. We killed two of these Japs, but one got away. Apparently they do not mind a sacrifice in order to get information. They are tricky bastards." *2d Lt. D. A. Clark, 7th Marines.*

The cruelest, most unforgiving instructor of the 1st Marine Division was combat itself:

"Teach your people that when a man is hit in the assault to leave him there. Too many of our men suddenly become first-aid men." *Sgt. Maj. B. Metzger, 5th Marines.*

"I think the snipers look for BAR men." *Plt. Sgt. F. T. O'Fara, B company, 5th Marines.* "No doubt about it. In one engagement, in one platoon, every BAR man was hit." *Col. Merritt Edson, 5th Marines.*

"Unnecessary firing gives your position away, and when you give your position away here, you pay for it." *Cpl. J. S. Stankus, E Company, 5th Marines.*

"If the numbers on the mortar sight were luminous, we would not have to use a flashlight. This flashlight business is dangerous." *Sgt. T. E. Rumbley, I Company, 5th Marines.*

"You must crawl in the advance, unless you are charging. The reason for this is that all men are hit from the knees up, except for ricochets." *Sgt. O. J. Marion, L Company, 5th Marines.*

"Sergeant Dietrich of I Company recently used his head. One night when the Japs advanced, a Jap jumped into Sergeant Dietrich's foxhole. Sergeant Dietrich pulled the pin of a hand grenade and jumped out. There was a hell of an explosion and one less Nip." *Cpl. Fred Carter, I Company, 5th Marines.*

The lessons learned were summed up by a sardonic Old Breed marine: "Your men have to be rugged and rough, and to win they must learn to disregard politeness and kill." *Sgt. Maj. B. Metzger, 5th Marines.*[2]

He Would Accept Vandegrift's Surrender

On 4 October, Admiral Yamamoto issued the operational orders that would launch what was seen by the Japanese high command as the final solution to the Guadalcanal problem. For two weeks, troops had been fed nightly into Japanese positions west of the marine perimeter via "ant" and "rat" Tokyo Express runs. By mid-October their number would total twenty-six thousand. Daily attrition strikes by the 11th Air Fleet, including fighter sweeps designed to downsize the Cactus Air Force, were making life doubtful for Capt. John Smith's and Capt. Bob Galer's Wildcat pilots, fewer of whom were returning from the midmorning scrambles. This time the commanding general of Japan's 17th Army, Lt. Gen. Harukichi Hyakutake, under whose aegis the previous two campaigns had miscarried, would land on Guadalcanal. There he would relieve the disgraced Kawaguchi of command, and personally supervise delivery of the blow that would humble Vandegrift and his marines. With Hyakutake would come 22,500 seasoned veterans of the Sendai Division, who had conducted the rape of Nanking; with them would arrive three additional infantry battalions and tanks, together with large stores of rice and other logistical supplies, the lack of which had contributed to previous failures. Commanding the Sendai Division in the field would be Lt. Gen. Masao Maruyama. He would accept Vandegrift's surrender on 15 October at the mouth of the Matanikau, where the marine general would be ordered to appear with a white flag.

Get off Your Duff

Scouting SBDs were bringing back ominous photographs from their flights over western Guadalcanal. These revealed a growing concentration of enemy troops along the coast and inland, confirming what the 1st Division had learned at the Second Matanikau in exchange for its bloody nose. Vandegrift was worried. If the Japanese were to cross the river in force, it would threaten the entire perimeter: from the near bank, their artillery could reach Henderson Field. Clemens's native scouts were already reporting scattered Japanese activity on the east bank. Vandegrift ordered a preemptive attack. This time the marines would be familiar with the terrain, and they already knew that the Japanese were there, if not exactly where.

The attack jumped off at dawn on 7 October. Two battalions of the 7th Marines marched to a point near the Nippon bridge, where the Raiders had previously come to grief. Their commanding officer, Col. Amor L. Sims, ordered them to dig in and wait for morning, when his regiment would cross the Matanikau into Japanese-held territory. Sims himself would remain behind. A second force consisting of Edson's 5th Marines, together with the Raiders, advanced to the Matanikau's mouth and found the Japanese had gotten there first. After a scuffle, the Japanese withdrew to a pocket next to the sandspit. Edson ordered one company of the Raiders to keep them penned up, then backed off and dug his regiment in. That night the penned-up Japanese burst out, yelling, shooting, and throwing hand grenades. The Raiders, by now accustomed to this sort of thing, fought them hand to hand, backed them against the barbed wire, and annihilated them to a man.

The next day a storm broke over the lower Solomons, a gale blew, and the rain marched through in ragged gray battalions. Edson's 5th Marines and the Raiders stayed put. Back at 1st Division HQ, Vandegrift was handed a decoded message from Naval Intelligence. It was an official warning of Hyakutake's new offensive—the previous day's push across the Matanikau by the Japanese had been its kickoff. Vandegrift immediately ordered Edson to pull his battalions out and return to the perimeter. Early that morning, however, Colonel Sims's 7th Marines had already crossed the Matanikau upriver, minus Colonel Sims, and were deploying on the far side. Bringing up the rear was Chesty Puller's 1st Battalion, by now thoroughly blooded. Ahead of Puller was the 2d Battalion, and ahead of them an advance scouting force that was feeling its way down the Matanikau's west bank toward the sea. The scouts found no Japanese—they had vanished like smoke. The 2d Battalion widened the search. They, too, drew a blank. Then Puller's battalion fanned out farther yet, and suddenly there they were—an entire battalion of Japanese troops closely packed into two deep ravines, their weapons trained on the coast road and their rear totally unprotected. Grabbing a radio-telephone operator, Puller rang up the 11th Marines and requested that an immediate artillery barrage be dropped into the first ravine. "On the way," confirmed the 11th Marines. With the same breath, Puller ordered his mortar sections to rapid-fire into the second ravine.

Soon shells were crashing into both, and as the Japanese began frantically to scramble out, 1st Battalion machine-gunners cut them down. It was a grisly business. Within minutes, the lips, sides, and bottoms of the two ravines were stacked with Japanese dead—690 of them, a captured diary later revealed.

As the shells moaned overhead and the machine guns hammered, Puller's radio operator announced that Colonel Sims was on the radio-telephone. Capt. Regan Fuller, standing next to Puller, took it all in. From his command post on the other side of the river, Sims said, "Puller, we've got a change in orders." He then told Puller to return by way of Kokumbona, making a reconnaissance in force en route. "How the hell can I make a reconnaissance when we're engaged down to the last man," Puller shouted into the receiver. "We're fighting tooth and nail, man. If you'd get off your duff and come up here where the fighting is, you could see the situation."[3] So saying, Puller abruptly ceased transmission and handed the walkie-talkie back to the RTO man. On the following day the entire attack force returned to the perimeter. The butcher's bill for the three-day operation came to 65 marines killed, 125 wounded.

Crossing the T

On 5 October Ens. John Taurman, who had been rescued after ditching his torpedo bomber on 24 August, found himself lost and running out of gas on a night flight over the Slot. When his engine quit, he put his nose down, trimmed for glide, and raised a buddy, Bruce Harwood, on his radio. "I think I've used up all my luck," he said. Taurman and his crew were never found.

On 7 October Col. Louis Woods, Gen. Roy Geiger's number two, was made a brigadier general.

On 9 October the 164th Regimental Combat Team of the Americal Division shipped out of Noumea for Guadalcanal. The 164th was a good choice. A U.S. Army National Guard unit recruited from western Minnesota and the Dakotas, its rank and file of Swedish and German farm boys had the right stuff for the desperate work to come.

On that same day, Lieutenant General Hyakutake, commander of Japan's

17th Army, landed at Cape Esperance on the northwest coast of Guadalcanal. His commander in the field, Lieutenant General Maruyama, had already issued a general order to the Sendai Division: "This is the decisive battle between Japan and the United States, a battle in which the rise or fall of the Japanese Empire will be decided. If we do not succeed in the occupation of this island, no one should expect to return to Japan alive."

On the afternoon of 9 October a squadron of twenty new F4Fs appeared over Henderson Field, got the OK to land, and one by one touched down on its infamous surface. The new squadron was met by Capt. John Smith, veteran CO of Marine Fighter Squadron 223. Smith acidly informed its squadron leader, Maj. Leonard "Duke" Davis, that he had landed on the wrong field; a second field was now designated as Guadalcanal's fighter strip. The new airstrip, Fighter One (known familiarly as "the cow pasture"), had been recently completed by the 6th Seabees. It lay two thousand yards east of Henderson. Somewhat abashed, Squadron 221 took to the air and relanded. The squadron's exec was a lanky Dakotan, Capt. Joe Foss, destined in the coming months to win the Medal of Honor. Old at twenty-seven for fighter work, Foss was referred to by the squadron's mostly twenty-one year olds as "Old Foos." The squadron itself would yield more aces than any other squadron to fight on Guadalcanal.

On 11 October Maj. John Smith and Capt. Marion Carl took their leave of Guadalcanal, having become two of the historic air battle's most celebrated figures. Now only four pilots remained of the Cactus Air Force's original fighter squadron, VMF-223.

On 12 October Maruyama's engineers began cutting a trail through the rain forest. Coyly dubbed "the Maruyama Trail" by the general, it would snake from Kokumbona in the west through deep jungle to the southern sector of the marine perimeter and hopefully deliver the Sendai Division to battle. Other Japanese units would strike simultaneously across the Matanikau and attack the marines' western perimeter.

That night, the U.S. naval task force covering the convoy that bore the 164th Infantry Regiment to Guadalcanal was alerted to the presence of a Japanese force in the Slot, making swiftly for Guadalcanal waters. The Japanese had obviously spotted the U.S. convoy and were out to sink it. Rear Adm. Norman Scott, commander of the U.S. covering force, had hoped for just such an opportunity to even the score for the U.S. Navy's humiliation at the Battle of Savo Island in August. Scott had spent the previous three weeks training his captains and crews in the night-fighting skills so badly bungled at Savo—gunnery, torpedo attack, communication, maneuvering, and nighttime recognition of Japanese and American warships.

Scott now got what he wanted when the two forces collided in the dark off of Cape Esperance. Cutting across the leading warships of the enemy column at right angles in a classic "crossing of the T," Scott enfiladed the Japanese line of battle and as each U.S. warship came to bear, its gunners raked the length of the enemy column. The only Japanese ship that could effectively return fire was the lead vessel, using just its forward guns. Scott's "T" crossing then turned into a general melee. The Japanese rear admiral, Aritomo Goto, was killed on the bridge of his flagship, after which his task force lost two warships with most of their crews, and sustained damage to several others. The surviving Japanese ships then broke off the action and sped north before dawn could reveal their position to the Cactus Air Force. Scott's task force lost one destroyer; a second destroyer and a cruiser were damaged. There were several American muddles in the course of the battle, but no matter, Scott had severely punished the Japanese and sent them packing. Later, a few contentious historians would label Scott's success as more luck than judgment. The U.S. press, however, famished for good news, hailed Scott's victory at the Naval Battle of Cape Esperance as brilliant and Scott as a hero. He would enjoy the role for only a month before dying in a holocaust of shellfire on the bridge of his ship at the Naval Battle of Guadalcanal.

On the morning of 13 October the convoy bearing the 164th Infantry Regiment anchored in Iron Bottom Sound and began unloading twenty-eight hundred American GIs. When it departed, it took with it the skinny, battle-happy survivors of the 1st Raider Battalion. They had "served their time in hell" but would not go home. They would fight again in the mid-Solomons campaign of New Georgia, then merge with the 1st Raider Regiment and the 4th Marines to shed their blood in subsequent battles. Their inspired and enigmatic commander, Merritt "Red Mike" Edson, would later be promoted to brigadier general, and a few years after the war, back in civvies, he would inexplicably take his own life.[4] His Raiders, who had loved and occasionally hated him, would always wonder why.

That evening, a battery of Japanese long-barreled, 105-millimeter artillery pieces situated west of the Matanikau opened fire on Henderson Field.[5] Until they burned out their barrels, they would continue to shell the airstrip around the clock. The marines, quick to nickname their enemy's various harassments, christened the new battery "Pistol Pete."

Chesty Puller's men needed clothes. Their socks had dissolved, their skivvies were see-through and their dungarees were out at the knees and elbows. So, when Puller saw several of them dressed in brand new army issue, he knew that the 164th Infantry Regiment had landed. "Where'd you get em?" he inquired. "Colonel, the beach is loaded," he was advised. Never one to pass up a foraging opportunity, Puller and his first sergeant jumped in a jeep and drove down to the beach. There they found great stacks of GI supplies. But no guards. The guards, they noted, had prudently taken cover when several shells from Pistol Pete strayed into the area. Just as Puller and Pennington had stacked their jeep to capacity, an army MP yelled at them from a nearby foxhole, "Leave that stuff alone, dammit, that's Army gear." Puller yelled back, "If you're guarding this stuff, get the hell out here and guard it."[6]

Flying Boxcars

At 1:40 A.M. on 14 October the naval phase of Admiral Yamamoto's all-out plan to recapture Guadalcanal kicked in. Two of the world's most formidable battleships, *Kongo* and *Haruna*, swung their ponderous guns, sixteen of them, until they bore on Henderson Field. Their first salvo hurled illumination shells that burst on the runway and outlined everything—the Pagoda, sitting aircraft, outbuildings, and fleeing marines—in stark black and white. Then, with the perimeter lit up like a night baseball game, the Japanese gunners began ramming massive high-explosive shells up the breech. The recoil from these monsters tipped the huge ships sideways, great smoke rings blew from the guns' mouths, and the vast basso *ba-boom* reverberated from Guadalcanal's distant hills as the 14-inch shells thundered on their way. To the marines on the beach, they sounded like flying boxcars chasing each other through the heavens. The explosive effect was near-nuclear. Throughout the perimeter, terrified men dove from their tents into dugouts as the whirlwinds of concussion sent palm trees straight up out of sight, shredded whole tent settlements, drove two-by-fours through jeep hoods, and raised a fog of airborne particles consisting of earth, wood, metal, humanity, and dense black smoke from burning aviation gasoline. At Henderson the Pagoda took a near miss and toppled over. Blazing aircraft ringed the field. Ammunition dumps blew sky high in colossal orange fireballs that beggared modern Hollywood's most ambitious special effects. The view from shipboard was spectacular. "The night's pitch dark was transformed by fire into the brightness of day," recalled Admiral Tanaka. "Spontaneous cries and shouts of excitement ran throughout our ships."[7]

The bombardment lasted for seventy minutes. When it lifted, men crawled blinking and trembling from their holes. The sun rose on catastrophic damage. Dozens had been killed and maimed, others were buried in their dugouts. Part of the hospital was leveled. Blankets, mess kits, boondockers, burst cans of Spam, and every kind of personal effect littered the area. On surviving coconut palms sea bags hung like strange fruit. Henderson Field was nearly totaled. The airstrip was thickly cratered, but by first light the 6th Seabees were hauling fill to repair it. Nearly all of the stored aviation gas had gone up in flames; all but five SBDs were damaged or destroyed; all of VT-8's torpedo planes were junk. A couple of the 67th Fighter Squadron's P-400s and new P-39s had survived. Miraculously, few shells had fallen on Fighter One some two thousand yards east, and all of the F4Fs were intact. Evidently the Japanese were unaware of the airstrip's presence.

By the following day, the men of the 1st Division had shaken off some of the shock and were hard at work on repairs. Smoke from burning gasoline still hung over the perimeter and cartridges went off like popcorn in the smoldering ammunition dumps, but the Henderson runway was now usable, barely, and the mess kitchens were serving hot chow. Over the perimeter appeared a PBY, its wheels down, making an approach on Fighter One. The Dumbo was Gen. Roy Geiger's personal PBY, the "Blue Goose," flown in from Espiritu Santo by his aide, Maj. Jack Cram.

In it were two torpedoes for the navy's Torpedo Squadron 8, which had just been demolished. Thinking, perhaps, to lighten the mood, Cram ordered the two torpedoes rigged under the PBY's wing with a toggle release in the cockpit. Torpedoes on a Dumbo, of course, looked like socks on a rooster, but Cram took off, escorted by a lone F4F, and headed for Kokumbona, where a Japanese transport lay in shallow water. Five Japanese destroyers prowled nearby as Cram and the PBY began a majestic, swanlike approach. The destroyers, fearing some new kind of marine trick, peppered the apparition and its crazy pilot with antiaircraft fire, but Cram stayed the course and, on a note of triumph, pulled the toggle releases at the appropriate moment. The torpedoes splashed into the sea and made for the transport. One missed and ran up the beach. The other struck the transport amidships, exploded in a towering plume of water, and broke its back. Cram banked away gracefully and headed for home. When he landed, he was met by an angry looking Geiger who had been told of his aide's plans. Surveying the PBY, which now had more than fifty holes in its fuselage, Geiger icily dressed Cram down, spoke of a possible court-martial for destruction of government property, then stomped off to his temporary office. There he wrote out a recommendation that his aide be awarded the Navy Cross for one of the most intrepid assaults in Marine Corps history. Cram had lightened the mood.

CHAPTER TEN

You Can't Live Forever

THE 13 OCTOBER BOMBARDMENT of the marine perimeter by Japanese battleships was the most destructive hurricane of high-explosive shells yet to be dropped on an enemy ground position by any naval force. In minute-by-minute intensity, it equaled the artillery bombardments of such World War I battlegrounds as Verdun and Paschendaele. The shelling had killed or maimed seventy Americans, shredded food and equipment stocks, and demolished acres of tentage and quonset huts. It had crippled the striking power of the Cactus Air Force, destroying forty-eight SBDs and torpedo bombers and reducing aviation gasoline reserves to a two-day supply for the few planes still flyable. Henry Keys of the *London Daily Express* called it "a most unenviable experience." Another correspondent wrote, "It is almost beyond belief that we are still here, still alive. . . . We cannot write in this madness, but we keep notes with shaking hands."

By the following day, six of the eight civilian correspondents covering the campaign had arranged to exit Guadalcanal. That afternoon Col. Toby

Munn of General Geiger's staff dropped by the bivouac area of the army's 67th Pursuit Squadron and rounded up everyone in sight. "I want you to pass the word along," he told them, ducking for an incoming artillery shell, "that the situation is desperate. We don't know whether we'll be able to hold the field or not. There's a Japanese task force of destroyers, cruisers, and troop transports headed this way. We have enough gasoline left for one mission against them. Load your airplanes with bombs, go out with the dive bombers and hit them. After the gas is gone, we'll have to let the ground troops take over. Then your officers and men will attach themselves to some infantry outfit. Good luck and good bye."[1] That evening, Vandegrift radioed Ghormley, "Urgently necessary this force receive maximum support of air and surface units. Absolutely essential aviation gas be flown here continuously."

As night fell on the perimeter, every man found a hole in which to sweat out the naval bombardment that was sure to follow. It did, beginning at 2:00 A.M. This time it was the cruisers *Chokai* and *Kinugasa*, which mounted sixteen 8-inch guns between them. Firing at the rate of sixteen rounds every forty-five seconds, they walked their 8-inchers back and forth across the perimeter, 752 rounds in half an hour. The bombardment was seconded by well-aimed 105-millimeter rounds from Pistol Pete. Fighter One as well as Henderson was hammered by the angry guns.

The following morning, 15 October, marines near the beach beheld the heart-sinking sight of six Japanese transports in their curious orange and white camouflage paint anchored a few miles up the shoreline, boldly unloading four thousand infantrymen of Lieutenant General's Hyakutake's Sendai Division. "They're landing 'em faster'n we can kill 'em," groaned one marine. Over the Japanese landing site flew an uncontested air umbrella of carrier-launched Zeros. This up-your-nose audacity was inspired by the belief, substantially correct, that the Cactus Air Force had been destroyed. The Japanese 11th Air Fleet, wheeling like vultures over the perimeter, continued its all-out attack on Henderson Field. In Hawaii, Admiral Nimitz estimated the situation: "It now appears that we are unable to control the sea in the Guadalcanal area. Thus our supply of the position will only be done at great expense to us. The situation is not hopeless, but it is certainly critical." Navy lieutenant "Swede" Larsen, CO of Torpedo

Squadron 8, grimly surveyed the shambles of his torpedo planes, then led his pilots, aircrews, and mechanics up to Edson's Ridge, where they scrounged some marine rifles, dug in alongside the ground-pounders, and hunkered down facing the jungle's edge. Over at the 1st Pioneer Battalion area, the commanding officer, marine major Robert Ballance, issued his order of the day:

> The time has come for all good men to show their guts. . . . Now, what the hell, you joined this racket to fight, and fight I have every confidence that you will. Forget about this dying business; you can't live forever. Think instead about killing, squeezing off those shots, making every round land in one of the little yellow bastards. . . . Sure we'll get bombed, sure we'll get shelled, sure it's tough to take it, but I want every god-damned son-of-a-bitch in this outfit to stay in his position and keep thinking, "Let 'em come, brother, let 'em come," and when they do, acquit himself like the man and Marine he is. If die we must, we'll do it with our boots on and our face to the Japs. Keep cool and good luck.

As the situation worsened, the words of combatants such as Major Ballance had become grittier, while those of the editorial writers increased in eloquence. On the sixteenth the *New York Herald Tribune* brooded: "The shadows of a great conflict lie heavily over the Solomons. All that can be perceived is the magnitude of the stakes at issue." Not to be outdone, the *New York Times* printed an editorial that read suspiciously like a funeral oration: "Guadalcanal. The name will not die out of the memories of this generation. It will endure in honor." Back at Henderson Field, however, the issues were grubbier. There, the hunt was on for the aviation gas reserves that had been squirrelled away in the jungle against such a day. Each fifty-five-gallon drum represented one hour in the air for one Wildcat. Louis Woods, who had supervised the dispersion job, was off the island on official business, so it was anybody's guess where most of the hoarded avgas was. One of the first "bingos!" occurred when someone thought to siphon the gas from the tanks of two crippled B-17s that had landed at Henderson. Meanwhile, marines fanned out into the jungle, beating through marshes and thickets where the precious distillate was likely to be hidden, turning up some four hundred drums and wrestling them back to the field.

The seabees and marine engineers had sweated since dawn to repair the damage to Henderson and Fighter One. That forenoon, marine and army transports from Espiritu Santo began slipping in over the treetops, loaded to the maximum with drums of avgas. By midday, a cobbled-together assortment of marine, navy, and army air power, including air force B-17s from Espiritu, had begun to harass the Japanese transports anchored up the beach from the perimeter.[2] High in the sky over Henderson, F4Fs of the newly arrived Marine Squadron 221, with the help of antiaircraft fire, carved up that day's air raid, accounting for twelve Bettys and five Zeros. By late afternoon the action over the Japanese unloading site had become so furious that three of the transports, severely holed by bombs, had to be beached. The remaining three hoisted anchor and fled before they could finish unloading. But the Imperial Japanese Navy still ruled Guadalcanal waters and that night demonstrated this again with a third bone-jarring bombardment from Iron Bottom Sound, which the marines had begun calling "Sleepless Lagoon." In the process, another fifteen hundred shells were flung into the perimeter.

That morning in Hawaii, Admiral Nimitz had called his staff together and, with scrupulous objectivity, put a question to them: should Admiral Ghormley be replaced? After each man had been heard from, Nimitz thanked them and said he would consider their opinions. Late in the evening as he was getting ready for bed, his phone rang. One of his staff members asked permission to call on him, despite the hour. He arrived with the rest of the staff. The admiral received them in robe and pajamas and was told that his staff felt strongly that Ghormley should be replaced, a conclusion which Nimitz himself had already reached, and which was now confirmed by the men who knew nearly as much about the Pacific war as he did. After the meeting broke up, Nimitz sat down and wrote out an order. He then picked up his telephone and summoned his communications officer.

Victory Is Already in Our Hands

Harukichi Hyakutake, commander of the emperor's 17th Army, was on Guadalcanal to make certain that this attack, unlike the two previous attempts, would not fail to obliterate the U.S. presence on the island. The hand he held looked like a winner. Inundation would be the key to success. Nightly bombardments by the Imperial Japanese Navy would continue to neutralize the Cactus Air Force. The Bettys and Zeros of the 11th Air Fleet could bomb the airfields and perimeter almost at will. And he had more than enough strength on the ground—twenty-six thousand of the emperor's finest to hurl against the flimsy marine lines, including the battle-hardened Sendai Division. A reserve infantry element—the Koli detachment—was still afloat, to be landed if needed. The attack plan was based on well-established Japanese military principles. Tanks, troops, and artillery would strike east across the Matanikau and advance on Kukum, a deserted village between the Matanikau and the Lunga, now a marine stronghold. A second force would cross the Matanikau upstream and hook back, trapping any U.S. forces in the Kukum pocket. The Sendai Division, commanded by Lieutenant General Maruyama, would proceed down the Maruyama Trail to a concealed position near Edson's Ridge and, in a surprise night attack, burst through the perimeter to seize Henderson Field. When the mop-up was complete, Maruyama would accept Vandegrift's surrender at the mouth of the Matanikau. The marine general and his staff would then be flown to Tokyo and placed on public display.

On 16 October the leading elements of the Sendai Division shouldered their equipment and set off down the Maruyama Trail. Attached to them were the remnants of General Kawaguchi's defeated brigade, including the chastened general himself, who had marched west with his survivors and joined Hyakutake's newly arrived regiments. Kawaguchi, a sadder but wiser man, was the only commander present with firsthand knowledge of the diabolical Guadalcanal jungle. On the eighteenth the remainder of the force followed in their footsteps. The attack would jump off on 22 October. In a situation appraisal radioed to Rabaul, the 17th Army concluded its report with the words, "The victory is already in our hands. Please rest your minds."

Jesus Christ and General Jackson

On the afternoon of 18 October a four-engine Coronado amphibian aircraft touched down on the dancing waters of Noumea Harbor and swanned to a stop. Out climbed a man with a face like a bulldog. Vice Adm. William F. Halsey had arrived to assume command of a carrier task force. His boss would be an old friend, Vice Adm. Robert Ghormley. As Halsey stepped into the bobbing whaleboat that would take him to Ghormley's flagship, he was handed a sealed envelope. Opening it, he drew out a second envelope, marked "Secret." Inside, Halsey found a slip of paper. He read it, then exclaimed, "Jesus Christ and General Jackson, this is the hottest potato they've ever handed me!" On the slip of paper was printed an order from Nimitz: "You will take command of the South Pacific Area and South Pacific forces immediately."

The sixty-year-old Halsey was ideally qualified for the job. A seagoing Chesty Puller, his style, whatever the occasion, had always been "Full speed ahead, commence firing!" Nor was his manner exactly mild. And like Puller, his name throughout the Fleet and the Marine Corps had become synonymous with bold and decisive action. Therefore, no one was surprised at his first moves. Instead of settling into Ghormley's suffocating quarters on the elderly *Argonne*, he helped himself to the former Japanese Embassy ashore, ignoring the outraged protests of the local French government. He then moved U.S. Fleet Headquarters into the combat zone, from New Zealand to Noumea. To meet its needs he demanded and got from the French authorities a million square feet of floor space. After which he issued a directive forbidding neckties to be worn by naval and marine personnel in the South Pacific. His less than subtle mission statement, "Kill Japs, kill Japs, kill more Japs!" soon appeared in letters two feet tall on a billboard overlooking Tulagi Harbor.[3] All of this suggested to his command that Halsey was there not to administrate but to fight. Having set the stage, Halsey then declared his priorities. The first was to supply Archer Vandegrift with enough men and logistical supplies to secure Guadalcanal. Number two was to derail the Tokyo Express, making it impossible for the Japanese to land reinforcements. The third was to sink as many enemy ships and kill as many Japanese as possible.[4] To make these priorities perfectly clear, he called for a conference of all concerned, Marine Corps, U.S. Navy and Army, at Noumea on 23 October. On the morning of 20 October, Vandegrift flew to Noumea to prepare for the meeting.

It is recorded that when the marines on Guadalcanal got word that Halsey was now in charge, they jumped for joy. When the same news reached Japan, it touched off a frenzy of speculation. The changeover, concluded one Japanese news medium, foretold the "withdrawal of all American naval forces from the South Pacific."

A Half-Ration of Cold Rice

As the discredited Kawaguchi knew it would, the Guadalcanal jungle welcomed the 17th Japanese Army like a Venus flytrap. To begin with, the soldiers were cruelly overburdened. Each man carried, in addition to a full field pack, rifle, bayonet, ammunition, and full canteen, another twenty-some pounds of metal on his back—mortar or artillery shells, bits and pieces of field artillery, machine-gun barrels and tripods, mortar tubes and base plates. It was a staggering burden for men whose average weight was around 140 pounds. The practice had been feasible in northern China's temperate climate, but the soggy, prickling heat of Guadalcanal's rain forest now sucked at each man's energy, while the mucouslike mud of the jungle floor sucked at his feet. Soon the sixty pounds on each man's back felt like a grand piano, and the column was forced to stop and pant every few hundred yards.

The trail hacked out by Maruyama's engineers was single-file and undulating. It led down choked, slithery ravines and up 45-degree grades to razor-back ridges. Maruyama used his white cane to pull himself along. After day one the trail to the rear was strewn with equipment, and officers could do nothing about it. No amount of tongue-lashing or kicking could make an exhausted man shoulder an impossible load. To worsen matters, each soldier's daily nourishment consisted solely of a half-ration of cold rice.[5] Kawaguchi saw it as a rerun of his September trek to Edson's Ridge. As the sweating column toiled on and its progress slowed to a crawl, Maruyama was forced to radio Hyakutake with postponements of the attack date from 22 to 23 October, and finally to the twenty-fourth. (It is unlikely that Hyakutake or the Matanikau attack force ever received the message.) Still, Maruyama took heart from what Hyakutake had told him on the eve of departure: that the naval bombardments had been "a great shock to the enemy," and that their strength and morale were "gradually weakening." But fatigue and privations notwithstanding, the 17th Army coiled onward down its narrow jungle path, still the most formidable force the Marine Corps had yet to face on Guadalcanal.

At sea with his battleships and advised by 17th Army of the delay, the impatient Yamamoto withdrew north to refuel.

I Can Hold

Halsey's conference convened at Noumea on 23 October. Present were Maj. Gen. Archer Vandegrift; Maj. Gen. Alexander Patch, U.S. Army; Rear Adm. Kelly Turner; Maj. Gen. Millard Harmon; and Lt. Gen. Thomas Holcomb, commandant of the Marine Corps, who had flown in to view the situation and huddle with his old friend A. A. Vandegrift. At the meeting, Halsey called on each area commander to speak his piece. Vandegrift painted a realistic, but not pessimistic, picture of his situation. Halsey then asked him, "Are we going to evacuate or hold?" "I can hold," Vandegrift said, "but I've got to have more active support than I've been getting." Harmon's story reinforced Vandegrift's. Kelly Turner inventoried his problems—a critical shortage of cargo ships and enough warships to protect them. After Turner's recital, Halsey looked at Vandegrift and said, "Go on back, I'll promise you everything I've got." Halsey had one yardstick for measuring the caliber of his commanders—aggressiveness. If they attacked and lost, okay, as long as they had done their best. If in the process of attacking they made mistakes, that was okay, too: even the best officers make mistakes. But if they hesitated, went over to the defensive or, God help them, quit the field while still able to fight, Halsey would promptly have their guts for garters—and every naval officer in the South Pacific with "scrambled eggs" on his hat knew this.[6]

Blood for Eleanor

Despite their preoccupation with the U.S. landings in North Africa, the Joint Chiefs of Staff in Washington were finally beginning to understand that Vandegrift, Nimitz, and King were not just crying "Wolf." To the contrary, the fate of Guadalcanal was indeed hanging by a slender thread that the Japanese were now poised to snip. An alarmed Franklin Roosevelt blew the whistle. On 24 October, in a presidential memo to Gen. George Marshall, chairman of the Joint Chiefs, Roosevelt directed him to "make sure that every possible weapon gets into that area to hold Guadalcanal." It had the desired effect. Marshall immediately ordered fifty of the new Lockheed Lightning P-38 fighters flown to Henderson Field, and the army's 25th Infantry Division, twenty thousand strong, dispatched from Hawaii to the South Pacific. But there was no way in which these reinforcements could reach Guadalcanal in time to influence the impending battle.

On 20 October the Japanese permitted the marines a glimpse of their muscle. The object was to mislead, to make the marines think that the main assault would come from the west, across the mouth of the Matanikau, rather than out of the jungle on the perimeter's vulnerable southern front. Gen. Tadashi Sumiyoshi, commander of the Matanikau force, had not gotten word of the attack postponement. Acting on his original orders, he dangled two of his tanks at the far end of the Matanikau sandspit. It was a sacrificial bunt. One tank was punctured with antitank fire and the other withdrew, together with its supporting infantry ("like a dog with its fleas," in marine ground-pounder idiom). On the night of the twenty-first, Sumiyoshi again put on his sideshow—this time, nine tanks with their "fleas." Again the marine antitank guns opened up, disabling one tank. The rest, treads clanking, spun around and waddled back into the jungle. Meanwhile, Maruyama continued his efforts to raise Sumiyoshi on the radio and advise him of the delay, with no luck. To complicate matters, Sumiyoshi was languishing in the grip of a severe malarial attack and barely rational. Around midnight on the twenty-third, he committed all of his tanks to a genuine attempt at crossing the Matanikau's mouth. Twelve of them were destroyed before they could reach marine lines, and several hundred of his men met their maker in the shallows before the marine wire. Sumiyoshi had shot his bolt, and with this the western attack collapsed.

Back at 1st Division Operations, Lt. Col. Thomas, acting in Vandegrift's absence, weighed up the noisy Japanese demonstration at the mouth of the Matanikau. Worrying that it might indeed signal the main thrust, he moved the 2d Battalion, 7th Marines from the southern defense sector to the Matanikau. This left half of the southern perimeter unmanned, including Edson's Ridge. The remaining battalion on that sector, Chesty Puller's, spread out to take up the slack and were now thin on the ground—seven hundred men along a fourteen-hundred-yard front, roughly a two-man foxhole every twelve feet, not at all comforting when the Japanese are coming at you six deep and virtually shoulder to shoulder. Puller personally walked the lines, checking the position of every marine and his weapon. He was confident of his firepower; a few days ago he had sent a scrounging party to the Cactus Air Force bone yard to strip wrecked F4Fs and SBDs of their machine guns, which were now rigged alongside his other automatic weapons. Puller's lines were partly buried in jungle, and his marines with their usual gallows humor referred to the angle formed by the jungle's fringe and their battalion front as "Coffin Corner." Tied in on Puller's left flank was a battalion of the army's still-green 164th Infantry. Another battalion of the 164th was in reserve behind their lines. As yet, Thomas at 1st Division Operations had no reason to believe that a Japanese attack would be sprung against Puller's southern front.

On 23 October, in the jungle maze south of Henderson Field, Maruyama's units left the trail and began hacking their way north through the tightly woven jungle growth, each wing moving toward its assigned jump-off point south of Henderson Field. Earlier in the day, Kawaguchi, the only Japanese officer present who knew what they were up against, had approached Maruyama with a recommended change in plans. He was summarily fired, and command of his right wing given to Col. Toshinaro Shoji. To his credit Shoji objected, pointing out that sacking General Kawaguchi on the threshold of battle "was not the way of the samurai."

He was sternly overruled,[7] and Kawaguchi was shipped back to a Rabaul hospital under a cloud. The main attacking force now consisted of a right wing under Shoji, who was ailing with malaria, a center commanded by Maruyama, who was suffering from severe neuralgia, and a left wing commanded by Gen. Yumio Nasu, who was feeling far from well himself. All bore their afflictions stoically, as did their men. The left and right wings would launch their assaults against the southern marine sector at 5:00 the next afternoon, 24 October. After which Maruyama's force would drive through the middle of the marine line, then cut and thrust its way to the airfield.

At 3:00 the following afternoon a line of towering black thunderheads drifted slowly over Guadalcanal and shed its contents on the belligerents. Rain fell in solid gray sheets, drenching Japanese and Americans impartially. The forest floor was trampled to gumbo by thousands of Japanese feet, visibility in the jungle was near-zero, units mingled with other units like minnows in a bucket, and communications fizzled out. The 5:00 P.M. zero hour came and went as Japanese officers tried to reshape their scrambled commands. Four hours later in the blacked-out jungle, Colonel Shoji and his men were still not in position. Finally an exasperated Maruyama commanded Nasu's left flank to attack without waiting. Nasu, advised by his scouts that "Coffin Corner" was vulnerable, ordered it stormed.

At 9:30 P.M. a marine outpost of forty-eight men concealed on a little knoll three hundred yards in front of Puller's wire was bypassed by Nasu's silent skirmishers as they filtered into the no man's land between the marines and the Japanese. Puller's field telephone orders to the jittery men were to keep their heads down, let the skirmishers pass, then one by one steal through the bush toward the safety of the army's adjacent lines. At midnight, Puller's dripping ground-pounders were jerked to attention by the sight of a red flare rising from the jungle to their front and arcing through the wet sky. Rising with it from a thousand Japanese throats was the flesh-crawling chant of "Banzai! Banzai! Banzai!" as Nasu's men, bayonets at the ready, flooded out of the jungle and into the tall kunai grass that would take them to Puller's lines. On they came at the trot like a Zulu impi, shrieking and taunting. But the marines had learned their lessons well at the Tenaru and Edson's Ridge, and now had the hang of it. They drenched the oncoming waves of Japanese with mortar shells, punctuated with 105-millimeter howitzer rounds from the 11th Marines. To give their fleeing outpost time to reach the army lines, Puller's men held their fire as long as possible. Then, as the range closed, they opened up with machine guns, BARs, and rifles, thickening the air with snapping, chirping lead into which the Japanese bravely charged, shoulders hunched, backs bent, like men bucking a blizzard. Their leading ranks disintegrated, and as fast as following ranks could take their places, they in turn were struck down. Progress against the flailing lead became impossible, except at two points where the momentum of the charge breached the marine wire. There it was bayonet to bayonet, with men jerking and jabbing like video-game figures as exploding grenades strobe-lit the action. One of the breaches was quickly sealed and the intruding Japanese mopped up. Through the second breach, before it could be plugged, ran Colonel Furimiya and his color guard, one hundred men of the 129th Infantry carrying their regimental colors. Once inside the perimeter, they escaped notice and were swallowed up in the darkness and confusion.

At this point, Chesty Puller got on the field telephone to Division Operations and told Thomas that what was happening on his front was no sideshow but a major effort. His seven hundred marines badly needed reinforcement. Thomas told him to use the 3d Battalion of the army's 164th Infantry, the untested Dakota and Minnesota farm boys who had been hunkering down in reserve behind Puller's lines. The GIs were led forward through the rain, bedlam, and darkness and fed into the marine lines by the tens and twenties—a squad here, a platoon there. The mud-plastered, adrenaline-drunk marines quickly gave them the scoop, and when the next howling wave of Japanese struck, the army nineteen year olds proved steady under fire, giving good account of themselves with rifle, grenade, and bayonet. In minutes they were veterans. It is recorded that during these all-night attacks there was much trading of insults between the Japanese and the Americans. When the Japanese yelled, "Blood for the Emperor!" the Americans would yell back, "Blood for Eleanor [Roosevelt]!" And when the Americans taunted, "The Emperor eats shit!" the Japanese would counter with "Babe Ruth eats shit!"[8]

The hellish night wore on. Rain squalls lashed the battlefield, soaking the living and rinsing the dead. Hordes of Japanese continued to emerge from the darkness and fling themselves at the marine lines. Each time, with hoarse yells and frenzied energy, the marines and GIs stopped them at the barbed wire. At the very center of Puller's lines was marine Plt. Sgt. John Basilone, dug in with his section of water-cooled 30-caliber machine guns. Basilone was know as "Manila John" for the years he had soldiered there with the army. Several times during lulls he had sent men forward to unsnag the bodies that hung on the barbed wire and blocked his field of fire. Still the Japanese came, and Basilone's guns ran short of ammunition. Shucking off his boondockers (they had finally come apart in the mud), Manila John became a one-man bucket brigade, sprinting barefoot up and down the path between the front and the battalion command post with boxes of belted ammo and new barrels for his scorched out 30s. Returning with a load, he found that a knot of attackers had surged through the wire and surrounded two of his guns. Quickly he pulled together a rescue squad of riflemen. Then Basilone, not a large man, hoisted a hundred-pound machine gun onto his shoulders and dashed with the rifle squad to his overrun section, forcing the Japanese back and recapturing the guns. By dawn's somber light, an entire company of the Sendai Division's 129th regiment lay scattered in front of Basilone's section. The barefoot machine-gun virtuoso from Raritan, New Jersey, became the first enlisted marine on Guadalcanal to be awarded the Medal of Honor. "Manila John" Basilone would later be killed in action on Iwo Jima.

It is unclear what happened to Colonel Furiyami and his men once they entered the perimeter. It appears that they got as far as the outskirts of Henderson Field, then attempted to fight their way out of the perimeter, but were killed. However, Furiyami did succeed in getting a runner with a message back to Maruyama, who passed it on to Hyakutake, who radioed it to Rabaul. Furiyami's message was "Banzai!"—the code word for "Henderson Field taken." It was received in Rabaul with rejoicing, and a Betty bomber was dispatched by the 11th Air Fleet to take possession of the prize. The Betty arrived early the next morning and made a belly-scraping victory pass down the Henderson runway. When every marine and GI within range emptied his weapon at the presumptuous Betty, it spurted flame, rolled over, and slammed into the jungle.

Six times the Japanese came in force. Except for Shoji's right wing, still wandering in the blacked-out rain forest, the entire Sendai Division took part in the attack. During the night, General Nasu fell in battle, and at first light the remains of the division withdrew into the jungle to bind their wounds and regroup. The next morning, Puller's marines and GIs counted 941 bodies in front of their lines, scattered helter-skelter for acres and looking like disjointed, tossed-about window mannequins. The only ground lost was a salient the size of a football field punched into Puller's lines, which was mopped up at dawn. One colonel of the Sendai Division had committed suicide after the attack. In his diary, the colonel had bequeathed his watch to Captain Suzuki and his glasses to Sergeant Yamakawa. He offered his apologies for humiliating the Sendai Division commander and for staining his regiment's name with his failings.

All day, Puller's marines and the soldiers of the 164th worked to strengthen their positions, knowing that the Japanese would be back that night. A mile away at Fighter One airstrip, Capt. Joe Foss took a bold step —disregarding policy, he instructed his fighter pilots to tangle one on one with the Zeros. Foss reasoned that the hard-pressed Japanese 11th Air Fleet, in making its all-out effort against the Cactus Air Force, had been scraping the bottom of their barrel. Accordingly, most of its pilots were newly fledged with none of the aerobatic and gunnery skills of their predecessors. The expertise now belonged to the Americans. "Dogfight 'em," ordered Foss, which his F4F pilots promptly did.

That night the Sendai Division again attacked "Coffin Corner," but their hearts were not in it. The marine and army defenders threw them back with minimum losses to themselves. Four miles west of "Coffin Corner," however, this was not the case. There the 2d Battalion, 7th Marines were fighting a spirited battle with the forces of Col. Akinosuka Oka. The migratory colonel and his detachment had appeared from nowhere after missing the 23 October jump-off date. In a vicious engagement during which the Japanese attacked all along the marine front, the day was saved first by a lone marine machine-gunner and finally by a hastily recruited team of rear echelon personnel. The lone machine-gunner was Plt. Sgt. Mitchell Paige, an "Old Breed" marine who stuck to his gun until all other machine guns in his section had been silenced. Paige then ran from gun to gun, squeezing off bursts, and finally picked up one of the ponderous, water-cooled 30s, cradling the blistering hot weapon in his arms like a fire hose.[9] Backed up by a handful of riflemen, he advanced on the Japanese spitting bullets at the rate of six hundred rounds per minute.[10] The sight of this oncoming phenomenon dismayed and scattered the Japanese, buying time for Paige's section to be reinforced. Paige then made his way back to the battalion aid station for treatment of his agonizing burns. For this day's work, Paige was awarded the Medal of Honor. The second such phenomenon occurred when the Japanese occupied a strategic hill and began firing down on marine positions, making them untenable. Unable to spare riflemen from the line, the battalion commander, Lt. Col. H. H. Hanneken, rounded up a collection of marine cooks, typists, and bandsmen and pointed them at the Japanese. Up the hill they went, pelting the Japanese with hand grenades, and down the other side went the surprised Japanese. The next day, rumor had it that one of the cooks had decked a Japanese officer with a pancake.[11] (The fact that a flung-together detachment of cooks, typists, and bandsmen could run veteran Japanese infantry off a hilltop is no reflection on the Japanese: every marine, whatever his specialty, is fully trained and maintained as a combat-ready rifleman.)

At this juncture, what the Japanese had hoped would be the decisive battle for the island of Guadalcanal simply fizzled out. Their three major assaults had been thrown back, first by the jungle and then by the Americans. Nothing had been learned from previous defeats and, for the third time, large numbers of Japan's willing young men had been fed into the meat grinder by inflexible and vainglorious commanders. Their butcher's bill for the week totaled thirty-five hundred men of the Sendai Division, dead, wounded, or missing, with many yet to die of starvation in the jungle. Marine and army casualties amounted to two hundred killed and two hundred wounded, a ratio versus the Japanese of nearly nine to one. The outnumbered Cactus Air Force, living from hand to mouth on scanty avgas and ammunition rations, nevertheless had stood off Japan's 11th Air Fleet and sunk an enemy cruiser for good measure. When the smoke cleared it was reckoned that the Japanese had lost more than one hundred planes and pilots over the lower Solomons, crippling the 11th Air Fleet so severely that it was now a broken reed. Geiger, down to twelve F4Fs, eleven SBDs, and six P-400s, was only marginally better off,[12] but this for the Cactus Air

Force was simply business as usual, seeming to confirm the old cracker-
barrel observation that "what matters is not the size of the dog in the
fight, but the size of the fight in the dog!" If the marines had wondered
whether the army's untested 164th Infantry Regiment would acquit itself
well in action, they now had their answer. Col. Clifton Cates, who commanded the 1st Marines, voiced marine sentiment in a letter to Col. Bryant
Moore, CO of the 164th: "The officers and men of the 1st Marines salute
you for a most wonderful piece of work. . . . Will you please extend our
sincere congratulations to all concerned. We are honored to serve with a
unit such as yours."[13]

Attack—Repeat—Attack

When Admiral Yamamoto was advised, incorrectly, by the 17th Army that
Henderson Field was finally in Japanese hands, he called off the naval
bombardment of the airfield and headed southeast toward the Santa Cruz
Islands to execute phase two of his plan, the final destruction of the U.S.
Pacific Fleet. But U.S. Naval Intelligence had already cracked a coded
Japanese radio transmission spelling out Yamamoto's plans. Halsey, therefore, knew what was coming—four Japanese carriers escorted by sixty-
three battleships, cruisers, and destroyers. To oppose this daunting array,
Halsey could field only one operational carrier—the *Hornet*. His other two
were thousands of miles away. The *Saratoga* was laid up in a West Coast
shipyard with severe torpedo damage, and the *Enterprise* had been under-
going repairs at Pearl Harbor until the lucky code cracking, when an
alarmed Nimitz ordered *Enterprise*'s captain to sprint for the South Pacific
and damn the repairs.

The "Big E" arrived just in time for the slugging match. Commanding
the U.S. task force was Rear Adm. Tom Kinkaid, who on the morning of
the twenty-fifth was sharing with his opposite number, Adm. Chuichi
Nagumo, the anxiety of not knowing where his adversary lurked. In carrier battles, he who gets in the first punch has a distinct edge. Later that
morning, a patrolling PBY sighted several ships of Nagumo's force near
the Santa Cruz Islands (celebrated in the Broadway musical *South Pacific* as
"Bali-Hai"). Kinkaid immediately launched a strike, but when it arrived

the sea was empty. Then in the predawn hours of the twenty-sixth, Kinkaid
was handed reports of new enemy sightings, including two carriers. On
Noumea, Halsey read the same reports and promptly radioed Kinkaid an
unequivocal order—"Attack—repeat—attack." The *Enterprise* already had
a search mission in the air, two SBDs armed with five-hundred-pound
bombs. Banking onto their new heading, they soon sighted the small carrier *Zuiho*, threaded their way through the blossoming flak, and planted
both of their bombs on her flight deck. The *Zuiho* was out of the fight, but
her strike had already been launched. Nagumo, having gotten a fix on
Kinkaid's position, launched dive bombers, torpedo planes, and Zeros
from all four carriers. The U.S. and Japanese strikes passed within a few
miles of each other en route to their respective targets, exchanged stares,
but flew on.

The Japanese were first over their target and chose the *Hornet* as their
victim. One bomb penetrated *Hornet's* flight deck. A crippled dive bomber
hurled itself at the carrier's stack, glanced off, and crashed through the
flight deck with two five-hundred-pound bombs that exploded below
with disastrous effect. A pair of surface-skimming torpedo planes loosed
their steel fish against *Hornet's* bow. These exploded in the engine rooms
and the carrier slowed to a halt, listed heavily, and disappeared under a
sky-high mushroom of black smoke. Then three more five-hundred-
pounders slammed into her flight deck. Another suicidal pilot in a torpedo plane crashed into the bow gun gallery, and the detonation took
out the forward elevator shaft. The *Hornet* was in extremis, but her crew
refused to give her up. They battled the boiling, leaping flames as bravely
as any marines ever stood off a banzai charge. Now the *Enterprise* swam
into the bombsights of the bat-winged Vals. Antiaircraft bursts measled
the sky above her, but three Japanese dive bombers slipped through to
put their bombs into the Big E's still unrepaired flight deck. Forty-four of
her crew died, but the ship survived. Many miles away over the Japanese
carrier force, four SBDs from *Hornet* revenged their mother ship. With
their rear gunners still squeezing off bursts at pursuing Zeros, each pilot
in turn pushed over, split his flaps, put his right eye to the bombsight,
and lined up the cross-hairs on *Shokaku's* flight deck. At two thousand feet
he pulled the bomb release toggle, closed his dive brakes, flattened out,

shoved his throttle to the stop and had the satisfaction of hearing his rear gunner shout, "A hit!" into the intercom. The *Shokaku* would not sink, but would be out of the war for nine months.

The *Hornet* would sink. It was obvious to her captain that the ship could not be saved, and he ordered her crew taken off by the escorts. But the big carrier refused to die. She was taken in tow by the cruiser *Northhampton*, but after three more hits by late-appearing dive bombers she was cut adrift and the U.S. task force steamed away, leaving her to wallow and burn in the Solomon sea. When the Japanese arrived, two of their destroyers torpedoed her, and, with a great sigh of escaping air, down she went to oblivion. The battle was over. Japan, having sunk the *Hornet*, had achieved a tactical victory, leaving the U.S. South Pacific fleet with only one carrier, the *Enterprise*—damaged and barely operational. But for their efforts the Japanese had been severely hammered, so much so that, after the Naval Battle of Santa Cruz, Japan would never again risk her carriers in head-to-head confrontation with U.S. flat tops. In Hawaii, Admiral Nimitz cautiously acknowledged that "the general situation at Guadalcanal is not unfavorable."

There was a bitter aftertaste to the battle. *Hornet's* abandonment to the enemy was viewed by many Americans who flew and fought there as the most shameful page in U.S. naval history.

We Haven't Eaten in Three Days

The Japanese may have been inexpert strategists, but they were definitely not quitters. Their optimism undimmed by three calamitous defeats, the Imperial General Staff in their faraway Tokyo headquarters made ready for a fourth time to wrestle Guadalcanal from the Americans. There would be no change in procedure. Victory would be guaranteed by an even greater use of force majeure. Accordingly, on 27 October the IGHQ informed the 17th Army at Rabaul that the Japanese troops on Guadalcanal would again be heavily reinforced by the Tokyo Express; Henderson Field and the perimeter would for a second time be devastated by bombarding battleships; and the Cactus Air Force would once more be set upon by superior numbers. The assault date—coded "Z-day"—was fixed for 13 November, seventeen days away. Defeat would be unacceptable, the 17th Army was coldly advised. Taking no chances, Admiral Yamamoto independently assigned the 8th Fleet to escort the transports that would deliver 14,500 fresh troops to Guadalcanal. This time, however, there were dissenters among the Japanese officers who had taken part in the previous fiascos. One of them, Admiral Mikawa, made bold to suggest that the plan as it stood still did not guarantee enough Japanese airpower to shield the troop transports from the Cactus Air Force, the carrier-launched dive bombers, and the B-17s from Espiritu Santo. "To our regret," he later recorded, "the Supreme Command stuck persistently to reinforcing Guadalcanal."

While the IGHQ was issuing their new attack orders, the Sendai Division's right wing, lead by Col. Toshinaro Shoji, was retreating eastward on the Murayama Trail toward Koli Point. The rest of the division had withdrawn to the west, making for the upper reaches of the Lunga River. There they would rejoin the units that had fought along the Matanikau. If their earlier march into battle had been painful, their retreat from battle was agonizing. "October 27: I never dreamed of retreating over the same mountainous trail through the jungle we crossed with such enthusiasm. . . . We haven't eaten for three days and even walking is difficult. On the uphill my body swayed around unable to walk. I can't imagine how the soldiers carrying the artillery are doing. I must take rest every two meters. It is quite disheartening to have only one tiny teaspoon of salt per day and a palmful of rice porridge." This from the diary of Lt. Keijiro Minegishi.

The Scales of War

On 29 October, making good his promise to support Vandegrift to the hilt, Halsey ordered the 8th Marines to Guadalcanal. On their heels would arrive the 2d Raider Battalion, another regiment of the army's Americal Division, five hundred seabees, additional marine antiaircraft, and coastal defense units. Also adding muscle was the chronically outnumbered Cactus Air Force. With the arrival of Marine Scout-Bomber Squadron 132 and Fighter Squadron 112, five squadrons would soon be operating out of the perimeter's three airstrips. En route from Hawaii was the army's 25th

Infantry Division of twenty thousand men. The accounts of war were finally beginning to balance as both sides poured men and material ashore, the Japanese with nightly Tokyo Express runs and Turner with his daylight dashes across the Solomon sea from Espiritu Santo and Noumea.

For the first time since 7 August, Vandegrift found himself in the novel position of having enough manpower. He would employ it to solve two problems. The first problem was Pistol Pete—actually a battery of four long-barreled Japanese 105s.[14] Pete was a twenty-four-hour menace at Henderson Field, cratering the airstrip, damaging parked aircraft, and blowing away anyone unlucky enough to be near the shattering explosion. Firing from somewhere west of the Matanikau, Pete had never been pinpointed. The second problem was reported by Vandegrift's native scouts, who had spied remnants of the Sendai Division retreating westward through the jungle. If the retreating Sendai Division could be intercepted and successfully brought to battle, it could be written off. And if Pistol Pete could be located in his western lair and pushed back out of range, he could be neutralized. Consequently, in the last week of October, Vandegrift drew up plans for an operation that would strike west to accomplish both of these ends.

CHAPTER ELEVEN

A Certain Ruthlessness

BRIG. GEN. ROY GEIGER, commanding officer of the Cactus Air Force, had presided over an epic air battle in which a handful of exhausted marine, navy, and army pilots had taken on the entire Japanese 11th Air Fleet and fought it to a standstill. In the process the 11th Air Fleet lost an estimated 667 aircraft, together with most of their pilots and air crews. The battle had cost the Cactus Air Force 101 aircraft and 84 pilots and air crewmen.[1] Given the circumstances, this three-to-one ratio in favor of the Cactus Air Force was a stunning victory. To win it had required of Geiger a certain ruthlessness in motivating his command. Those who knew Geiger well, however, speculated that the losses suffered by his young flyers had imposed upon the white-haired, tight-lipped general an intolerable burden of silent grief. He had died a little with each of them, and this was consuming him physically and emotionally. Whatever the reason, during the first week in November, Brigadier General Geiger was relieved of command of the Cactus Air Force, not without acrimony, and replaced by his former number two, Brig. Gen. Louis Woods.

That same week, as if in tribute to Geiger, the Japanese 11th Air Fleet was judged by its superiors to be a spent force, having lost one-third of its strength. The fleet's surviving personnel and aircraft were withdrawn from Rabaul, and a new 11th Air Fleet was formed under the aegis of the 21st Air Flotilla.[2] Geiger would go on to new honors as commanding general of the 3d Marine Amphibious Corps in the battle for the Marianas. In the meantime, Cactus Air Force reinforcements continued to arrive. On 12 November an advance echelon of the army's 68th Pursuit Squadron landed at the newly completed Fighter Two airstrip. A day later it had already been blooded—on the ground: three of its members were wounded in an after-dark naval bombardment. When the rest of the squadron arrived, it brought with it the long-range, twin-boomed Lockheed Lightning P-38s, as well as P-39 Airacobras, P-40 Kittyhawks, and more of the long-nosed P-400s. The outfit was a direct descendent of Capt. Eddie Rickenbacker's 94th "Hat in the Ring" squadron of World War I fame.

Just Band-Aid Wounds

During this first week of November, Archer Vandegrift found himself at war on two fronts. In the west he had already launched his attack to push Pistol Pete out of firing range and cut off the retreating Sendai Division. Unlike the circuitous strategies of his opponents, Vandegrift's plan was dead simple—a straightforward thrust at the Japanese west of the Matanikau, or, in marine parlance, "Hey diddle-diddle, straight up the middle." Carrying the can were the 5th Marines, supplemented by a battalion of the 7th Marines, plus two battalions of the unblooded 8th Marines, until now in reserve on Tulagi. Merritt Edson was running the show. Jumping off on 1 November, the thrust got as far as Point Cruz then stalled. One obstacle was the ferocious resistance of the Japanese defenders. Another was the predictably slow progress of the 8th Marines, virgins to jungle fighting. At Point Cruz, three hundred Japanese were sealed off and killed, but little else accomplished to justify heavier-than-expected marine casualties. The retreating Sendai Division eluded its pursuers and continued on its way west. Edson was recalled to the perimeter, and Col. John M. Arthur, commander of the 8th Marines, was left in charge of the western front.

Meanwhile, a threat to Vandegrift's eastern front had materialized. Colonel Shoji, after trekking eastward through the jungle from Coffin Corner, had eventually reached the coast near Tetere with twenty-five hundred men. There Radio Rabaul had advised him that reinforcements would arrive near Tetere the night of 3 November, via the Tokyo Express. Simultaneously, Vandegrift was alerted by Naval Intelligence to the time and approximate place of the Tokyo Express delivery. Shoji's presence, however, was an unknown. Vandegrift dispatched a battalion of the 7th Marines eastward under Colonel Hanneken to ambush the newcomers. Hanneken's eight hundred marines arrived at twilight and waited for the Tokyo Express to show up. Less than a mile away, Shoji's twenty-five hundred Japanese did likewise. Neither spotted the other. At midnight, Hanneken's men made out the dim shapes of a transport and several destroyers close onshore. But to their dismay, the ships glided by and disappeared in the direction of the undetected Shoji. There they off-loaded reinforcements and supplies. As the night was moonless, Hanneken decided to stay put. He would move to the attack at dawn. Then as military matters will, this one began to unravel. No sooner had the sun risen and Hanneken's battalion set off in quest of the newly landed reinforcements than they bumped headlong into their quarry, coming their way. The Japanese were quicker on the draw. They showered the marines with mortar and howitzer fire, and the marines backed off. As they did, they heard firing behind them. From nowhere had arrived yet another Japanese delegation to attack them from the rear. Leaving the converging Japanese forces to shoot at one another, Hanneken's battalion scrambled out sideways and took cover on the far bank of a handy river. There they radioed for help. Vandegrift sent the Cactus Air Force to bomb and strafe the Japanese, but there was a snafu, as revealed by Hanneken's radioed comments entered in the 1st Division log:

1717. Friendly planes bombing and strafing.
1735. Planes are bombing us. Please stop them.
1755. Request all planes stop bombing until things can straighten out.

The plot continued to thicken as Vandegrift sent Puller's battalion and the army's 164th Infantry to the rescue. Command of the rapidly expanding force was turned over to marine Brig. Gen. William Rupertus, who had been hastily boated over from Tulagi. Puller's battalion was pushing in from the west when, without warning, enemy artillery and machine guns took them under fire. Puller heard the screech of an approaching shell, knew his name was on it, and ducked. It exploded just in front of him. For the first time in his long career, the indestructible marine nearly bought the farm. The blast of hot metal fragments blew him off his feet, riddling his legs and lower body. As Puller lay bleeding, he yelled to a marine crouching nearby with a field telephone, "Call headquarters, old man." "I can't, sir," said the marine, "the line's been cut." Puller got unsteadily to his feet, only to be shot twice through the arm by a sniper. Down he went for a second time.

Sgt. Maj. Frank Sheppard was up front with the machine-gunners when word reached him. He ran back to where Puller lay. "Are you able to stay in command, sir?" he asked. "Of course," snorted Puller, "I'll be okay—I can't leave these men." A foxhole was dug and Puller lowered into it on a poncho. Meanwhile, the phone line was repaired. From his hole in the ground, Puller told Sheppard to call in an artillery mission against the Japanese positions. When it arrived, howling overhead, the Japanese pulled in their necks and went quiet for the rest of the evening. Puller, his bleeding stanched by a corpsman, tried getting to his feet again, but without success. Calling up 1st Division HQ, he grudgingly confessed that he was unable to continue in command. Division sent Maj. John C. Weber to relieve him. When Weber arrived, Puller made a another desperate effort to stand and this time succeeded. Shaking off all assistance, he tottered away down the one-thousand-yard trail to the beach where a Higgins boat awaited. Back at the perimeter, he was met by Red Mike Edson, who asked if he was okay. "Hell," exclaimed Puller, "these are just Band-Aid wounds." He was then informed by the doctors that it was impossible to dig out all of the shrapnel—he would have to fly to Australia. Puller flatly refused, observing, "When I was a boy in Virginia, half the old men in the county carried enough Yankee iron in their bodies to open junkyards." Eight days later he got out of bed and reported himself fit for duty.[3]

While the wounded Puller was lying in his foxhole, Colonel Shoji received a radio order from 17th Army. It directed him to pull his reinforced contingent out of action and march west through the jungle to a rendezvous with newly arrived Japanese reinforcements on the upper reaches of the Lunga River. When an intercept of the message reached Vandegrift, he ordered the 2d Marine Raider Battalion to pursue, and so began one of the most remarkable feats of guerrilla warfare in the Pacific theater. Leaving behind a strong rear guard, Shoji and his men vanished into the twilight of the rain forest, the 2d Marine Raiders padding quietly on their heels. Back at the scene of action, two battalions of the army's 164th Infantry, having spent the previous night mistakenly shooting at each other, closed in and sealed off Shoji's rear guard of five hundred men. Nearby, Gen. William Rupertus, the officer newly in charge, collapsed with dengue fever, and the whole muddled enterprise began unraveling. Nevertheless, Vandegrift had secured his eastern front and the 2d Raiders were on their way to making military history.

Send in the Cook

On 8 November, three weeks after taking command, Adm. William F. Halsey made good on something that Adm. Robert Ghormley had neglected to do. He visited Guadalcanal. Vandegrift recorded that his visit was "a wonderful breath of fresh air." Halsey, said Vandegrift, radiated enthusiasm and confidence as he was taken to the island's already historic sites—the Tenaru, Edson's Ridge, Henderson Field, and the Matanikau. He met and spoke with marines, soldiers, and seabees of all ranks, praised them for their courage and fortitude, and, more important, recorded Vandegrift, "Halsey saw their gaunt, malaria-ridden bodies [and] their faces lined from what seemed like a nightmare of years." The admiral was welcomed ashore by the Japanese as well. Washing Machine Charley paid his usual wee hours visit to the perimeter, and a couple of destroyers on detached duty from the Tokyo Express run lobbed in some shells. After the war, Halsey confessed that it had made him a bit nervous. "It wasn't the noise that kept me awake; it was fright. I called myself yellow—and worse—and told myself, 'Go to sleep, you damned coward!' but it didn't do any good; I couldn't obey orders." Halsey's enthusiasm at one point proved excessive. Taking his evening meal with Vandegrift in the officer's mess, the admiral expressed his satisfaction with Guadalcanal's chronically substandard fare. "Send in the cook," he demanded. When the flustered mess sergeant, "Butch" Morgan, arrived at tableside, Halsey complimented him on the tasty meal. Butch, searching for a suitable reply, finally stammered, "B-b-bullshit, Admiral, b-b-bullshit!"

Two days after Halsey's departure, Vandegrift called off the attack west of the Matanikau. Intelligence reports were ominous and Vandegrift needed all of his marines back in the perimeter, preparing to face another Japanese onslaught.

Z-day

Japan's Z-day plans to once and for all eradicate the U.S. presence on Guadalcanal would entail a greater and more complex effort than any to date. Had some all-seeing U.S. war correspondent with a ringside seat at the developing battle been filing terse eyewitness dispatches to his editor in the states, they might have read as follows:

> TUESDAY, 10 NOVEMBER—In the last eight days the Tokyo Express has landed sixty-five destroyer loads and two cruiser loads of infantry on western Guadalcanal.

> THURSDAY, 12 NOVEMBER—Reinforcements continue to arrive at Lunga Point: yesterday, additional elements of the army's 147th Infantry and five hundred marine replacements, and today Admiral Turner delivered the 182d regiment of the Americal division. In spite of this, Japanese outnumber Americans on Guadalcanal.[4]

> Shepherding our troop transports and now standing offshore are two naval escort groups, one commanded by Rear Adm. Norman Scott, victor of the Battle of Cape Esperance, and the other by Rear Adm. Daniel J. Callaghan. Heading for Guadalcanal waters but still some distance away is a task force of U.S. Navy heavies, including two battlewagons—the USS *Washington* and USS *South Dakota*. Admiral Halsey knows the Jap navy is coming in strength, and he is loaded for bear.

> To supply much needed air cover, the fast carrier *Enterprise* is sprint-

ing up from Noumea. The *Big E* was attacked by Jap dive bombers on 26 October, and navy shipwrights are hastily completing her repairs at sea. With *Hornet's* sinking, the *Enterprise* is our only operational carrier in the South Pacific.

7:00 P.M.—Naval intelligence reports the movement of a large enemy naval force down the Slot toward Guadalcanal. According to aircraft sightings, tonight's Tokyo Express run consists of eleven troop transports, plus a powerful warship escort, including two battleships, four cruisers, and many destroyers. Our own battleships are not close enough to intercept. It is believed that the enemy battleships are on their way to bombard Henderson Field and knock out the Cactus Air Force, which will enable the Japanese to land reinforcements at will.

Admiral Halsey has ordered Scott and Callaghan to combine their escort groups and intercept the Japanese battleships, with Callaghan in command. Scott and Callaghan are steaming north toward Savo Island but will be heavily outgunned.

1:41 A.M., FRIDAY, 13 NOVEMBER—The Japanese force was sighted in Iron Bottom Sound by our lead destroyer, the USS *Cushing*, which turned broadside to launch torpedoes. The unexpected move threw Callaghan's column into confusion. Eight minutes were lost before the order to fire was given. The delay enabled the Japanese battleships, *Hiei* and *Kirishima*, to exchange their high-explosive bombardment shells for armor-piercing, ship-killing ammunition.

As Admiral Scott's ship, the USS *Atlanta*, began firing, she was illuminated by Japanese searchlights. A hurricane of shells from both Jap battleships struck the U.S. cruiser, disabling it. On the bridge, Admiral Scott was killed instantly.

Holed a dozen times by *Hiei's* 14-inch shells, our lead destroyer, *Cushing*, sank rapidly as her crew frantically abandoned ship.

The *Hiei* drew even with the destroyer USS *Laffey*, but too close to depress her guns. Little *Laffey* raked *Hiei's* bridge with machine-gun fire, killing her commanding officer. Moments later, *Laffey* was struck by a torpedo and took the plunge. The *Hiei* was afire from stem to stern and dead in the water but continued to fight. Her sister battleship *Kirishima* had taken only one hit.

On the *San Francisco*, Admiral Callaghan, concerned about hitting his own ships, ordered a cease-fire. As he did, Kirishima salvoed a full broadside that struck San Francisco's bridge, killing Callaghan, Capt. Cassin Young, and the entire bridge complement.

Ashore in the perimeter, thousands of eyes and ears took in the sea battle that could decide the outcome of the U.S. venture on Guadalcanal. The guttural thunder of naval cannon fire and distant sputter of machine guns was accompanied by a celestial light show of great orange flashes and undulating tracers that lit up the low-hanging clouds. It was impossible to know who was winning.

The skipper of the USS Helena, Capt. G. C. Hoover, inherited command of the U.S. force and ordered a withdrawal through Sea Lark Channel. Only the San Francisco, Juneau, and three destroyers were able to comply. The remaining Japanese ships were ordered to retire northward by their commander, Vice Adm. Hiroake Abe.

This savage sea battle has cost both sides dearly. Two American admirals have been killed in action and a large number of American seamen have been killed or wounded. The United States has lost two cruisers and four destroyers versus Japanese losses of two destroyers sunk and the battleship Kirishima mortally wounded. But for the United States it is a strategic victory. Henderson Field was not bombarded last night by the Hiei and Kirishima. The Cactus Air Force can now take to the skies and strike back at the remaining Japanese warships and transports.

DAWN, FRIDAY, 13 NOVEMBER—Both sides are now girding themselves to renew this critical sea battle. If the Japanese are successful in dominating Guadalcanal waters and grounding the Cactus Air Force, their transports will put ashore many thousands of fresh troops, unopposed.

Our two battleships, the Washington and South Dakota, are closing rapidly on Guadalcanal waters; the Enterprise will soon be within air striking range. Her decks are loaded with dive and torpedo bombers, welcome reinforcements for the Cactus Air Force.

11:00 A.M.—The U.S. cruiser Juneau, severely damaged in the battle, has been torpedoed by a Japanese submarine. Following a huge explosion, the ship literally disappeared, taking down with it nearly all of its crew, including five members of the same family, the Sullivan brothers.

NOON—Torpedo bombers from the *Enterprise,* on their way to bolster the Cactus Air Force, have torpedoed the battleship *Hiei.* Arriving at Henderson Field, they were quickly rearmed and have taken off again to give the huge Japanese battlewagon another dose. The U.S. Army Air Force has also gotten into the act. B-17s have flown up from Espiritu Santo to plaster the *Hiei* with sticks of five-hundred-pound bombs.

8:00 P.M.—The Japanese battleship *Hiei* has sunk! It is the first Japanese battleship to be sunk in the Pacific war, and the first time in any war that U.S. forces have sunk a battleship.

DAWN, 14 NOVEMBER—The Cactus Air Force together with dive bombers and fighters from the *Enterprise* are attacking the incoming Tokyo Express. Six transports, crowded with troops, are sinking.

Admiral Tanaka, in command of the Tokyo Express run, has pressed on with his remaining transports and run them aground on the beach west of the perimeter to debark troops.

Five thousand survivors of the Tokyo Express sinkings in the Slot have been plucked from the sea by their escorting destroyers.

8:15 P.M.—The U.S. battleships *Washington* and *South Dakota* have arrived in Guadalcanal waters with their escorts. Commanded by Rear Adm. Augustus "Ching" Lee, they have entered Iron Bottom Sound to mop up any lingering Japanese.

Storming down from the north to intercept Lee is Japanese admiral Nobutake Kondo in the battleship *Atago,* accompanied by the battleship *Kirishima.*

Two destroyers at the head of Lee's column, the USS *Preston* and USS *Walke,* have been surprised and sunk in Iron Bottom Sound by Japanese destroyers. The *Washington* and *South Dakota* threw life rafts to their crews in the water as they charged by in search of the Japanese.

MIDNIGHT—*Washington* has locked onto the *Kirishima* with her radar and opened fire at a range of 8,400 yards, scoring forty-nine hits.

12:07 A.M., 15 NOVEMBER—The Japanese battleship *Kirishima*, burning fiercely and unable to steer, has given up the fight!

12:25 A.M., 15 NOVEMBER—Admiral Kondo in the battleship *Atago* has thrown in the towel and quit the scene.

DAWN, 15 NOVEMBER—Air reconnaissance reports that the battleship *Kirishima* has been scuttled, and with it, Japan's hopes for victory in this pivotal battle.

An Exchange of Punches

The Naval Battle of Guadalcanal was won by the U.S. Navy and the Cactus Air Force. In ten furious hours of battle, navy losses had come to within two hundred men of the total number of marines who would die in action during the entire Guadalcanal campaign. Japan's fourth and most strenuous attempt to recapture Guadalcanal had failed. It remained to be seen if her leaders would mount another. In Tokyo, the shocking news intensified already strained relations between the Army High Command and the War Ministry. There followed heated debates and at times an exchange of punches between the two Imperial staffs over the question of ship requisition. In order to resupply Guadalcanal, the army now insisted on four times the amount of shipping that had already gone to the bottom of the Slot in November. Prime Minister Tojo refused the army demand. Instead, he replaced the vociferous army officers with men less likely to obstruct him. But among top Japanese naval officers were heard, for the first time, murmurs of Japan's need to abandon the struggle for Guadalcanal.

Events Great and Small

Something new was in the air. Everyone breathed a little easier. Men cautiously allowed themselves to believe that they might someday see home again. Troops and supplies poured into Guadalcanal. The action became kaleidoscopic. Events great and small tumbled over one another as the final phase of the campaign gathered speed:

Medical facilities on Guadalcanal were much improved. On 13 November the army's 101 Medical Regiment had landed and set up for business in time to succor the wounded from the Naval Battle of Guadalcanal—1,156 American casualties from two and a half days and nights of fighting.

Japanese troops on the island continued to hold U.S. forces in contempt. U.S. victories were written off as the result of a "material" advantage. The individual Japanese soldier still believed that in the end Japan's "spiritual" superiority would triumph.[5]

One of Admiral Nimitz's aides in Hawaii noted, "Now is the time to move in more supplies and relieve the tired Marine amphibian troops."

Seventeenth Japanese Army headquarters on Guadalcanal made the decision to go over to the defensive. As they had at Tulagi, Gavutu, and Tanambogo, the Japanese dug deeply, creating near-impregnable positions, expertly camouflaged, that took every advantage of the terrain. These positions were defended by light and heavy machine guns, mortars, grenade launchers, and 77-millimeter mountain artillery, capable of creating a holocaust of gunfire into which the new U.S. Army units would soon be advancing.[6]

In mid-November, Admiral Halsey issued orders to bring the 6th Marines up from New Zealand to Guadalcanal.

On 18 November U.S. Army Air Force colonel "Blondie" Saunders was leading a flight of eighteen army B-17s up the Slot on a bombing mission when set upon by a flock of Zeros. His left engines were shot out, his pilot killed, and his copilot badly wounded. Saunders jumped into the pilot's seat and ditched the flaming aircraft in the sea, deep in Japanese-controlled waters. In a hair-raising escape from the sinking bomber, he got the survivors, most of them wounded, into a life raft and made for a nearby island. The copilot died en route. Ashore, Saunders buried the copilot, then spied a canoe approaching from another island. It contained non-English-speaking natives, one of whom shinnied up a tree, fetched down a coconut, and presented it to Saunders. The canoe then departed. Time passed and a second canoe appeared. This one contained a white man, Australian coastwatcher Jack Keenan, who stepped out of the canoe and, with a flourish, presented Saunders with his card. Then began an odyssey in the course of which Saunders and his companions were spirited from island to island via the good offices of various Samaritans, all of whom were risking their lives in the doing. These included several Catholic missionaries and a Methodist nurse. Meanwhile, the downed airmen's plight had been reported via coastwatcher radio to 1st Division HQ. At 3:00 P.M. the following day a PBY escorted by three Wildcats set down offshore, the shaky and bloodied survivors were loaded aboard, and a short time later were between clean sheets at the army's 101 Medical Hospital in the perimeter. Scores of American airmen were fished out of the water and returned safely to duty by this clandestine network of natives, coastwatchers, and missionaries.

On 18 November, Vandegrift again sent his forces west of the Matanikau. Designed to exploit the enemy's Z-day disaster, the plan was to push up the coast as far as possible, then dig in on the new front. Elements of the army's 182d and 164th Infantry Regiments, advancing with a marine company, got a hot reception from the still-feisty Japanese, who pounded them with mortar fire. This was followed by fierce counterattacks against weak points in the U.S. line. Heavily pressured and lacking artillery of their own, the Americans pulled back to a more tenable position near Point Cruz. For the next fifty-four days this new front line would remain static.

The third week in November found Japanese engineers secretly constructing a new airfield midway up the Slot at Munda. Scaling new heights of camouflage, the Japanese cleared the land tree by tree, suspending the de-trunked treetops by wire above the runway as they worked. Photo-recon experts at Henderson Field saw through it, and for weeks to come the Cactus Air Force blasted the phony palm grove and the runway beneath it. Undaunted, the Japanese persisted under fire until, by 19 December, the disputed airfield was home to several squadrons of Zeros.[7]

In the second half of November, the Cactus Air Force grew by nearly 50 percent. Newcomers included eight army B-17s and five long-range reconnaissance Hudsons of the Royal New Zealand Air Force.

By 24 November the famous George Medal project was well in hand. Designed by a sub rosa committee of marine officers, the medal depicted on one side the hand and sleeve of a navy admiral dropping a hot potato into a marine palm. On the other side, a cow with upraised tail backed up to an electric fan. The medal's motto, *Faciat Georgius*, meaning "Let George do it," was contributed by Lt. Herb Merillat. Later minted in Australia, the medal was distributed to select members of the U.S. Armed Forces involved in the planning and execution of the Guadalcanal landings.

On 26 November, Lt. Gen. Hitoshi Imamura took command of the Japanese 8th Area Army, of which the 17th Army was a part. His message to the troops suggested that the emotional pain of their terrible struggle was being felt in high places: "Your loyalty and bravery is enough to make even the gods weep. I should like to express my hearty respect and gratitude to you officers and men for your brave fighting, and, at the same time, my regret to the souls of those who died of wounds and disease."

On the same Thursday, Thanksgiving Day, Halsey saw to it that all hands afloat and ashore got plenty of turkey and cranberry sauce.[8] Halsey was then notified that he had been promoted by an impressed President Franklin Roosevelt to four star admiral.

Estimates by 1st Division intelligence as to the number of Japanese troops on Guadalcanal at this time varied from nine thousand to sixteen thousand. Postwar estimates by Japanese historians put the number at twenty-five thousand.

Chief of Staff Gen. George Marshall directed the army's 25th Division to proceed to Guadalcanal. It would replace the 1st Marine Division, through whose tattered ranks rumors of "shipping out" were wildly flying.[9]

Native friendlies in twelve-man war canoes haunted the nighttime inlets and lagoons of New Georgia, an island midway up the Slot which lay in the path of Japanese barge traffic en route to Guadalcanal with reinforcements and supplies. Highly skilled "irregulars," the Solomon Islanders struck silently and swiftly at Japanese transients, taking no prisoners and beheading corpses with the captured samurai swords belted to their lava-lavas. In all probability, the heads were then smoked and mounted in the New Georgians' ceremonial "head houses" as trophies of war, according to centuries-old Solomon Islands tradition.[10] Commanded by Maj. D. G. Kennedy of the Solomon Islands Defense Forces, they were known as "Kennedy's Boys" and dreaded by the Japanese.

A navy pilot, whose SBD was heavily shot up during a mission over the Slot, headed for Henderson with a persistent Zero banging away at his tail. In the course of shooting back, the SBD's rear gunner ran out of ammunition. The navy pilot used every ounce of his expertise to shake off the obnoxious Zero, ducking into clouds, flat-hatting over the waves, then contour-skimming island ridges, but still the Zero pursued. The chase by now had taken the two aircraft so far south that Guadalcanal was in sight. Over the Russell Islands it dawned on the SBD pilot that his pursuer was also out of ammunition. At this point the Zero pilot pulled up alongside the SBD, waggled his wings in salute and peeled off for home. For a moment, the air war had been friendlier.[11]

On 30 November, after lengthy repairs in a stateside shipyard, the carrier *Saratoga* was on her way back to the South Pacific. The *Enterprise* was still on active duty in the area, despite her seized-up forward elevator. Battleships *Washington*, and the USS *North Carolina* and USS *Indiana* were also close at hand, while the *Maryland* and *Colorado* stood by in the Fijis, a day and a half from Guadalcanal.

The Tokyo Express continued to ply its trade, running supplies and reinforcements down the Slot to offload west of the perimeter. On the night of 30 November, one of these runs was intercepted by a vastly more powerful U.S. Naval force. The result was the Battle of Tassafaronga, a mortifying defeat for the U.S. Navy. Six Japanese destroyers, their decks encumbered with troops and supplies, nevertheless got the drop on a U.S. force composed of the heavy cruisers *Minneapolis, Pensacola, New Orleans*, and *Northhampton*; the light cruiser *Honolulu*; and four destroyers. In the bloody twenty-minute fracas that followed, both sides fired torpedoes. None of the U.S. "fish" connected, but six of the Japanese Long Lance torpedoes struck home, knocking out four U.S. cruisers and sinking one of them, *Northhampton*. Loss of life on the U.S. ships was considerable. One Japanese destroyer was sunk. Much of the blame could be pinned on the U.S. task force commander, Rear Adm. Carleton H. Wright, whose inexplicable four-minute delay in opening fire gave the Japanese time to get their accurate and potent torpedoes in the water.[12]

The Cactus Air Force now dominated the skies over Guadalcanal, unchallenged by the 25th Air Flotilla. The four-month battle for air supremacy in the lower Solomons had made good on Rear Adm. John "Slew" McCain's 11 September prophecy that "Guadalcanal would become a sinkhole for enemy air power." The Japanese had poured their irreplaceable pool of world-class pilots down the drain at Midway and Guadalcanal and would fight the rest of the war with novices at the controls.

The Tokyo Express still ventured down the Slot most moonless nights, trying urgently to resupply hungry Japanese forces west of the perimeter. The resourceful Admiral Tanaka sealed food, ammunition, and medicines in watertight drums, lashed them together, and heaved them over the side as close to shore as he dared venture. He then high-tailed it north before daylight and the Cactus Air Force overtook him.[13] In spite of Tanaka's enterprise, few of the drums were recovered, and the food they contained was often eaten by the shore parties who fished them out of the surf. As a result, the 17th Army was in starving condition. Rations for front-line soldiers had been cut to one-sixth, for others to one-tenth. Men were surviving on roots, coconuts, and grass. Consumed with malaria, skeletal, their bodies scourged by boils and jungle rot, many died daily. Second Lt. Yasuo Ko'o recorded in his diary the grim countdown by which he reckoned the approach of death from starvation:

> Those who can stand up—30 days
> Those who can sit up—3 weeks
> Those who cannot sit up—1 week
> Those who urinate lying down—3 days
> Those who have stopped speaking—2 days
> Those who have stopped blinking—tomorrow[14]

On 7 December, the first anniversary of Pearl Harbor, the 1st Marine Division's artillery regiment loosed an anniversary bombardment at Japanese positions west of the Matanikau. On each shell was chalked "Tojo—Dec. 7th, 1942."[15]

That night an especially urgent delivery by the Tokyo Express was frustrated by U.S. PT boats operating out of Tulagi. Eight of the high-speed wave-skimmers, manned by a special breed of naval crazies and armed with torpedoes and 50-caliber machine guns, stormed out to intercept an equal number of Japanese destroyers. Metaphorically, it was like a gang of kids with slingshots attacking eight M1-A1 Abram tanks. The PT boats blazed away with their machine guns and fired twelve torpedoes, all misses, but raised so much merry hell that the Japanese officer in command of the destroyer escorts thought better of his mission and retired northward.

CHAPTER TWELVE

Gung Ho

THE FIRST WEEK IN DECEMBER also marked the completion of the 2d Raider Battalion's thirty-day marauding expedition behind Japanese lines. For sheer viciousness of fighting and damage done to the enemy deep in his own turf there is nothing quite like it in Marine Corps annals. The 2d Raider Battalion's leader, Lt. Col. Evans F. Carlson, forty-seven, was a bone-lean career marine who had seen action in France, Nicaragua, and China during the course of a twenty-eight-year career. In China, he served as an observer with Mao Tse-tung's ragged army and studied close up the successful guerrilla tactics employed by the man who would later head that communist nation.

During three tours of duty, Carlson learned to speak fluent Chinese and became convinced that Mao and his unconventional guerrilla tactics were China's best weapon against the invading Japanese. For his somewhat unorthodox support of Chinese communism, Carlson was viewed in Marine Corps circles as slightly "pink," but nonetheless respected. "He

may be red, but he's not yellow," observed one marine colonel. So it was
that when the first two Marine Raider Battalions were formed in the
spring of 1942, Carlson was an obvious choice to command one of them.
He proved to be a charismatic and mystical leader in the stamp of other
such military nonconformists as "Gordon of Khartoum," Stonewall Jackson, and the British guerrilla leader Orde Wingate of the "Chindits" in
Burma. Carlson's maxim and the battalion's motto was "Gung Ho," Chinese for "work together." His nineteen-year-old Raiders loved him and
would have marched cheerfully to hell behind him, which in fact they
did while on the battalion's thirty-day slog through Guadalcanal's satanic
jungle in pursuit of a bone-tough enemy.

The first three companies of the 2d Raider Battalion arrived at Guadalcanal on 4 November, after weathering a violent tropical storm and losing a day en route. Their landing site was Aola, a jungly beach forty miles
east of the perimeter. The Raiders were met on the beach by Martin
Clemens, British coastwatcher turned scouting chief, who quipped, "I say,
what kept you chaps?" The three leading companies—C, E, and Headquarters Company—set up housekeeping in the jungle and awaited orders.
Their wait was an introduction to the rigors of jungle living. Lowell V.
Bulger, Raider corporal, takes up the story: "[There were] eerie jungle
noises, huge crawling land crabs, two-foot tree lizards, and millions of
insects. We each carried a small, black mesh headnet to pull over our helmet and protect our face on watch. We [stuffed] our pants legs inside our
socks and slept rolled up in a shelter half. Our hands and wrists were protected by wearing a pair of socks over them, but those blood-sucking
demons could easily penetrate any lose woven material and drink their
fill."[1]

While the Raiders swatted mosquitoes, Vandegrift issued marching
orders to Lieutenant Colonel Carlson. His three companies would set off
on an inland guerrilla patrol to assess the number of Japanese in the area.
The patrol would last two to three days and exit the jungle at Taivu, fifteen
miles west of Aola. As the patrol was a short one, rations were drawn for
only four days. C and E companies and a Headquarters detachment entered
the jungle at dawn on 6 November. All day the rain sluiced down through
the triple canopies of the forest, and the swearing marines slipped and

slid on the mud-slick trails. There was no sign of the Japanese. At dusk the column halted, having covered less than five miles. There could be no cooking fires and no smoking. The exhausted Raiders wrapped themselves in their shelter halves and lay down in the soaking rain. For security, one man in three stayed awake. At dawn the next day the sodden procession pressed on through the jungle half-light. Ahead of the column trotted a thirty-seven-man point squad, led by Colonel Carlson. It traveled light and fast, crossing and recrossing the meandering Bokokimbo River, until coming to a five-hut deserted village.

Lowell Bulger remembers: "We found much evidence of recent enemy presence. We hurriedly searched each grass hut and one large communal-type grass meeting hall. A strange stillness raised the hairs on the back of my neck. Even the macaws and minah birds were silent. The Japanese had shredded English bibles and bibles printed in the Solomon Island dialect, scattering the pages throughout the huts. Empty Japanese ration boxes and cigarette packs indicated that the enemy was well supplied and equipped."[2]

Carlson posted sentries and decided to wait for the main body. One of the native scouts disappeared into the jungle and returned with a huge bundle of ngali nuts. They tasted like avocado, and the Raiders wolfed them down. Food in any form was already becoming a preoccupation, and the nineteen-year-old marines' rumbling bellies never let them forget it. At 4:00 P.M. a single rifle shot sounded somewhere ahead—a Japanese Arisaka 6.5, which had a higher flatter crack than the Raiders' new 30-06 M1s. Without waiting for the main body, the point squad took off up the trail. As Lowell Bulger recalls,

> Moving at a trot, we entered a small glade and ran into ten or twelve Japanese who were gathered around a wild pig. They were busy skinning the dead animal. Our heavy automatic fire rapidly scattered the enemy into the bush. Two dying Japs were quickly isolated, and blood-stained leaves two hundred yards up the trail indicated more wounded. "Red" Meland and I dragged one of the wounded Japanese out to the trail. He was gut-shot, and his intestines dragged in the brush behind him. Colonel Carlson searched him and found an oil-skin packet of money and papers sewn inside his uniform. He kept talking and begging for water, which we were forbidden to give any

gut-shot man. As the Raiders were nearly out of food, we made short work of the freshly killed wild pig. The main body arrived about dark and a restless night was spent wondering if a Japanese army was about to rush our positions.[3]

With only hot tea for breakfast, the Raiders headed for the coast. Arriving there, they were transported by Higgins boat to Tasimboko, where their orders had promised them a rendezvous with supplies and reinforcements. The area was spooky and deserted except for the spoiled and stinking remains of the Japanese supply dump gutted by the 1st Raider Battalion in August. With hunger teething on their vitals, the Raiders crawled into abandoned Japanese foxholes and spent a trigger-happy night, punctuated by sporadic rifle shots and apologetic cries of "Accidental!" The next morning they were reinforced by B, D, and F Companies, newly arrived from Espiritu Santo, and food rations were issued.

Bulger recalls that "a half sockfull of rice, a half pound of bacon, one sock of tea, a few raisins and some sugar was supposed to last three men for four days, but could easily have been wolfed down in one day's sitting." From this point on, food in any form became the number one obsession and constant topic of conversation. "Raiders will eat anything that doesn't bite first," observed one Raider wit. A case of food thievery occurred, and Colonel Carlson warned, "If any Raider is caught stealing food from another Raider, I hereby authorize you to shoot him dead—or if you can't shoot a buddy, bring him to me and I'll shoot him!"[4]

His Raiders now six hundred strong, Carlson left Tasimboko and marched inland to Binu. With him went Sgt. Maj. Jacob Vouza, together with one hundred native scouts and bearers. At Binu, Carlson set up a base camp, planning to headquarter there for several days and send out patrols in all directions. On 11 November, one company-strength patrol of Raiders unexpectedly bumped into a force of seven hundred Japanese who were fleeing the same action in which Chesty Puller had been wounded. Pete Arias, a Mexican American Raider remembers:

> I was in J. D. Bennett's squad. He was blasted across the chest by a Jap machine gun. J. D. had ordered us into a skirmish line, and then all hell broke lose. Larry Spillan and Joe Harrison were killed. Man, I

never heard so goddamn much firing. I couldn't get close enough to the ground. One machine gun didn't sound too friendly directly in front of me. Lieutenant Maitland ordered "Okay men, let's get up and charge them." Sergeant "Bulldog" Evans said "Okay, Lieutenant, you get up first and we'll follow you," and that ended any foolish charge talk. I was one of those who didn't get the word when we withdrew. "Happy" Sanchez and everybody thought I was killed, but "Happy" kept saying "Nobody can kill that goddamn Mexican!"[5]

At 11:00 A.M., E Company of the Raiders was ordered to cross the Metapona River and hit the enemy from the rear. The confrontation was equally brutal. Lt. Cleland Early's platoon was pinned down by a diehard machine-gun nest. Early recalls:

This was one hell of a skirmish, as each time we killed one Jap another took his place on the Nambu. I was informed that Pfcs Gerald Miller and Lorenzo Anderson had been hit. Corpsman Westley Proctor came forward. We moved forward with him and found both Raiders. Both had been shot in the head. Miller was still alive, but Anderson had been hit between the eyes and was dead. Miller died soon afterward. . . . We moved forward to take the machine gun nest. Several bodies were around the gun and a [dead] sergeant was holding the gun. I turned him over and narrowly escaped death when a grenade he was holding went "puff" and was activated. I was hit in the left hand with shrapnel. When we started to take mortar fire, Captain Dick Washburn decided that we would get the hell out of there. Joseph Auman had been killed at his machine gun, we had no mortars with us and could not reach Carlson by radio. Also, we were out of food and water.[6]

On the next day, B company renewed the attack, but the Japanese had vanished. Thus far, Carlson's Raiders had been dueling with the newly landed Japanese reinforcements, but now they made first contact with their assigned adversaries. Col. Toshinaro Shoji's regiment, back on its feet after October's Battle of "Coffin Corner," was withdrawing through the jungle under orders to rendezvous with Japanese forces west of the perimeter. Sergeant Major Vouza and his scouts picked up the scent and on 12 November led a Raider patrol along narrow jungle trails to a village on the Metapona River. Staking out a nearby shallows, the Raiders bushwhacked a company of oblivious Japanese, most of whom were bathing, killing 120 of them before they could react. This hit-and-run tactic became the pattern for Raider success—native scout–led patrols would fan out along Guadalcanal's vast internal network of trails to locate unwary Japanese bivouacs; a larger body of Raiders, filtering silently through the jungle, would close in and tighten the noose. Then, at a signal, all hands would blaze away until no one in sight was standing. After which the Raiders would quickly mop up and vanish back into the bush as silently as they had come. By 24 November, Carlson had set up a base camp on the Tenaru River, a few miles southwest of the perimeter. Patrols were sent out but did no business. The next day, Carlson received orders from Vandegrift to locate and destroy a battery of Japanese mountain guns that were shelling the perimeter from high ground to the south, which the now-efficient Raiders did without a hitch. On the thirtieth of November, the Raiders again scaled the high ground, this time in torrents of rain, and headed for the Lunga River. Lowell Bulger recalls:

> When we reached the top, moved down the ridge and prepared to descend the Lunga River side, heavy firing broke out at the bottom. We half ran, half slid in the steady rain, finally just sat and slid down the hill on our rumps like a bunch of otters. The F Company lead squad under Cpl. John Yancey charged into the middle of about one hundred Japanese in their bivouac area. The enemy's arms were stacked! The surprised Japs bolted and dove into the river. The Raiders had a field day with their automatic weapons. Our native scouts bayoneted some of the enemy who played dead, and other Raiders picked off swimming Japs in the river. When it was quiet again we dragged the dead into the nearest foxholes and covered them up. As space was limited in this jungle glade, we erected lean-to shelters on top of the graves. I awoke in the night to find the protruding hobnail boot of a dead Jap poking me in the back. On this day, 30 November 1942, the Raiders and our native scouts suffered not a single casualty, while destroying upwards of eighty Japanese.[7]

On 3 December, Carlson assembled his men and told them that their long, unspeakably difficult mission was over; the next day they would return to the perimeter. He then asked them to perform a simple ceremony, one with which few of today's nineteen year olds would identify—young Americans were that different in 1942. "Let us all stand," Carlson said, "and sing 'The Marine Hymn.'" Lowell Bulger remembers that "with our chests bursting with pride, we sang the hymn at the top of our voices." "Now," Carlson said, "let us sing 'Onward Christian Soldiers' so our native scouts can join in." Bulger recalls, "Again we sang at attention with our hearts pounding. To those of us who were there, it was the proudest moment of our young lives."[8] The next day, the battalion made its way down the valley to the perimeter, fighting as it went. For the 2d Marine Raiders, the Guadalcanal campaign was over. Two weeks later the battalion embarked on USS Neville for the six-hundred-mile voyage back to Espiritu Santo. They had pulled off one of the most remarkable combat exploits in World War II history.

The Army Takes Over

On 8 December, the last of the Americal Division's infantry regiments— the 132d Regimental Combat Team, fresh and unblooded—arrived at Lunga Point, Guadalcanal.

On that same day a pinch-faced, mosquito-blotched, raggedy-assed regiment of fighting men formed up on the same beach. There they began climbing into the Higgins boats that would ferry them out to the transports. The 5th Marines were leaving Guadalcanal. They had, with the rest of the 1st Marine Division, taken the worst punishment that the Japanese Empire and the Guadalcanal jungle could dish out. By dint of fidelity, marine cool, and sheer cussedness, they had outfought both. Day by day the remorseless law of averages had whittled down their chances of survival. Cell by cell their exhaustion had grown. Now many of them had to be assisted up the same wobbly cargo nets they had clambered down four months ago. They left behind them a battle essentially won and their share of the 1st Division's 1,242 dead.[9] Their brother regiments, the 1st, 7th, and 11th Marines, would shortly follow them to Australia for recuperation and replacements. After which the 1st Marine Division would hound the Japanese closer and closer to their homeland, from Cape

Gloucester to Peleliu to Okinawa, until the atomic bomb ended the Pacific war and the division was diverted to China.

As there soon would be more U.S. Army troops than marines on Guadalcanal, it was time for the marine's Maj. Gen. Alexander Archer Vandegrift to pass his baton to the army and move on with his division. Therefore, on the day following the 5th Marines' embarkation, Maj. Gen. Alexander M. Patch of the U.S. Army assumed command of all ground and air forces on Guadalcanal and Tulagi. General Patch, fifty-two, was a West Point graduate who had fought in France during World War I. Prior to Pearl Harbor, he had served as commanding officer of the Basic Infantry Camp at Camp Croft, South Carolina, where many of his National Guard soldiers from Illinois had trained. Patch was a firm believer in the West Point Cadet Corps credo of "Honor, Duty, Country," and he would appoint only professional army officers to command his "civilian army" of National Guardsmen.[10] With the arrival of the army's 25th Division from Hawaii, Patch would have at his disposal more than fifty thousand American fighting men.[11] Overhead flew a powerful and accomplished Cactus Air Force. At sea in and around Guadalcanal waters was a burly U.S. Navy. What had begun on 7 August 1942 as a white-knuckled holding action was now a military pile driver.

A Discreet Examination

On 12 December there were indications that the powers that be in Tokyo, some of them at least, were nibbling at the concept of abandoning Guadalcanal. An order was handed down to 8th Army HQ directing that the 51st Infantry Division be routed, not to Guadalcanal, but to New Guinea. This contradicted without explanation the official IGHQ strategy that identified Guadalcanal as the number one priority of Japanese arms. On the same day there appeared at 8th Army HQ in Rabaul a senior naval officer who proposed a discreet examination of the problem of withdrawal from Guadalcanal, and in the next breath the launch of a new, all out effort to retake the island. At Imperial General Headquarters the naval branch announced to the Combined Fleet that it was in accord with the growing sentiment to abort Guadalcanal and implied that the Imperial Japanese

Army shared its opinion. This the army declined to confirm, as it was still under orders to renew the offensive.[12]

The Gifu

On 9 December 1942, almost a third of Guadalcanal was still in Japanese hands, and there remained a lot of killing and getting killed to be done. In anticipation of this further bloodletting, the Japanese had selected Mt. Austen as one of their defensive citadels. The mountain had proved invaluable as both an artillery site and an observation post from which every inch of Henderson Field and the perimeter could be surveyed, as well as ship movements in Iron Bottom Sound. Its peak was covered with tall kunai grass and braided jungle growth, making the position an attacker's nightmare. It was also a potential thorn in the side of any U.S. thrust west of the Matanikau. Japanese engineers, working without detection, had constructed a fifteen-hundred-yard-long fortification, studded with forty-five sunken log bunkers, each of which supported its neighbors with interlocking machine-gun fire. The design anticipated the virtually impregnable defenses that the Marine Corps and U.S. Army would confront in Pacific island battles to come. Manning the fortifications were three Japanese regiments—the 124th, 228th, and 10th Mountain Artillery Regiment, fighting as infantry. They were commanded by the ubiquitous Col. Akinosuka Oka. All had been weakened by hardships but were staunch in their determination to fight to the death, taking with them as many Americans as possible.[13] Most men of the 228th were from Gifu, a district on the Japanese island of Honshu. It followed that they would name their awesome defensive position "the Gifu." The U.S. Army troops that would soon be assaulting the Gifu also shared common origins. Nearly all were from the Chicago area.

On 10 December, General Patch issued orders for the American Division's 132d Regiment, commanded by Col. Leroy Nelson, to seize and occupy Mount Austen. Patch's reasons were twofold: the attack would shut down the pestiferous Japanese observation post and launch what was to be a major enveloping move against the Japanese west of the perimeter. The regiment's 3d Battalion drew the Gifu assignment, which was thought by Patch and his adjutant, Brigadier General Sebree, to be rather small potatoes, unworthy of a full regiment's attentions. Prior to jumping off into the jungle foothills on 17 December, a patrol from the 3d Battalion reconnoitered the immediate front. There was no sign of the Japanese, and the rest of the battalion was ordered to advance. Soon the jungle had clasped the unacclimated GIs in its steamy embrace, and the advance slowed to a shuffle. Without warning, a Japanese Nambu took the leading elements under fire. They had bumped into the Gifu's suburban defenses. Those GIs in the line of fire hit the deck. The 3d Battalion halted, caught its breath and dug in for the night. On the following day, the battalion commander, Lt. Col. William Wright, called for an artillery barrage on the expertly camouflaged Japanese positions. When it lifted, three platoons from L Company attacked, unable to see what they were attacking. It was entirely possible in the finely woven jungle to tread within a few feet of the firing slot in a Japanese bunker without spotting it. The popping popcorn fire of many Nambus, their 7.7-millimeter slugs whipping through the underbrush, brought the GIs to an abrupt halt. Obviously the artillery barrage had not dented enemy defenses. The GIs, breathing hard and sweating like water bags, were too exhausted to continue. Another artillery barrage was ordered, with K and L companies moving forward the moment it ceased. Again, the fiercely ratcheting Nambus stopped them in their tracks. The battalion then pulled back for the night.

Death in the Morning

On the morning of 19 December, the 3d Battalion's commander, chaffing at the slowness of his battalion's advance, went forward to reconnoiter. Lt. Col. William Wright of Oak Park, Illinois, was greatly admired by his men for his fearlessness and offensive spirit. With his messenger, radio operator, and three other men to cover him, Wright worked his way out in front of his troops for a firsthand look at the situation. Their progress was slow in the dense tangle of ferns and creepers. A few minutes after 9:00 A.M. the party was blindsided by a concealed Nambu. The colonel fell, his leg ripped open by the burst. Next to Wright his messenger lay dying in the mud. The colonel's radioman also lay nearby, one hand shot away. Men from K and L companies struggled through the undergrowth to the rescue, but the Nambu opened up again, wounding five of them. Wright called to his radioman, Pvt. John DiCicceo, to heave a grenade at the bunker concealing the Nambu. DiCicceo tried, but with only one hand could not pull the pin. Seeing this, the wounded colonel struggled to his feet and tried it himself, only to catch another machine-gun burst in the arm and abdomen. The other three men in his party crawled to the badly bleeding Wright, who was slipping into shock. When they attempted to drag him back, more Nambus opened up and made it impossible for them to raise their heads. Nevertheless, one man, Lt. Benjamin McGahey, wriggled his way out of the field of fire and sprinted back to battalion lines, where he encountered Major General Patch and his adjutant, Brig. Gen. Edward Sebree, who had come up to observe. They discussed Wright's rescue, but Sebree was not optimistic. He worried about losing more men. McGahey reassured him that a rescue was possible—a twelve-man patrol could manage it.

A volunteer patrol that included the wounded colonel's brother, Lt. Howard Wright, was formed. Into the lethal jungle went the green GIs, every nerve twanging, careful not to snap twigs or clink their equipment, pausing after each cautious step to listen. The battalion waited. Hours later, the patrol reappeared with its burden. Lt. Col. William Wright was examined by the surgeon and pronounced dead. The Gifu had killed their battalion commander.

On 21 December the regiment's commanding officer, Colonel Nelson, asked permission to commit a second battalion to the attack. His request was flatly denied by General Sebree, who told him to forget about reinforcements. Sebree and Patch believed that only one company of Japanese defended the Gifu; if an entire U.S. Army battalion couldn't do the job, Nelson's leadership must be at fault. The chastised Nelson then requested artillery preparation for the next day's attack. The following morning, the 3d Battalion withdrew one hundred yards to make room for the heaviest U.S. artillery barrage in the campaign to date. It was delivered to Japanese positions by both army and marine batteries, then followed up with Cactus Air Force strikes. The event was a plentiful waste of ordnance. So utter was the exhaustion of the 3d Battalion that most of the day was spent in regaining the original position. After six days of fighting in the stupefying jungle heat, the GIs were in no better shape to attack uphill against a furiously defended position than the marines had been during their first week on Guadalcanal. The soldiers' bodies, already weakened by fatigue and dehydration, were now feeling the onset of malaria. Dysentery, too, had surfaced and was sending men by the dozens on frequent trips to the bushes. The result was plummeting morale and in many cases near collapse.

Lead for Christmas

Sebree finally relented, and on 22 December the 3d Battalion was joined in the jungly hills of Mt. Austen by the 1st Battalion. By now the weary GIs of the 3d Battalion had clawed their way under fire up the baking, crazy-quilt slopes to a point where Battalion Intelligence could estimate the general outlines of the Gifu itself. With each yard gained the fight had grown more savage and personal. All day the Nambus ripped. Invisible snipers fired into battalion lines from every angle. At times, casualties were carried into the battalion aid station faster than the medics could handle them. Patrols went forward early each morning to feel out the Japanese positions, and some of their members never returned. But combat savvy was coming to the 3d Battalion with every drop of sweat and bullet fired.

Not so the 1st Battalion. On Christmas Eve, an eighteen-man patrol from the newly arrived battalion was briefed on the following day's mission by their platoon leader, 2d Lt. Albert Swacina. It would be their first brush with the Japanese. They were ordered to "search the area in front of C Company for a thousand yards." After the briefing, they settled down in their foxholes and reflected on the irony of their Christmas Eve. There was no peace on the bit of earth in which their foxholes were dug, and precious little good will toward their enemy. One of the men, Pvt. Robert Hensley, the platoon's medic, had gotten a "Dear John" letter from his wife. She was leaving him for another man. Hensley was heartbroken and told his buddies that if any of them were to be killed the next day, he wanted to be the one.

At 10:30 on Christmas morning the patrol left the 1st Battalion's front and word was passed up and down the line, "Patrol going out." They headed south through the jungle, painfully aware of their vulnerability, trying their best not to make a sound. Off in the distance they could hear the faint *pop, pop, pop* of a firefight on the 3d Battalion's front. Sweat ran smarting into their eyes and soaked their green GI fatigues. Tiny buzzing things vectored themselves at their ears and nostrils. Branches whipped across their faces. The heat was appalling. But there was no sign of the Japanese. The jungle was empty.

When the patrol had reached its farthest point, Lieutenant Swacina ordered a halt. He appeared exhausted. They would return to the lines, he ordered, by the same route. Pvt. Elmo Hutchinson, who carried the compass, reminded the lieutenant that this violated patrolling regulations. The same route should never be used twice. Swacina overruled him. The tired men started back to the battalion perimeter. Hutchinson spotted a vine hanging across the trail that shouldn't have been there. Before he could open his mouth, a hand grenade sailed through the air and exploded in their midst. Rifle and machine-gun fire flogged the jungle foliage. A bullet fired at close range struck Lieutenant Swacina's neck, slicing through his jugular and splattering him with blood. In moments he was dead. Pfc. George Drobnik took a burst in the abdomen and fell, screaming in agony to be shot again. Another burst thudded into him and he was gone. A second machine gun stitched Pvt. Russell Pence, who flopped down soundlessly and died. Sgt. Nick Vakola was machine-gunned to death in the mud. A grenade landed near Hutchinson's left foot and exploded. His legs felt as though they had been fed into a meat grinder. The pain was awful, but he somehow kept himself from screaming. Forcing himself to look down, he saw that his legs were still there, but torn and bleeding. At this moment, a Japanese poked his head through the undergrowth and stared at Hutchinson, who grabbed his rifle, fired one shot, and saw the Japanese topple backward into the bushes. He had looked about fifteen years old.

Strung out along the snaking jungle path, the rest of the patrol listened to the terrifying noises of ambush and slaughter. It sounded as if the whole Japanese army were attacking. No officer was there to tell them what to do. Their one noncom, a sergeant, was mute with fear. The rest of the patrol turned and legged it back toward the 1st Battalion front. The jungle was silent again. Hutchinson's legs had gone numb. He wormed his way on his elbows to the concealment of a big fern, where he spent a terrified night wondering if the Japanese would come back. In the morning they did, but Hutchinson wasn't spotted. He could hear them stripping the dead Americans of their rifles, ammunition, and dog tags. Suddenly a covey of artillery shells fluttered overhead to explode farther up the slope. Army and marine batteries were registering on the Japanese positions. The Japanese souvenir hunters departed in haste as the shellbursts grew nearer. Confronted with this new menace, Hutchinson began dragging himself back down the slope toward U.S. lines. As he neared C Company's barbed wire, two wary GIs fired at him, but missed. Then one of them yelled, "Hey, it's Hutch!" He was carried to the company mess area, given a cup of coffee, an apple, and debriefed. After which he was evacuated to the base hospital in the main perimeter. A patrol was dispatched to recover the bodies but collided with the friendly fire of the U.S. batteries, so came back empty handed. After a sojourn in the base hospital, Hutchinson rejoined his outfit. Six weeks later, when U.S. lines had leapfrogged the area, he led a search party to the spot where the ambush had taken place. The bodies lay where they had fallen, identifiable by the names on their fatigue jackets. They were recovered and sent to the main perimeter cemetery for burial. The 1st Battalion had been taught a valuable lesson in the art of jungle warfare. Hutchinson would remember it as the Christmas from hell.

They're All West Pointers

Valuable lessons notwithstanding, Col. Leroy Nelson's command was in bad shape. Not only were its members dead beat and burning with malaria, but 313 of them had been lost to death, wounds, and illness, leaving only 1,541 men fit for duty—barely. Nelson himself was grieving over the sacrifice of so many of his young men in blind frontal attacks against the invisible Japanese. Adding to his woes was his own exhaustion, compounded by malaria.

Finally, on 29 December, the 2d Battalion was sent up the slopes to join the 1st and 3d. With his regiment now complete and his impatient superiors demanding results, Nelson drew up a new plan of attack. Before it could be launched, however, he was informed by Patch and Sebree that his time was up—he would no longer command the 132d. "They're sending me back to the states," Nelson told Sgt. Bob Muehrcke bitterly. "They're going to put a West Pointer, Lieutenant Colonel Alexander George, in command of the 132nd. . . . Here at headquarters they're all West Pointers. I'm National Guard and a civilian soldier. Colonel George is one of them. He's a professional. He speaks their language." Tears ran down his face as he spoke. "I've got to step aside for the good of my boys."

Colonel George put in an immediate and remarkable appearance. Clad only in shorts and a fatigue hat, he strolled up to the 132d's front line of foxholes and bunkers, toting a rifle and wearing no insignia.[14] Snipers were everywhere, and the grimy, combat-savvy GIs crouching in their holes yelled at him to take cover.[15] Undismayed, the colonel strode the length of the regimental line, greeting his men and ignoring the occasional 7.7-millimeter slugs that whizzed past his ear. It was an impressive display of poor marksmanship by the local Japanese. The GIs, devoted to their former commander and sorry to see him go, didn't buy Colonel George's act. "Most of us regarded him as a Hollywood showman," recalls Sergeant Muehrcke. Like him or not, the 132d continued to fight its way up the slopes, running on ragged nerve and motivated by the shining emotion of loyalty to one another, which explains why men will go forward together into machine-gun fire. During the next three days, the regiment fought to within pistol shot of the Gifu's eastern flank. Along the way the 2d Battalion took Hill 27, a strategic elevation from which the Japanese could fire down on anything that moved. At its top, the GIs surprised the crew of a Japanese artillery piece, killing them all.

The three days had been studded with instances of everyday courage: On Hill 27, Capt. Philip Cecala, 2d Battalion surgeon, set up his aid station, calling it "the little hospital on the hillside." The Japanese soon mounted a series of screaming counterattacks, alternated with barrages, to drive the GIs off the hill. For seventy-two hours, Cecala got no sleep. Litter bearers arrived at his aid station day and night with bleeding wounded, or soldiers who had folded under the emotional strain. Japanese infiltrators were fought off hourly. Snipers fired at litter bearers, medical staff, and wounded alike. Only desperate cases were evacuated down the hillside under the enemy's guns. But the little hospital on the hillside stayed open for business.

Plt. Sgt. James Fornelli, twenty-one, shot seven snipers out of their trees. Not content with this, he located a machine gun manned by three Japanese and, like Sgt. Alvin York of World War I fame, picked off all three. He then bumped into a Japanese at the battalion water hole and killed him in a hand-to-hand struggle. Asked where he had learned to shoot so well, he explained, "Killing rats from my back porch . . . on the west side of Chicago."

Pvt. Stanley Kras and three others left the Hill 27 perimeter to relieve an outpost. The other three were out of sight twenty yards ahead when one of them called Kras's name. Before he could answer, a concealed Japanese yelled, "I am Kras!" The three GIs moved toward the voice and were instantly shot down. Kras hid behind a rock. When the ambush party headed in his direction, he opened up with his BAR, killing all twelve. Kras stayed put all night. The next morning when five Japanese showed up to strip the dead GIs of weapons, Kras killed them as well. He was awarded the Silver Star for valor.

Pvt. George Riley had been a supply sergeant, but was busted to private for making "Raisin Jack" moonshine. Reassigned to a line company, he was filling canteens at the water hole and passing them out along the front line when a machine-gun burst killed him instantly.

Some of the action had its lighter moments. PFC Jack Berry of LaGrange, Illinois, was digging his foxhole when he was wounded by machine-gun fire. Evacuated to the perimeter hospital, he was lying on his cot when a party of VIPs approached him. One of them was "Bull" Halsey, South Pacific Area commander. After a handshake and a few questions, Halsey reached into his shirt pocket, pulled out a bag of Bull Durham tobacco, and rolled himself a cigarette. Seeing this, it dawned on Pfc. Berry that "Bull" Halsey had come by his nickname honestly.

On Hill 27, E Company was hard-pressed and short of ammunition. Its CO requested an airdrop. When the parachuted ammo cases floated to earth they were found to include a generous bonus of chocolate bars. For the next three days the embattled company lived and fought entirely on chocolate.

At this point the 132d's battle casualties had risen to 387 men, plus an extensive malarial toll. In exchange, the regiment had gained footholds on three sides of the Gifu. As an effective fighting unit, however, the 132d was a spent force. On 4 January the flamboyant Colonel George was ordered to dig in and sit tight until a relief arrived.[16] This he did until 9 January, when a battalion of the army's 25th Division, fresh from Hawaii, made its way up the battle-tattered jungle slopes and took over. It would be nearly three weeks and many casualties later, however, before the riddle of the Gifu would be cracked, and then with the simplest of solutions.

The Once
Unthinkable Decision

I︎F TOKYO'S DETERMINATION to repossess Guadalcanal was eroding, word of this had not trickled down to the officers and men in the South Pacific who were still under orders to get the job done. On the contrary, Lt. Gen. Hitoshi Imamura, who headed the 8th Army, had assembled fifty thousand men at Rabaul and was planning yet another all-out assault on the U.S. presence in the Solomons. There would be no piecemeal commitment of troops—he would inject two full divisions into the attack, scheduled for the first of February. Keenly aware of the patient misery of his soldiers on Guadalcanal, he impressed on his commanders that "this time it is necessary to arouse the officers and men to a fighting rage."

Imamura himself had been tipped off to Tokyo's ambivalent frame of mind. In mid-December he had been approached by an emissary from the IGHQ, who hinted to him the possibility of a withdrawal. Imamura replied that it was Tokyo's business, not his, to decide such matters, but in no case would he go along with the abandonment of his men to the enemy. Rather, he would make every effort to save them. Moreover, if word of a withdrawal leaked out, he warned, every man on Guadalcanal would feel obliged to commit suicide. By the last week in December, the subject of withdrawal had moved out from behind closed doors at the IGHQ and was being candidly debated in the conference rooms. Then on 26 December the once unthinkable decision was taken: Guadalcanal would be written off and the Imperial Japanese Army would quit the field. Survivors of the doomed campaign would be rescued by the Imperial Navy. Plans were drawn up. In place of the usual barges and small boats, the Imperial Navy reluctantly agreed to provide a large number of destroyers for the evacuation of troops. On the twenty-eighth Emperor Hirohito was ruefully advised of the decision. His response was twofold: he wished to learn of the operational plans for the withdrawal and be briefed on the next major offensive move to be taken by the IGHQ. Then on New Year's Day, he issued his annual Imperial Rescript to the people of Japan: "The Emperor is troubled by the great difficulties of the present war situation. The darkness is very deep, but dawn is about to break in the Eastern sky. Today the finest of the Japanese Army, Navy and Air units are gathering. Sooner or later, they will head toward the Solomon Islands where a decisive battle is being fought between Japan and America."[1] On 4 January the IGHQ committed the order to paper: "The troops in the Solomon Islands will give up the task of recapturing Guadalcanal and will withdraw to the rear. After withdrawal, they will hold New Georgia Island and the Solomon Islands from Santa Isabel north, including the Bismark Archipelago."

No inkling of Tokyo's decision to withdraw from Guadalcanal was gleaned by U.S. Naval Intelligence. Instead, there was every indication that the Japanese would soon be at it again. As early as 1 December an intelligence analyst at Nimitz's headquarters in Hawaii had prophesied, "It is still indicated that a major attempt to recapture 'Cactus' is making up."

On 9 January a detailed plan for the evacuation of Guadalcanal, coded "KE," was finalized by the Japanese Combined Fleet and General Imamura's 8th Army Command. A fresh battalion of infantry, six hundred men, would be shipped to Guadalcanal on 14 January to act as rear guard. On the fifteenth, provisions for twenty-three days would be assembled at a strategic location. A unit by unit withdrawal to western Guadalcanal by the 17th Army would begin on 25 or 26 January. On the twenty-eighth the army and navy air forces would launch a campaign to suppress the Cactus Air Force. The Russell Islands, lying just northwest of Guadalcanal, would serve as a staging area. Destroyers and landing craft would accomplish the three evacuation lifts. Submarines would pick up any stragglers. The number of men to be recovered was estimated at thirteen thousand. By 10 February, the last of the troops would have been rescued from the island of death and starvation.[2] The grievously sick and wounded would be left behind. Also spelled out in the KE plan were the particulars of an intricate charade with which the Japanese hoped to disguise the operation. If the deception worked, U.S. Naval Intelligence would interpret Japanese withdrawal preparations as the buildup for another major attack. The scam would include phony radio messages and diversionary air raids. Old hands at doing one thing and making it look like another, the Japanese would spare no detail in perfecting the illusion.

Hobbling the Horses

By 7 January 1943, Gen. Alexander Patch's strength on Guadalcanal had increased to 50,666 men with whom to smite the Japanese. Included in this number were the U.S. Army's Americal Division, the 25th Infantry Division, and the 147th Infantry Regiment; also present were the 2d, 6th, and 8th Marines of the 2d Marine Division, now assembled in one place for the first time. In the army's table of organization, this many divisions under one roof constituted a "Corps," and it was so designated—XIV Corps. The object of this military pile driver's attention would be the thirteen thousand Japanese still holding out in the perpendicular hills of western Guadalcanal, few of whom were ready to say "Uncle." Patch's battle plan called for a four-pronged attack. Three of the prongs would encircle and subdue the Japanese defenders on three strategic hills: "Galloping Horse" and "Sea Horse," both named for their fanciful shapes, and the cruelly defended Gifu. Assaulting these malevolent hills would be the job of the Army's 25th Division, commanded by Maj. Gen. J. Lawton Collins.[3] The fourth prong would proceed westward along the coast, pushing the Japanese toward Cape Esperance on the northwestern tip of the island.

The latter assignment was handed to the 2d Marine Division. In contrast with earlier days on Guadalcanal, the shoe was now firmly on the other foot: the Americans were attacking and the Japanese were defending.

If the army's assault on the three hills went according to plan, it would create three separate enclaves, each of which could be reduced without interference from the others. The attack on the first of these was launched at dawn, 10 January. By way of introduction, a broad river of steel flowed over the heads of the waiting infantry in the form of six thousand artillery rounds en route to Japanese positions on Galloping Horse. This cloud-burst of metal was followed by the dropping of forty-eight bombs by the Cactus Air Force, thirty-six of them naval depth charges of the sort usu-ally sent down after submarines. Three battalions of the 27th Infantry Regiment then set out to hobble the Galloping Horse. It was the same nasty story of scratching out an advance yard by yard up tangled terrain in the face of murderous fire while enveloped in smothering heat. Like so much of the fighting on Guadalcanal, progress depended on the initiative of individuals and small groups of men unafraid to bare their bodies to the snapping 7.7-millimeter machine-gun slugs or scything mortar rounds. For every medal won, there were dozens of undocumented candidates. The breakthrough came on 13 January, when a five-man patrol rushed a ridgetop stronghold, wiping it out in full view of hundreds of other GIs. The act empowered all who saw it. The spectators then rose and overran the remaining Japanese on Galloping Horse, securing the whole of that objective.

A different problem was posed by the fight for Sea Horse. The task was complicated by the difficulty of supplying the combatants as they made their way up the homicidal slopes. Borrowing a page from the Egyptian pyramid builders, the ingenious Gen. J. Lawton Collins solved the prob-lem by mass conscription of muscle power. A small army of GIs rolled up their pants legs and, disregarding the leeches, pushed countless boat-loads of logistical necessities up a shallow, zigzag fork of the Matanikau River to a collecting depot. From there, three hundred native bearers humped the food, water, ammunition, and medical supplies up steep jungle trails to the front lines. Wounded GIs were relayed back down by the same tortuous route. The Japanese had taken full advantage of the atrocious terrain, digging themselves invisibly into the jungle floor in pop-up "spider traps" from which to snipe or cutting knee-high fire lanes for their Nambus and waiting until the cautiously advancing GIs were within feet of their firing slots before squeezing off a burst. On 11 January the 1st and 3d Battalions of the 35th Infantry Regiment, with a supreme effort, finally tethered the Sea Horse. In the process they also sealed off the Gifu. Its scrawny and feverish defenders would receive one last supply of rations, smuggled through U.S. lines on the fourteenth by a daring Japanese working party. By the sixteenth both battalions had pushed farther westward in the teeth of more furious machine-gun fire and point blank 70-millimeter shells, completely encircling the Sea Horse pocket. Some forty Japanese managed to filter through the army cordon, but they left behind 558 of their dead.[4]

While this was happening on the ground, marine captain Joe Foss of the Cactus Air Force shot down three more Japanese aircraft, for a total bag of twenty-one, making Foss the ace of aces in the United States' pantheon of combat aviators. With this distinction came the Medal of Honor.

To Do the Impossible

There remained the Gifu to be dealt with. On 9 January the three badly mauled battalions of the 132d clinging to the sides of the Gifu had been relieved in a three-for-one swap by Lt. Col. Ernest Peters's 2d Battalion, 35th Infantry. The situation maps and estimates that the 132d turned over to the 2d Battalion proved highly inaccurate. According to the 132d's calculations, the Gifu contained only one hundred defenders and two machine guns. Peters's 2d Battalion would subsequently find that it had been dealing with 431 Japanese and forty machine guns, as well as twelve mortars, two hundred rifles, and thirty-eight swords. For the next five days Peters sent patrols forward to grope through the jungle for enemy strongholds, but each time they scrambled quickly back, having been expertly machine-gunned and grenaded by the Gifu's defenders. The fierceness of their resistance masked their wretched condition. Most were in the final stages of starvation and burning with fever. Many could barely crawl. Nightly dousings by army artillery and mortar fire multiplied their sorrows, were that possible. Nevertheless, their will remained unbroken and their minds content to die a soldier's death.

On the fifteenth, an attack by three companies of the 2d Battalion netted only fifty yards against venomous Nambu fire. A second attack fared no better. The 2d Battalion at this point was suffering the same rate of attrition that had shriveled the ranks of the 132d. One man in four had been struck down by death, wounds, or malaria, and the other three were wilting fast. Morale also was wobbly, as evidenced by a paragraph in the official U.S. Army history: "About 1630 the battalion executive officer ordered one badly shaken platoon from G Company to withdraw, but as the order was passed verbally along the line, the soldiers misinterpreted it as an order to the entire battalion to retire, and all fell back."[5] The battle for the Gifu was also proving to be a graveyard for the careers of battalion commanders: on the sixteenth, after just seven days on the job, Lieutenant Colonel Peters was replaced by Maj. Stanley R. Larsen. The new commander immediately sent out patrols, which returned with encouraging news that the western face of the Gifu was lightly defended, held only by scattered infantry units and a few machine guns. On the strength of this, Larsen decided to attack the western face on the following day, after a massive artillery bombardment had stunned the Gifu's defenders.

While Larsen's patrols were still reporting in on the sixteenth, a loudspeaker in U.S. lines began broadcasting an invitation to the Gifu's occupants to surrender. A few sickly stragglers did so. The high-decibel harangue continued until dusk, resuming the next morning as most of the 2d Battalion withdrew three hundred yards in expectation of the deluge of shells on the Gifu. The loudspeaker blitz persisted for another five hours, then went off the air as the first of seventeen hundred artillery rounds arrived to pulverize the Gifu's interior and concuss its dwellers. Also left woozy by the pounding were many of the GIs on the eastern slope. By now it was midafternoon and too late to launch the attack, which was postponed until morning. On the eighteenth elements of the 2d Battalion attacked the west face, made minor progress, and dug in. The next three days also generated modest headway, but no breakthrough. Then, on the twenty-second, inspiration arrived in the form of three tanks on loan from the Marine Corps. Manned by army crews, two of them bogged down in the jungle muck en route to the scene of action. The third, shadowed by a small infantry escort, snuffled up the jungly slope and bashed its way into the Gifu's interior. Once inside, the tank ran amok, its machine guns spraying anything that moved while its 37-millimeter cannon fired into the unprotected rear of the bunkers. By 3:00 P.M. it had knocked out eight of them and opened a hole in the Gifu's defenses wide enough for the entire 2d Battalion to gush through. A new line was quickly formed within the horseshoe of bunkers, and the battalion dug itself in for the night. At 2:30 the next morning, about one hundred of the Japanese defenders banzai'd hopelessly into U.S. lines. After a brief shootout in the dark, lit by grenade flashes, eighty-five of them were dead, three captured, and the few survivors had vanished back into the darkness. Come morning, the GIs of the 2d Battalion formed a skirmish line and methodically swept the Gifu's interior, mopping up as they went. By evening it was over.

The riddle of the Gifu had been cracked between breakfast and dinner by a lone tank and a thimbleful full of army infantrymen. Had this obvious solution occurred to the army brass three weeks earlier, the lives of 175 GIs would not have been squandered in an attempt to do the impossible.

One Last Bit of Glory

Japanese resistance, wherever encountered by XIV Corps, was as steely as ever. The hollow-eyed soldiers of the emperor continued to prefer death to the dishonor of surrender and had to be silenced in their bunkers by the meanest, most dangerous kind of close-in work with BAR, grenade, and high explosive. Snipers continued to fire from "spider traps" into the backs of advancing GIs, or ping away invisibly from jungle tree tops, making for nervous going every foot of the way. Japanese morale, resilient in spite of war's terrors, was further stiffened by the thought that reinforcements would soon arrive, ushering in the ultimate offensive. Not one of them, including their commanding officer, Lt. Gen. Harukichi Hyakutake, suspected the truth.

The truth arrived, however, on 14 January in the person of Lt. Col.

Kumao Imoto. With a party of officers and enlisted men, Imoto came ashore at Cape Esperance bearing, in addition to the detestable evacuation orders, packages of "consolation gifts" in the form of cigarettes, sweets, and small bottles of liquor. After an eighteen-hour forced march, enlivened by Cactus Air Force strafing, they reached the 17th Army command post and there met first with the chief of staff, Maj. Gen. Shu'ichi Miyazaki. After hearing their unpalatable news, Miyazaki countered, "If the army cannot be strengthened and sufficiently supplied, then we have no other choice but to cut our way into the enemy lines and bring into our own one last bit of glory." They debated the issue until sunrise, then Imoto was conducted to the commanding general, Hyakutake, who sat like a Buddhist patriarch in a small recess under the roots of a tree. He listened to the orders, then said he wished to consider the matter. Imoto withdrew and returned at noon. The general addressed him with closed eyes. Under the circumstances, he told them, it was a difficult matter to evacuate the army. "But," he said, "the orders of the Area Army, based on orders of the Emperor, must be carried out at any cost. Therefore, I will respectfully comply with the conditions of the order."[6]

Word of the withdrawal was kept the strictest of secrets, privy only to commanding officers and their staffs. The troops were told that the 17th Army was still engaged in a holding action, pending reinforcements and a new offensive. The arrival from Rabaul of the fresh battalion detailed to guard the retreating army's rear strengthened this impression. The battalion was quickly dispatched to the front. Also sent forward from the rear area's feeble ranks was anyone yet able to pull a trigger or lob a grenade. In deference to the ever-present Cactus Air Force, all movements were carried out at night. Top secret orders were cut for the disposal of war materials not critical to the withdrawal. These would be executed on the eve of departure. Artillery pieces, trucks, and tractors would be buried or demolished. Portable weaponry—machine guns, mortars, antitank guns, and their ammunition—would be ferried out to sea and dumped. Unlike the burning U.S. carrier *Hornet*, which had been abandoned to the Japanese navy in October, nothing of value, real or symbolic, would be left to the enemy.

Like a Miles-Long Centipede

As January drew to a close, U.S. Naval Intelligence sifted through their clues to Japanese activity and found convincing evidence of preparations for a renewed offensive. The Japanese deception was working. In addition to the carefully planted disinformation, there were other persuasive indications. Rabaul had recently become host to fifty thousand fresh troops. Transports had sailed from Rabaul and Truk for the Shortlands, a Japanese marshaling point at the head of the Slot. Three newly arrived carriers and a battleship had been detected at Truk. An unusual number of Japanese submarines had been spotted in southeastern Guadalcanal waters, the usual tip-off to an impending fleet action. Moreover, U.S. radio intelligence was intercepting frequent mentions in Japanese radio traffic of an "Operation KE." The mysterious letters stood for the Japanese withdrawal, but to U.S. code analysts they sounded suspiciously like the cryptonym for another Z-day. The Japanese then changed all of their radio codes, making it impossible for U.S. intelligence eavesdroppers to snoop. This further heightened American paranoia. Advised of these sinister developments, Halsey and staff began thinking in terms of bracing for yet another assault on Guadalcanal—the fifth.

On 17 January, Patch launched phase two of his western thrust. Thus far, Galloping Horse and Sea Horse had been overrun and the Gifu surrounded by Collin's 25th Division, while the 2d Marine Division had successfully fought its way up the shoreline and reached its phase one objective. Now the 25th would advance by the inland route and hook north toward Kokumbona, a Japanese stronghold on the coast. The 2d Marine Division would continue its trek up the shoreline. Patch also cut orders for the 2d Battalion of the 132d Infantry, commanded by the picturesque Lieutenant Colonel George, to sail around the island's tip and land on the far side at Verahue Beach, which it would do on 1 February. Its mission was to act as a blocking force should the Japanese attempt to escape by the southern route. It would also be on hand to repel any Japanese attempt to land reinforcements there. On 23 January, after sorting out a slight interservice snafu, Kokumbona fell to the 1st Battalion of the army's 27th Infantry. The snafu had occurred when the 1st Battalion nearly walked into the fire of the 2d Marine Division, which was zeroing in on Kokumbona from the east.

To continue the shoreline push, Patch reshuffled his assets. He grafted the 6th Marines onto the army's 147th and 182d Regiments and created the CAM (Combined Army and Marine) Division, later augmented by the army's 161st Infantry. A rendezvous between the 25th and the CAM Division took place on 24 January east of Kokumbona, sealing the fate of any remaining Japanese in the crotch between the two divisions. From this point onward, the coastal terrain dictated the tactics. Here the steep coral ridges of Guadalcanal overlooked the shore, leaving a corridor between ridges and sea through which the CAM Division, like a miles-long centipede, would have to squeeze. Either that, or move inland and clamber over the razor-back ridges. On the twenty-sixth, Patch, who shared Halsey's worry that the Japanese would strike at Guadalcanal a fifth time, pulled the entire 25th Division back into the perimeter to beef up defenses. That same day, the newborn CAM Division set off westward along the narrow coastal corridor. Japanese defenders skillfully exploited the wicked terrain. They arrayed machine guns along the towering ridge tops to spray down at the exposed Americans, who could do little but duck and double-time through the worst of it. Casualties resulted.

Running interference for the CAM Division with offshore gunfire were a number of destroyers, including the USS *Anderson* and USS *Wilson*. The concept of warships providing close infantry support was a novel one, but their 5-inch naval shells outperformed the army's 75- and 105-millimeter howitzers and soon won the approval of the troops. (On one occasion when CAM ground-pounders complained via field telephone that the destroyer salvos might land uncomfortably close, their battalion commander bawled into the mouthpiece, "Don't call me 'til it falls in your mess kits!") The CAM Division pressed on, meeting spotty but determined resistance, until on the afternoon of the twenty-sixth it finally banged heads with the Japanese rear guard battalion, commanded by Maj. Keiji Yano. A stiff fight ensued, with the six hundred Japanese of the Yano battalion slowly giving ground until they had pulled back across the Bonegi River and dug in. It took the CAM division three more days to dislodge the resolute battalion, accomplished only after the destroyer *Wilson* had pumped enough 5-inch shells into the Japanese positions.

An Ill-Starred Finale

While the CAM Division was slugging it out with Yano's rear guard battalion, a battle was shaping up at sea. It commenced with aircraft sightings of Japanese warship concentrations north of Guadalcanal. They were gathered there innocently enough to assist in the withdrawal, but Halsey, as the Japanese would have it, interpreted their presence as threatening. Accordingly, he dispatched four transport loads of infantry reinforcements to Guadalcanal. Riding herd on the troop convoy some distance off was a U.S. task force commanded by Rear Adm. Robert C. Giffen. Under his authority were sixteen warships, including two "baby flattop" carriers and *Chicago*, the only U.S. heavy cruiser to have survived the Naval Battle of Savo Island. Bringing up the rear some three hundred miles to the south was the *Enterprise*.

A veteran of Atlantic naval warfare, Giffen was up to date on German U-Boat methods, but scant of knowledge regarding Japanese aerial torpedo tactics. Thus it was that on 29 January, when his task force was suddenly attacked by torpedo wielding Bettys, Giffen found himself unready. His baby flattops with their combat air patrols had been outdistanced astern, and he had neglected to issue orders to his captains for dealing with aerial torpedo attacks. The Bettys struck repeatedly until, just after sundown, *Chicago* took a hit in her vitals, lost power, and stopped dead in the water. Giffen ordered her taken in tow by another cruiser, then proceeded slowly south toward the *Enterprise*. On the following day, the Japanese found Giffen again and, despite the best efforts of *Enterprise's* combat air patrol, the bold Bettys put four more torpedoes into the stricken *Chicago*. She sank a short time later in twelve thousand feet of water, taking with her sixty-one of her crew. The troop transports escaped Japanese notice, reached Lunga Point, and unloaded in safety. The Battle of Rennell Island was the last of seven naval engagements fought in Guadalcanal waters—for the U.S. Navy, an ill-starred finale.

They Could Eat Only Porridge

The Battle of Rennell Island had set the Japanese timetable back a day. Now, on the night of 1 February, the scarecrow remnants of the 17th Army were hobbling westward along the muddy jungle paths toward deliverance. Men unable to walk were helped by their friends to commit suicide. Their deaths, they were promised, would be honorably recorded as "killed in action." The appointed hour of 9:00 P.M. came and went, but there was no sign of the destroyers that would carry them away from what the soldiers now called "the island of death." The rescue mission had been delayed by a Cactus Air Force ambush, but got off lightly with one bomb hit on the Makinami that failed to sink her. Next, a squadron of U.S. PT boats, boiling out from Tulagi, had intercepted the destroyer force and given it a hard time. It was a sacrificial offering: after a ninety-minute scuffle in the dark no destroyers were torpedoed, but three of the fragile PT boats were blown to bits, one by a bomb from a Zero floatplane, and fifteen American sailors died. At 9:40 the eighteen destroyers materialized intact off of Guadalcanal's northwestern tip and at midnight the boarding process began. All night long the small boats plied between shore and ship with their woeful passengers. A Japanese naval officer recorded that the faces of the tattered, skeletal survivors were utterly blank with exhaustion, and their stomachs so wasted that they could eat only porridge.[7] Shortly before dawn the loaded destroyers weighed anchor and made for the Slot, where they rendezvoused with a covering force of Zeros. Again the Cactus Air Force spotted the racing destroyers and tried to intercept but was fought off. The following day, the five thousand evacuees were unloaded at Bougainville. The daylight portions of these comings and goings had been observed by coastwatchers and the Cactus Air Force, but the sightings had merely reinforced American convictions that they were witnessing the buildup for another Z-day attempt. As a result, Halsey continued to raise the level of preparedness. Two U.S. carrier task forces were positioned nearer to Guadalcanal, and MacArthur was asked to step up the B-17 bombings of Rabaul.

A Swift Death

On land, the Yano rear guard battalion continued to dispute the narrow front with the CAM Division, reinforced by the haggard complement of men plucked from the retreating 17th Army who still had strength to work their rifle bolts. Many of these were leftovers from bygone battles, dating back to the 7 August landing, including Zero pilots now toting a rifle, and sailors who had swum ashore from sinking ships in Iron Bottom Sound. Together with Yano's rear guard, they would be last to leave the island. Colonel Matsuda, the officer in charge of fighting the delaying action, had drawn up a plan for the evacuation of his hard-pressed people. It called for Major Yano to pull his battalion back from the line of fire, leaving an officer and seventy men to slow the U.S. advance. Yano disagreed, arguing that the withdrawal would result in an enemy breakthrough. He would prefer to stand fast and die with his entire battalion. Matsuda gave in and instead ordered Yano to fall back and establish a new line, leaving behind only those men unable to walk. They would be asked to fight to their last bullet, then kill themselves. Each would be given two fast-acting bichloride of mercury pills to expedite death.

Loaded and Under Way

On 3 February the evacuation force again headed down the Slot and was obliged once more to run the gauntlet of U.S. SBDs and torpedo bombers. Orbiting above the twenty destroyers and one cruiser was an air umbrella of Zeros. As usual, the Cactus Air Force was waiting for them like bullies on a street corner, but luck again favored the Japanese. All twenty-one ships reached the evacuation point unscathed, although a number of Zeros were splashed. The PT boats, still licking their wounds from the previous battle, stayed home. Some of the Japanese troops had already departed the loading zone. They had barged out the previous night and landed in the Russell Islands, thirty miles northwest of Guadalcanal. From there destroyers would lift them up the Slot. By dawn of the fourth, the evacuation ships were loaded and under way. With them went Major Generals Kawaguchi and Miyazaki. This time the destroyers sped back to Bougainville by a different route and faked out the Cactus Air Force, which searched for them in vain. The searchers did, however, spot several dozen landing boats adrift off of Cape Esperance. This oddity was reported to authorities, but still no one in the American camp saw through the masquerade. Instead, Halsey's task forces continued on full alert, expecting Yamamoto's Combined Fleet to strike at any moment.

The Country of the Dead

As the crunch approached, the pace quickened. The U.S. forces now resembled the jaws of a vice, methodically closing on the two thousand Japanese squeezed onto Guadalcanal's northwestern tip. The CAM Division continued to shoulder its way up the west coast with its sights on Cape Esperance, spearheaded by the 161st Infantry. Resisting the American advance were the emaciated diehards of Colonel Matsuda's rear guard. Meanwhile, Colonel George's 2d Battalion—the vise's lower jaw—had landed at Verahue Beach on the far side of Guadalcanal and was slogging its way up the south coast toward Cape Esperance, virtually unopposed. The evacuation of Major Generals Kawaguchi and Miyazaki had left Matsuda in charge of all Japanese forces on Guadalcanal. His southern front now threatened, the new commander promptly sent a blocking detachment to the south coast to contest the way with Colonel George's oncoming 2d Battalion. On 4 February the colorful colonel reached the village of Titi and halted, uncertain of how many Japanese barred the way. There his 2d Battalion lingered until the sixth, seeing from afar the Japanese movements and the drifting barges, but unsure of their significance.

That same day, the vise's upper jaw bit off another two miles of coastline, and Matsuda got some bad news. He was advised by radio that the Imperial Navy would only evacuate men who were waiting offshore in landing craft. This suggested to Matsuda that the navy was wavering, reluctant to risk its valuable destroyers a third time for a mere two thousand men, many of them unfit for further duty. In war's callous logic, it would make sense. Taking no chances, Matsuda drew up contingency plans to load his men into the last of their landing craft and set out up the Slot. It would mean an open sea voyage in small boats. The slightest foul weather would swamp and sink them, and there was no knowing how long their fuel would last. On 7 February, General Patch, who had been badly briefed by his intelligence sources, stated his belief that the two Tokyo Express runs had delivered a fresh regiment to Guadalcanal, while retrieving some headquarters personnel. On the same day, the American upper jaw bit off another twenty-six hundred yards of shoreline as GIs of the 161st Infantry edged warily forward into what now resembled the country of the dead. The Cactus Air Force and the shells of division artillery had preceded them. So had disease, starvation, and suicide. The way ahead was strewn with the wasted corpses of Japanese soldiers. Some, faithful unto death, hunched over rusting weapons. The shriveled eyes of others peered out like curious spectators from their burrows under fallen trees. Many were frozen in agony. A few rested stiffly on their backs, their ragged uniforms squared away and puttees neatly wound, as if on horizontal parade. The bellies of most were too shrunken to bloat, and scarcely enough flesh clung to their bones for the flies and maggots to bother with. Putrefaction's gagging odor hung everywhere. Here and there the advancing GIs saw an arm or leg move, stopped to look, and then moved on, leaving death to complete its work.

The CAM Division was now only ten miles from Cape Esperance. Also on 7 February, Lieutenant Colonel George, who had resumed his push up the south coast, demonstrated that he was not altogether bulletproof. He stopped a 7.7 slug with his shin and turned over his command to Lieutenant Colonel Ferry. Ferry pressed on to Marovovo, where his battalion was taken under fire by Matsuda's blocking detachment and brought to a halt. He ordered his artillery to bombard the enemy positions, then dug his battalion in for the night.

Blue Lights Glimmered

From one direction Colonel Matsuda could hear the crash of artillery shells; from the other came reports of machine-gun fire. The crunch was at hand. At 9:30 he marshaled his men, those who could walk, and began loading them into the landing craft. For once, conditions were ideal—

the sea was flat and the night moonless. The little flotilla moved out onto the dark waters and waited. Rendezvous time was 11:00. It passed, and Matsuda steeled his mind to the alternative—a sea voyage in open boats, with the Cactus Air Force waiting to pounce at dawn. Then through the darkness blue lights glimmered, soon followed by the shadowy shapes of destroyers and the splash of anchors. One by one the small boats drew alongside the warships and their fragile passengers were helped up the boarding ladders to salvation. Shortly after midnight on 8 February, the loading was complete. Anchor chains scraped up hawsepipes, engine room bells clanged, white water boiled under the stern of each destroyer, and the evacuation force dissolved into the Pacific night.

Grinning and Yelling

On 8 February, Ferry's 2d Battalion and the 161st Infantry made good their objectives at a walk. The gap between them had narrowed to five miles. Organized opposition had ceased. In addition to the dead and dying, the coastline here was strewn with the litter of an army in full retreat: weapons, equipment, packs, anything that might have weighted down an exhausted man. It was blindingly obvious that the Japanese were in great distress and taking their leave of Guadalcanal, or may already have gone. Surmise of this had percolated through the U.S. command for the last twenty-four hours. Now Patch could confidently radio Halsey that the Tokyo Express runs had not been delivering fresh regiments to Guadalcanal, but extracting the survivors of a ruinous defeat.

On the next afternoon, the leading elements of Ferry's battalion and the 161st Infantry closed from opposite directions on the tiny coastal village of Tenaro. As each recognized the other's GI helmets and battle dress, the grinning and yelling began. Word flew down both converging columns, and officers hurried forward. The first to shake hands were Major Butler of the 2d Battalion and Colonel Dalton of the 161st. The time was 4:50 P.M., February 1943.[8]

Major General Patch immediately flashed the triumphant news to Halsey in Noumea, who forwarded it to Nimitz in Hawaii, who radioed it to Washington—to Ernie King, Franklin Roosevelt, and a waiting world: "Total and complete defeat of Japanese forces on Guadalcanal effected 1625 today. 'Tokyo Express' no longer has terminus on Guadalcanal."[9]

It was over. Six months and two days after the 1st Marine Division waded ashore at Beach Red, the Imperial Japanese Army, its will to fight broken, had withdrawn its forces from Guadalcanal and would penetrate no farther south. The winds of war had veered, unexpectedly and dramatically. Already, far to the north in Tokyo, Emperor Hirohito and his proud commanders were feeling the sudden chill.

After Guadalcanal, Japan would never again take the initiative in the Pacific War.

The Way We Were

The Battle of Guadalcanal was fought more than a half-century ago when America was a younger, more innocent nation. It was a battle we had no right to win, given the circumstances. One that any bookmaker would have bet against. It demonstrated what young and untried Americans can do when the need was great and the cause just. Its name recalls a way of thinking, feeling, and acting that may be missing from our national life today, but always returns with a rush when the chips are truly down. It reminds us of the way we were.

Chapter 1. The Problem

1. Prange, *Miracle at Midway*, 9.
2. Ibid., 10.
3. Lord, *Lonely Vigil*, 36.
4. Leckie, *Helmet for My Pillow*, 84.
5. Ibid., 234.
6. Lord, *Lonely Vigil*, 37.
7. Morison, *Struggle for Guadalcanal*, 12.
8. Frank, *Guadalcanal*, 33.
9. Vandegrift, *Once a Marine*, 18.
10. Thacker, *U.S. 1st Marine Division*, 4.
11. Griffith, *Battle for Guadalcanal*, 37.
12. Manchester, *Goodbye Darkness*, 204.
13. Griffith, *Battle for Guadalcanal*, 41.

Chapter 2. Thrust! Withdraw! Horizontal Butt Stroke!

1. Tregaskis, *Guadalcanal Diary*, 8.
2. Ibid., 20–21.
3. Miller, *Cactus Air Force*, 4.
4. Manchester, *Goodbye Darkness*, 195.
5. Merillat, *Guadalcanal Remembered*, 55.
6. Hoyt, *Guadalcanal*, 26.
7. Griffith, *Battle for Guadalcanal*, 54.
8. Stafford, *Big "E,"* 121–23.
9. S. Sakai speech to Cactus Air Force veterans at Nimitz Foundation gathering, Phoenix, Ariz., 1991.
10. Frank, *Guadalcanal*, 68.
11. Manchester, *Goodbye Darkness*, 206.

12. Hammel, *Guadalcanal*, 61.
13. Hoyt, *Guadalcanal*, 20.
14. Hoffman, *Once a Legend*, 172.
15. Hoyt, *Guadalcanal*, 21.
16. Peatross, *bless 'em all*, 39.
17. Hoyt, *War in the Pacific*, 2:174.
18. Griffith, *Battle for Guadalcanal*, 70.

Chapter 3. Under New Management

1. Merillat, *Guadalcanal Remembered*, 85.
2. Tregaskis, *Guadalcanal Diary*, 56.
3. Frank, *Guadalcanal*, 123.
4. Stafford, *Big "E,"* 127.
5. Hoyt, *Guadalcanal*, 54.
6. Thacker, *U.S. 1st Marine Division*, 6.
7. Hammel, *Guadalcanal*, 148.
8. Ibid., 134.
9. Tregaskis, *Guadalcanal Diary*, 97.
10. Jones, *Forgotten Warriors*, 14.

Chapter 4. Japan Man 'long Here?

1. Griffith, *Battle for Guadalcanal*, 99.
2. Richter, *Where the Sun Stood Still*, 175–80.
3. It was "the Tenaru" to my Parris Island drill instructor, Plt. Sgt. Robert Cally, who had fought in this battle with the 1st Marines.
4. Griffith, *Battle for Guadalcanal*, 102.
5. Sgt. Robert Cally, conversation with author, Parris Island Marine Boot Camp, April 1945.
6. Ibid.
7. Harry Horsman, National Historian, Guadalcanal Campaign Veterans, personal communication with author.
8. Frank, *Guadalcanal*, 154.
9. Morison, *Struggle for Guadalcanal*, 72.
10. Letter from Mantis Tani, Japanese historian, to Harry Horsman, National Historian, Guadalcanal Campaign Veterans, 23 February 1985.
11. Frank, *Guadalcanal*, 156.

12. Griffith, *Battle for Guadalcanal*, 104.
13. Richter, *Where the Sun Stood Still*, 172–80.
14. Miller, *Cactus Air Force*, 34.
15. Tregaskis, *Guadalcanal Diary*, 154.

Chapter 5. Yamamoto's Armada

1. Miller, *Cactus Air Force*, 34.
2. Ibid., 37–38.
3. Ibid., 39.
4. Stafford, *Big "E,"* 136.
5. Ibid., 142–43.
6. Miller, *Cactus Air Force*, 48.
7. Ibid., 49.
8. Griffith, *Battle for Guadalcanal*, 112.
9. Merillat, *Guadalcanal Remembered*, 118.
10. Morison, *Struggle for Guadalcanal*, 112.
11. Tregaskis, *Guadalcanal Diary*, 180–81.
12. Hoyt, *Guadalcanal*, 98–99.
13. Potter, *Nimitz*, 186.
14. Griffith, *Battle for Guadalcanal*, 193.
15. Mytinger, *Headhunting in the Solomon Islands*, 122.
16. Stafford, *Big "E,"* 203.

Chapter 6. Something Sobbed Like a Child

1. Griffith, *Battle for Guadalcanal*, 132.
2. Miller, *Cactus Air Force*, 86.
3. Vandegrift, *Once a Marine*, 152–53.
4. Hoyt, *Guadalcanal*, 113.
5. Ibid., 114.
6. Buell, *Dauntless Helldivers*, 146.
7. Hoyt, *Guadalcanal*, 114.
8. Manchester, *Goodbye Darkness*, 227.
9. Morison, *Struggle for Guadalcanal*, 128.
10. Hoyt, *Guadalcanal*, 270.
11. Buell, *Dauntless Helldivers*, 252.

Chapter 7. The Cactus Air Force

1. Buell, *Dauntless Helldivers*, 140–42.
2. Frank, *Guadalcanal*, 214.
3. Griffith, *Battle for Guadalcanal*, 120–21.
4. Miller, *Cactus Air Force*, 69.
5. Stafford, *Big "E,"* 160–61.
6. Miller, *Cactus Air Force*, 82.
7. Griffith, *Battle for Guadalcanal*, 128.

Chapter 8. Torpedoes on the Starboard Bow

1. Davis, *Marine!* 108–9.
2. Ibid., 111–12.
3. Merillat, *Guadalcanal Remembered*, 151.
4. Davis, *Marine!* 113.
5. Morison, *Struggle for Guadalcanal*, 140.
6. Davis, *Marine!* 118.
7. Ibid., 119.
8. Peatross, *bless 'em all*, 112.
9. Berry, *Semper Fi, Mac*, 120.
10. Hammel, *Guadalcanal*, 263.
11. Davis, *Marine!* 124.
12. Hammel, *Guadalcanal*, 267.
13. Davis, *Marine!* 126.

Chapter 9. An Old Friend of Chester Nimitz

1. Potter, *Nimitz*, 192.
2. All the marine quotations in this section are from *Fighting on Guadalcanal*, 1–49.
3. Davis, *Marine!* 130.
4. Hoffman, *Once a Legend*, 411.
5. Harry Horsman, personal communication with author.
6. Davis, *Marine!* 134.
7. Griffith, *Battle for Guadalcanal*, 181.

Chapter 10. You Can't Live Forever

1. Miller, *Cactus Air Force*, 121.
2. Morison, *Struggle for Guadalcanal*, 176–77.
3. Michener, *Return to Paradise*, 178.
4. Stafford, *Big "E,"* 197.
5. Hammel, *Guadalcanal*, 339.
6. Hoyt, *Guadalcanal*, 245–46.
7. Frank, *Guadalcanal*, 437.
8. Morison, *Struggle for Guadalcanal*, 193.
9. *Old Breed News*, October 1993, 32.
10. Interview with Mike Zello, September 1994.
11. Griffith, *Battle for Guadalcanal*, 204.
12. Hoyt, *Guadalcanal*, 174.
13. Griffith, *Battle for Guadalcanal*, 205.
14. Harry Horsman, personal communication with author.

Chapter 11. A Certain Ruthlessness

1. Miller, *Cactus Air Force*, 209.
2. Frank, *Guadalcanal*, 470.
3. Davis, *Marine!* 149–51.
4. Morison, *Two-Ocean War*, 197.
5. Griffith, *Battle for Guadalcanal*, 247.
6. Ibid., 247.
7. Frank, *Guadalcanal*, 525–26.
8. Griffith, *Battle for Guadalcanal*, 250.
9. Ibid., 250.
10. Johnson, *Bride in the Solomons*, 172–78.
11. Stafford, *Big "E,"* 219.
12. Morison, *Two-Ocean War*, 209–10.
13. Merillat, *Guadalcanal Remembered*, 235–36.
14. Frank, *Guadalcanal*, 527.
15. Merillat, *Guadalcanal Remembered*, 238.

Chapter 12. Gung Ho

1. Bulger, "Second Marine Raider Battalion," pt. 2, p. 2.

2. Ibid.
3. Ibid., 3.
4. Ibid., 6.
5. Ibid., pt. 3, p. 6.
6. Ibid., pt. 2, pp. 8–9.
7. Ibid., pt. 4, p. 11.
8. Ibid., 13.
9. Davis, Marine! 155.
10. Muehrcke, Orchids in the Mud, 47.
11. Frank, Guadalcanal, 543.
12. Ibid., 536–37.
13. Muehrcke, Orchids in the Mud, 105–30.
14. Frank, Guadalcanal, 533.
15. Muehrcke, Orchids in the Mud, 131–45.
16. Frank, Guadalcanal, 533.

Chapter 13. The Once Unthinkable Decision

1. Morison, Struggle for Guadalcanal, 317.
2. Frank, Guadalcanal, 541.
3. Morison, Struggle for Guadalcanal, 340.
4. Frank, Guadalcanal, 562–63.
5. Ibid., 564.
6. Griffith, Battle for Guadalcanal, 280.
7. Frank, Guadalcanal, 588.
8. Ibid., 582–97.
9. Morison, Struggle for Guadalcanal, 371.

Berry, Henry. *Semper Fi, Mac*. New York: Berkley Publishing Group, 1987.

Buell, Harold L. *Dauntless Helldivers*. New York: Dell, 1992.

Bulger, Lowell V. "The Second Marine Raider Battalion on Guadalcanal." *Raider Patch*. Pts. 1–4, May–November 1981.

Davis, Burke. *Marine! The Life of Chesty Puller*. New York: Bantam, 1964.

Fighting on Guadalcanal. Pamphlet. Washington D.C.: Government Printing Office, 1943.

Frank, Richard B. *Guadalcanal*. New York: Random House, 1990.

Griffith, Samuel B., II. *The Battle for Guadalcanal*. New York: Bantam, 1981.

Hammel, Eric M. *Guadalcanal: Starvation Island*. New York: Crown, 1987.

Hoffman, Jon T. *Once a Legend*. Novato, Calif.: Presidio Press, 1944.

Hoyt, Edwin P. *Guadalcanal*. New York: Jove, 1986.

———. *War in the Pacific*. Vol. 2. New York: Avon Books, 1990.

Johnson, Osa. *Bride in the Solomons*. New York: Garden City Publishing, 1944.

Jones, Arvil L. *Forgotten Warriors*. Paducah, Ky.: Turner, 1994.

Leckie, Robert. *Helmet for My Pillow*. New York: Bantam, 1992.

Lord, Walter. *Lonely Vigil*. New York: Viking, 1997.

Manchester, William. *Goodbye Darkness*. New York: Dell, 1987.

Merillat, Herbert Christian. *Guadalcanal Remembered*. New York: Avon, 1990.

Michener, James. *Return to Paradise*. New York: Random House, 1951.

Miller, Thomas G., Jr. *The Cactus Air Force*. New York: Harper & Row, 1969.

Morison, Samuel Eliot. *The Struggle for Guadalcanal*. Boston: Little, Brown, 1989.

———. *The Two-Ocean War*. Boston: Little, Brown, 1963.

Muehrcke, Robert C. *Orchids in the Mud*. Chicago: J. S. Printing, 1985.

Mytinger, Carolyne. *Headhunting in the Solomon Islands*. New York: Macmillan, 1942.

Old Breed News, October 1993.

Peatross, Oscar F. *bless 'em all*. Irvine, Calif.: ReView Publications, 1995.

Potter, E. P. *Nimitz*. Annapolis: Naval Institute Press, 1976.

Prange, Gordon W. *Miracle at Midway*. New York: Penguin, 1983.

Richter, Don M. *Where the Sun Stood Still*. Calabasas, Calif.: Toucan, 1992.

Stafford, Edward P. *The Big "E."* New York: Ballantine, 1990.

Thacker, Joel D. *U.S. 1st Marine Division, 1941–1945*. Washington, D.C.: Headquarters USMC Historical Division, 1949.

Tregaskis, Richard. *Guadalcanal Diary*. New York: Random House, 1943.

Vandegrift, A. A., with R. B. Asprey. *Once a Marine*. New York: Norton, 1964.

About the Author

Born in Chicago, Carl Hixon left DePauw University in 1943 to serve in the Merchant Marine and the U.S. Marine Corps. After the war he earned a B.A. in English literature and joined the Leo Burnett advertising agency, where he became a member of the board of directors. He was posted to Burnett's London office to oversee the creative quality of the company's British, European, and African units, returning to its Chicago headquarters in 1976 as an executive vice president. After he retired in 1980, Hixon worked as a magazine columnist and wrote a four-part series about Stalin for the Discovery Channel before embarking on the six-year task of writing this book.

The Naval Institute Press is the book-publishing arm of the U.S. Naval Institute, a private, nonprofit, membership society for sea service professionals and others who share an interest in naval and maritime affairs. Established in 1873 at the U.S. Naval Academy in Annapolis, Maryland, where its offices remain today, the Naval Institute has members worldwide.

Members of the Naval Institute support the education programs of the society and receive the influential monthly magazine *Proceedings* and discounts on fine nautical prints and on ship and aircraft photos. They also have access to the transcripts of the Institute's Oral History Program and get discounted admission to any of the Institute-sponsored seminars offered around the country.

The Naval Institute also publishes *Naval History* magazine. This colorful bimonthly is filled with entertaining and thought-provoking articles, first-person reminiscences, and dramatic art and photography. Members receive a discount on *Naval History* subscriptions.

The Naval Institute's book-publishing program, begun in 1898 with basic guides to naval practices, has broadened its scope in recent years to include books of more general interest. Now the Naval Institute Press publishes about one hundred titles each year, ranging from how-to books on boating and navigation to battle histories, biographies, ship and aircraft guides, and novels. Institute members receive discounts of 20 to 50 percent on the Press's more than eight hundred books in print.

Full-time students are eligible for special half-price membership rates. Life memberships are also available.

For a free catalog describing Naval Institute Press books currently available, and for further information about subscribing to *Naval History* magazine or about joining the U.S. Naval Institute, please write to:

Membership Department
U.S. Naval Institute
291 Wood Road
Annapolis, MD 21402-5034
Telephone: (800) 233-8764
Fax: (410) 269-7940
Web address: www.usni.org